Staging the Gaze

Staging the Gaze

POSTMODERNISM, PSYCHOANALYSIS, AND SHAKESPEAREAN COMEDY

Barbara Freedman

Cornell University Press

ITHACA AND LONDON

First published 1991 by Cornell University Press.

International Standard Book Number 0-8014-2279-5 (cloth)
International Standard Book Number 0-8014-9737-X (paper)
Library of Congress Catalog Card Number 90-55117
Printed in the United States of America

"Keeping Things Whole" is reprinted with permission of Atheneum Publishers, an imprint of Macmillan Publishing Company, from *Reasons for Moving* by Mark Strand. Copyright © 1964 by Mark Strand.

Librarians: Library of Congress cataloging information appears on the last page of the book.

⊗The paper in this book meets the minimum requirements of the American National Standard for Information Sciences—Permanence of Paper for Printed Library Materials, ANSI Z39.48-1984.

For Paul

In a field
I am the absence
of field.
This is
always the case.
Wherever I am
I am what is missing.

When I walk
I part the air
and always
the air moves in
to fill the spaces
where my body's been.

We all have reasons
for moving.
I move
to keep things whole.
—Mark Strand, "Keeping Things Whole"

Contents

Illustrations

Acknowledgments

Recognition and misrecognition, debts and acknowledgment, figure largely not only in Shakespeare's comedies but in the completion of any book. Since this book both records and enacts my fascination with knowing blind spots, even here I shall probably fail to recognize the many people who have helped me along my errant path. But at least I can record my gratitude to the exciting collaborative thinking in which I have participated, both with my students in the classroom and with scholars at the Center for Literary Studies at Harvard University, the Center for Renaissance Studies at the Newberry Library, the Center for the Psychological Study of the Arts at the State University of New York at Buffalo, the Institute for the Psychological Study of the Arts at the University of Florida, and the Shakespeare Association of America annual meetings. Specific individuals who have helped to shape my thinking in this work include Scott McMillin and a group of uncannily familiar strangers whose works have inspired mine from afar: Jacqueline Rose, Shoshana Felman, Ernest Gilman, Kaja Silverman, Samuel Weber, and Claudio Guillén. Grateful thanks are due to several scholars who have given generously of their time and thoughts on behalf of this book in its early stages—Marjorie Garber, Maurice Charney, David Willbern, Sidney Homan, and Norman Holland. I want to add special thanks for insightful suggestions on specific chapters offered by Marilyn Williamson, David Loewenstein, Richard Strier, Naomi Liebler, Paul Yachnin, Sue-Ellen Case, Bernard Paris, and J. P. Earls. My friend James Loftus read and reread the entire manuscript, and succeeded in making this a far better book through his painstaking

Acknowledgments

work and invaluable suggestions. Bernhard Kendler, my editor, was remarkably resourceful, patient, and good-humored during the lengthy time that it took me to get the manuscript into its final shape. Ellis Freedman, my father, tracked down citations and offered stylistic suggestions in addition to quietly providing encouragement over the years; Marilyn Freedman and Doren Greene shared with me both the humor and emotional support I needed while I was writing. Finally, I can only try to thank my husband, Paul Krueger, whose fascination with space and vision has spurred my own, and whose support on so many different levels can never be acknowledged in words.

This book could never have been written without the economic backing of the Andrew W. Mellon Foundation, which gave me the opportunity to teach and do research both at the California Institute of Technology and at Harvard University, and of the National Endowment for the Humanities for a fellowship at the Newberry Library. Saint John's University also provided me with a leave of absence and a McPherson Grant while teaching.

Because I have placed my earlier work in a larger theoretical context that subverts it, no chapter appears elsewhere in print. I am grateful to the editors of the following publications, however, for permission to refurbish sections of the following essays: "Egeon's Debt: Self-Division and Self-Redemption in *The Comedy of Errors*," *English Literary Renaissance* 10 (1980), 360–83; "Errors in Comedy: A Psychoanalytic Theory of Farce," *Shakespearean Comedy*, ed. Maurice Charney (New York: New York Literary Forum, 1980), 233–43; "Separation and Fusion in *Twelfth Night*," *Psychoanalytic Approaches to Literature and Film*, ed. Maurice Charney and Joseph Reppen (Rutherford, N.J.: Fairleigh Dickinson University Press, 1987), 96–119; "Frame-Up: Feminism, Psychoanalysis, Theatre," *Theatre Journal* 40 (October 1988), 375–97; "Misrecognizing Shakespeare," *Shakespeare's Personality*, ed. Norman Holland, Sidney Homan, and Bernard Paris (Berkeley: University of California Press, 1989); "Pedagogy, Psychoanalysis, Theatre: Interrogating the Scene of Learning," *Shakespeare Quarterly* 41 (Summer 1990), 174–86. I thank Mark Strand for being willing to let me reprint his poem "Keeping Things Whole."

BARBARA FREEDMAN

New York City

xii

Staging the Gaze

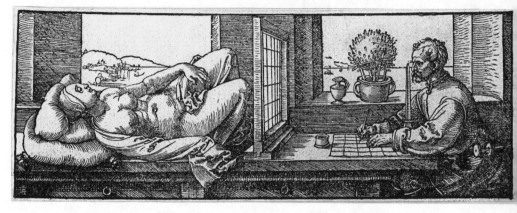

Figure 1. Albrecht Dürer's draftsman, woodcut from *Unterweisung der Messung* (Nuremburg, 1525), B. 149. Courtesy Kupferstichkabinett, Staatliche Museen Preussischer Kulturbesitz, West Berlin.

Introduction

What do we mean when we say that someone or something is theatrical? What we mean is that such a person is aware that she is seen, reflects that awareness, and so deflects our look. We refer to a fractured reciprocity whereby beholder and beheld reverse positions in a way that renders a steady position of spectatorship impossible. Theatricality evokes an uncanny sense that the given to be seen has the power both to position us and to displace us. Whereas Western narrative cinema is obsessed with the look, Western theater is fascinated by the return of that look, what psychoanalyst Jacques Lacan terms "the gaze." If the eye is that which sees, the gaze is that which elides the eye and shows us how we are caught out by our own look—displaced in the act of spectatorship.

Works that both confound the spectator's look and parade that fact are theatrical, as are paintings and films that expose their observers as voyeurs. Consider, for example, how Albrecht Dürer's woodcut of a perspective painter (figure 1) plays out, reverses, and so complicates positions of right and erring spectatorship. Dürer's multiplication of pictures within this picture creates the theatrical effect of a dramatic interplay of looks. Not only do the windows frame nature much as the artist would frame woman, but we in turn frame the painter as well. The painter as a privileged spectator is himself displaced by being made the object of our look. We no sooner see him as a Peeping Tom than we see ourselves as voyeurs who are similarly caught in the act of looking. The complex relay of looks among painter, model, and spectator not only stages our look, but reflects it back to us in a way that we cannot but identify as theatrical.

I

The very concept of right spectatorship and the conditions under which we identify with voyeur, exhibitionist, or both are at least partly a function of gender ideology. Since this famous woodcut documents the development of painter's perspective, we usually identify with the artist's point of view. In the process, however, we identify with the male as the appropriate bearer of the look, the female as the proper object of that look; we identify with reason against sexuality, activity over passivity, and seeing instead of showing. The scenes framed by the windows further encourage our identification with masculinity as culture against femininity as disorganized nature. The fullness of the potted tree framed by the artist's window suggests a disorderly nature made fertile by the artist's containing vision. In contrast to the strong vertical lines of the tree, the draftsman's posture, and his viewing rod, the horizontal lines of the woman's reclining body are reinforced by the low rolling hills seen through her window. These visual cues facilitate our identification with the painter and encourage the equation of right spectatorship with a controlling patriarchal perspective.

Once we adopt the woman's perspective, the picture neatly reverses itself. The woman lies comfortably relaxed; the artist sits upright, rigidly constrained by his fixed position. The woman knows that she is seen; the artist is blinded by his viewing apparatus, deluded by his fantasy of objectivity. The draftsman's need to order visually and to distance himself from that which he sees suggests a futile attempt to protect himself from what he would (not) see. Yet the cloth draped between the woman's legs is not protection enough; neither the viewing device nor the screen can delineate or contain his desire. The perspective painter is transfixed in this moment, paralyzed, unable to capture the sight that encloses him. Enclosing us as well, Dürer's work draws our alarm.

Like Dürer's woodcut, Shakespeare's comedies are notorious for games that reverse the look and entrap the audience. The comedies play upon the lure of a spectator consciousness; they no sooner tantalize us with a stable position of mastery than they mock this stance by staging audience, character, plot, and theme as sites of misrecognition. First, the role of spectator offers a group ego as a site of misrecognition, insofar as it tempts us with the illusory position of the privileged voyeur. Colluding with the stage fiction, the audience denies the place of its look and identifies with the relay of looks

2

between the play's characters. Without ever "offending the audience," Shakespearean comedy moves its outside within and displays it, exposing the audience's desire to perceive itself as constituted somehow outside of a reciprocal gaze. Onstage audiences in *The Taming of the Shrew* and *A Midsummer Night's Dream* physically enact the subversion of the stable position of viewer which occurs during the performance of these plays.

The actor's body, mask, and character offer another site of audience misrecognition. Following Freud's definition of the ego as a projection of the body's surface, Lacan describes our identification with the mirror reflection of the body image as the constitutive misrecognition through which ego identity is formed. The image of the body envelope serves as a lure for the infant's desires for unity and presence at a time when motor coordination is still undeveloped. Theater plays upon our specular captivation by corporeal images; the body as a vehicle facilitates identifications that evoke the illusion of self-presence. The use of identical twins in *The Comedy of Errors* and *Twelfth Night* and of visual disguise and illusion in *The Taming of the Shrew* and *A Midsummer Night's Dream* foregrounds visual appearance as a site of errors.

Plot misrecognition offers another site of misidentification; the relation between audience and performer is doubled at the level of narrative when each character seeks in the other its proper reflection. Both tragic and comic narratives stage misrecognition in the quest for recognition. Whereas Shakespeare's tragedies address the need and failure to find a place in another's eyes, the comedies are more concerned with dislocating perspective; they suggest that only a limited perspectival space defined by error constitutes identity. A fourth misrecognition occurs when the comedies thematize these physical and visual errors to demonstrate how gender, class, and ideology function as sites of misrecognition. In *The Comedy of Errors*, Shakespeare adds to broad physical, visual comedy an interrogation of the very possibility of a discourse of mastery. In *The Taming of the Shrew*, Christopher Sly's interpellation as a lord serves as model for the coercive system known as class identity. The construction of Sly's "madam wife," who is actually a male servant disguised as a female, highlights the constrictive system of gender against which Kate rebels. The comedies encourage us to question not only the master-servant relationships within the plots but the relations of power implicit in the conventions of "right spectatorship." They no sooner create ambiguous subject positions for their characters than they refer the tension of mistaken identification back to their viewers.

In question is how to read plays that stage reading as erring. Like the characters within *The Comedy of Errors*, readers of that play are torn between an interpretation of events based on an appealing fantasy of narrative closure and an interpretation that subverts the fantasy of a unified reading. Just as the characters within *Twelfth Night, or What You Will* cannot avoid seeing things as they will, so we as readers must fail in our attempts to read the play without projecting onto it what we will. The mockery of right spectatorship in *Twelfth Night* is cunningly staged in the portrait of "We Three"; two fools are pictured there, and the spectator stands perplexed before that work and struggles to decode the title. Malvolio's attempts to decipher a nonsense letter in the same play are enough to make any well-meaning critic cringe: "'M. O. A. I. doth sway my life,'" he reads aloud; "If I could make that resemble something in me!" (2.5.110, 119–20). But how do we read Malvolio misreading without also misreading?

Rather than deny the plays' resistance to interpretation, I suggest that we understand it in the context of a Renaissance tradition of learned ignorance, trick perspectives, and optical experiments, all of which answer to our paradoxical desire to see how we cannot see ourselves seeing. Among the most prominent works in this tradition are Nicholas of Cusa's *De docta ignorantia*, Erasmus's *Praise of Folly*, and Shakespeare's comedies, each of which studies that which resists knowledge as a form of knowledge. Unlike Shakespeare's tragedies, where misrecognition leads to a crisis of representation, the comedies take resistance to meaning as meaningful in itself. If the tragedies more directly critique the myth of self-presence, the play of representation in the comedies makes them more *useful* to that critique. Comedy claims as its province both the representation of illusion and the illusion of representation, both the forms of desire and the desire of form. Its divided voice allows it to comment on itself and so upon the structure and workings of the psyche as discourse. Its multiple perspectives enable it not only to interrupt its own construction but to stage that interruption in dizzying *en abyme* structures, in complex games of self-reference, and in paradoxical shifts in levels of representation. Shakespeare's comedies work at the boundaries between

4

what can and cannot be seen, known, or represented; in their concern with errors, dream, censorship, and illusion, they anticipate Freud's study of considerations of representability. Like dreams and jokes, the comedies display unconscious discourse, stage the relationship between desire and signification, and explore how the categories of knowledge and ignorance are generated.

Rather than apply an interpretive model to these plays from a position of mastery, this book adopts the more circular strategy employed within the plays. Since the comedies function as optical devices for staging distortions and blind spots, we can use them to subvert the place of our own look, to explore our own sites of misrecognition, and so to bring early modern and postmodern models of the mind into dialogue. The following chapters are less concerned to "apply" psychoanalysis to Shakespeare's comedies than to explore, from multiple perspectives, the myth of mastery and the play of denial as performed in their reception. Each chapter casts Renaissance theater, psychoanalysis, and critical theory in a dramatic interplay of reciprocally reflecting gazes. Similarly, each play is used to rethink the cultural production of spectatorship. The result is a series of agons, or contests, in which feminism, deconstruction, cultural materialism, and psychoanalysis confront, accuse, and displace one other. No one discourse is the master here, and no one object, such as Shakespearean comedy, is the primary text that the others are recruited to explain. This model of reading is essentially *theatrical* insofar as it works at the intersection of various theories in order to subvert the place of one's look.

Chapter 1 works with the relationship between models of history, sight, and knowledge and relates emerging models of Renaissance subjectivity to a tradition of learned ignorance and to developments in optics and perspective painting. Chapter 2 examines the use of psychoanalysis by film theory as a means of rethinking theatricality and its relationship to postmodern theory. Chapters 3 to 6 focus on four Shakespearean comedies often described as the farcical comedies—*The Comedy of Errors, The Taming of the Shrew, A Midsummer Night's Dream,* and *Twelfth Night*—and employ their games with spectatorship to interrogate and reverse perspectives in critical theory today. The end result is a series of readings that question the possibility of reading as mastery.

Shakespeare's comedies keep announcing that neither we nor

they can stand outside of these scenes of misrecognition. If we cannot avoid getting lost within their traps, we can employ theatrical strategies to dislodge them. Insofar as Shakespeare's comedies stage resistance to meaning, their study of censorship, denial, and displacement can teach us about how we construct, privilege, and censor meaning today. Our fascination with the game of uncovering meanings in the comedies is a tribute to their facility in subverting any fixed perspective. Our continued work with these plays, however, depends upon our willingness to displace our look, to stage it, and so to keep it on the move. For those engaged in this undertaking, the question is how and where theory will move today. If theory is theatrical and thereby offers a strategy by means of which we can posit and so displace our unknowingness, perhaps it can provide us with some answers.

I

Displacing a Spectator Consciousness: Theater, Psychoanalysis, and Renaissance Considerations of Representability

I cannot urge you too strongly to a meditation on optics. The odd thing is that an entire system of metaphysics has been founded on geometry and mechanics, by looking to them for models of understanding, but up to now it doesn't seem as though optics has been exploited as much as it could have been.
—Jacques Lacan, *Freud's Papers on Technique, 1953–1954*

I

A delight in sectioning off and comparing time periods proves as useful to people seeking to redefine themselves as to those who would pretend to study them. To inscribe itself temporally, a culture must freely deploy strategies of exclusion and revision. Barriers must be fortified and blinders put on. Renaissance mirror games arrange for a flattering self-portrait to come into focus precisely in that moment when a distorted image could be relegated to a field of erring sight. The concept of a fetish object and the carefully delineated field of vision it requires helps explain why the Renaissance as such was contemporaneous with the development of the perspective picture and the picture frame.[1] Disdaining and disowning what it

---

[1] In *Questions of Cinema* (Bloomington: Indiana University Press, 1981), Stephen Heath observes that the first recorded use of the word *frame* in an artistic sense occurs around 1600, and the first use of the word *easel* around 1634 (34). In *Shakespeare and the Arts of Design* (Columbia: University of Missouri Press, 1937), Arthur H. R. Fairchild argues that what is important in Shakespeare's Sonnet 24 is not the idea of perspective as an optical device but the idea of the frame as a window (127).

could of its past, relegating what it did not want to see to the aptly titled dark or middle ages, a culture refashioned itself in terms of idealized figures of the past. But amid that mania for classification and boundaries, for fetishized objects and dividing lines, were people ignorant or all too aware of the role played by exclusion in the formation of a cultural identity? And if we are aware that in studying the Renaissance we collude in these games of exclusionary self-fashioning, then how to rethink our position?

Erwin Panofsky points to "a curious inward correspondence between perspective and what may be called the general mental attitude of the Renaissance"; he maintains that "the process of projecting an object on a plane in such a way that the resulting image is determined by the distance and location of a 'point of vision' symbolized . . . a period which had inserted an historical distance—quite comparable to the perspective one—between itself and the classical past."[2] Rereading Panofsky today, we may question the extent to which perspective conventions have shaped Western models of historical inquiry. The precautions required to see the perspective picture correctly—a careful control over distance and location, a clearly delineated position of mastery for the individual viewer, a privileged single eye, and, above all, a blinded eye—are the same rituals observed in historical practice. Can we avoid inserting a carefully delineated perspectival distance between ourselves and others to construct our point of view? Whether we seek to uncover the past or to recover ourselves, in question is whether historically grounded studies can avoid partaking in Malvolio's quest to "make that resemble something in me" (*Twelfth Night*: 2.5.119–20).[3]

As an alternative, postmodern theorists propose that we interrogate the conditions under which explanatory narratives such as "the Renaissance" operate—what Freud termed, in another context, "considerations of representability."[4] Michel Foucault, for example,

[2]Erwin Panofsky, *The Life and Art of Albrecht Dürer* (Princeton: Princeton University Press, 1955), 261.

[3]This and all quotations from Shakespeare are from the Riverside Shakespeare, ed. G. Blakemore Evans (Boston: Houghton Mifflin, 1974).

[4]This phrase appears as the title to Section D of Chapter 6 of *The Interpretation of Dreams* (1900), 5:339–49. All quotations from Freud, unless otherwise noted, are from *The Standard Edition of the Complete Psychological Works of Sigmund Freud*, ed. James Strachey, 24 vols. (London: Hogarth Press, 1953–74).

charges historians with ignoring the constitutive role of negation in their construction of historical time periods: "where historicism sought for the possibility and justification of concrete relations between limited totalities . . . the analytic of finitude tries to question this relation of the human being to the being which, by designating finitude, renders the positivities possible in their concrete mode of being."[5] Rather than seek the truth of the Renaissance, Foucault focuses attention on the enabling conditions according to which a culture constructs, measures, or recognizes truth. Similarly, rather than try to decipher the Renaissance world picture, we might explore what is involved in conceiving of the world as a picture.

Accordingly, we may follow up on Heidegger's characterization of the early modern age as an effort to conceive of the world *as* a picture: "Where the world becomes picture, what is, in its entirety, is juxtaposed as that for which man is prepared and which, correspondingly, he therefore intends to bring before himself and have before himself, and consequently intends in a decisive sense to set in place before himself. Hence world picture, when understood essentially, does not mean a picture of the world but the world conceived and grasped as picture."[6] The Elizabethan world picture thus depends upon what we might term a spectator consciousness, an epistemological model based upon an observer who stands outside of what she sees in a definite position of mastery over it. Since we typically characterize the Renaissance in terms that reinforce this model, of interest here is a countertradition devoted to the subversion of a spectator consciousness, according to which the relationship between seeing and knowing takes a different turn.

The Renaissance preoccupation with undermining right sight through trick perspective pictures and paradoxes, unreason or folly, and theatrical games that confuse spectator and spectacle has been well documented, and we are now accustomed to reading Shakespearean comedy in this context.[7] But we have yet fully to appreciate

[5]Michel Foucault, *The Order of Things: An Archaeology of the Human Sciences* (New York: Random-Vintage, 1973), 373.

[6]Martin Heidegger, "The Age of the World Picture," in *The Question Concerning Technology and Other Essays*, trans. William Lovitt (New York: Harper and Row, 1977), 129.

[7]For this tradition see Walter Kaiser, *Praisers of Folly: Erasmus, Rabelais, Shakespeare* (Cambridge: Harvard University Press, 1963); Rosalie L. Colie, *Paradoxia*

how the comedies' games with a spectator consciousness offer a model of knowing unknowingness which requires us to rethink the reading process. Their notorious resistance to interpretation makes sense in the context of a rich cultural tradition of staging blindness and erring as a form of insight. Their interactive traps not only play upon our desire to see ourselves seeing but expose us as observed from a point of view within as well as from without with which we can never merge. Given their interest in a model of subjectivity which is not ego oriented but based on the inevitable play of blind spots and misrecognitions, given their concern with figuring how we cannot see and know as a form of positive knowledge, Shakespeare's comedies suggest less a field on which to prove the truth of psychoanalysis than a means by which to rethink issues facing it today. The Renaissance revival of traditions of learned ignorance and perspective optics provides a means of historicizing these games with a spectator consciousness; in the tradition of knowing unknowingness through the subversion of point of view and in the branch of faculty psychology known as optics, we may trace the basis of psychoanalytic theory and appreciate its importance to Shakespearean comedy. As we study the crossroads where learned ignorance, trick perspectives, and Shakespearean comedy meet, we may come to understand why Shoshana Felman suggests that "what Freud discovered in the Oedipus myth is not an answer but *the structure of a question*, not any given knowledge but a structuring positioning of . . . ignorance."[8]

II

In the *Meno*, Socrates boasts of his ability to avoid teaching: "I shall do nothing more than ask questions and not teach him. Watch

Epidemica: The Renaissance Tradition of Paradox (Princeton: Princeton University Press, 1966); and Barbara C. Bowen, *The Age of Bluff: Paradox and Ambiguity in Rabelais and Montaigne* (Urbana: University of Illinois Press, 1972). Its importance to Shakespearean comedy has been carefully explored by Ernest B. Gilman, *The Curious Perspective: Literary and Pictorial Wit in the Seventeenth Century* (New Haven: Yale University Press, 1978). I am much indebted to his work, especially to his chapters on Shakespearean comedy. For a more recent study which just came to my attention, see John Greenwood, *Shifting Perspectives and the Stylish Style: Mannerism in Shakespeare and His Jacobean Contemporaries* (Toronto: University of Toronto Press, 1988).

[8]Shoshana Felman, *Jacques Lacan and the Adventure of Insight: Psychoanalysis in Contemporary Culture* (Cambridge: Harvard University Press, 1987), 103.

whether you find me teaching and explaining things to him instead of asking for his opinion."[9] Whereas traditional pedagogy conceives of knowledge as a product or commodity, Socratic learning is a process of questioning that can never be satisfied. In traditional pedagogy, knowledge is cumulative and strengthens the stability of subject positions; the pedagogical countertradition implies a subject who is constituted by this continual shift in the relation of ignorance and knowledge and so finds herself only through displacement. Rather than *contrast* ignorance and knowledge, Socrates emphasizes their constitutive and dynamic relationship. Rather than define ignorance as the absence of attainable knowledge, he defines knowledge as an awareness of the inevitability of ignorance. The Socratic model moves beyond attacks upon the vanity of learning insofar as its stance of ignorance is generative; Socrates urges us to know *how* we don't know, to know *that* we don't know, if not to know *what* we don't know. His model is therefore less a particular stance than an imperative to displace any stance in a critique of the concept of "standing under," or understanding, a master as the "subject supposed to know." "At least I'm wiser than that one," explains Socrates. "Perhaps neither of us knows anything beautiful or good, but he thinks that he knows when he doesn't, whereas I don't think that I know, as indeed I do not. So at least I'm wiser than he in this one little thing—I don't think that I know what I don't."[10]

If this style of reasoning calls to mind the perverse style of some contemporary continental thinkers, this is because learned ignorance has a long and varied history whose cultural specificity cannot be ignored. For example, what distinguishes Renaissance forms of learned ignorance is an emerging model of subjectivity based upon a precise spatial relationship between observer and observed. With the Renaissance rediscovery and application of the measure or ratio, new ideas and techniques were generated in fields as varied as painting and architecture, navigation and cartography. By positing a human centric point and employing an arbitrary unit as a standard, Renaissance thinkers introduced theories of perspective which effectively reshaped their conceptualization of knowledge. The works of Leon Battista Alberti, for example, helped to popularize the central per-

[9]Plato, *Meno*, trans. G. M. A. Grube (Indianapolis: Hackett, 1976), 17.
[10]Plato, *The "Apology" and "Crito" of Plato and The "Apology" and "Symposium" of Xenophon*, trans. Raymond Larson (Lawrence, Kans.: Coronado Press, 1980), 29.

spective system and so to strengthen the stability of a position of mastery. The use of the ratio redefined both sight and knowledge as human centered, relative, and perspectival rather than God centered and absolute. But Alberti bracketed and so effectively repressed the doctrine of relativity he discovered in Protagoras, observing:

> All knowledge of large, small; long, short; high, low; broad, narrow; clear, dark; light and shadow and every similar attribute is obtained by comparison. Because they can be, but are not necessarily, conjoined with objects, philosophers are accustomed to call them accidents. . . . Thus all things are known by comparison, for comparison contains within itself a power which immediately demonstrates in objects which is more, less or equal. . . . This is best done with well-known things. Since man is the thing best known to man, perhaps Protagoras, by saying that man is the mode and measure of all things, meant that all the accidents of things are known through comparison to the accidents of man.[11]

By accidents Alberti means circumstances, and from circumstances he derives rules. "What Alberti had seen in the *measure* of Protagoras was a *standard*, a 'measure' by which the painter could find and reproduce the ratios of the scene he wanted to depict! Reading the classic statement of ancient subjectivism mathematically," Joan Gadol observes, "he had drawn from it, wonderful as it may seem, a directive for establishing the objectivity of the perspectival picture."[12] What is wonderful—or paradoxical—is the way that Alberti derives certitude from radical uncertainty. While accepting that knowledge is always limited by one's viewpoint, Alberti argued that the measurement of perspective could yield certain knowledge.

Advances in Renaissance cartography exemplify the revolutionary shift in spatial relations effected by the widespread use of the ratio. The spatial arrangements in medieval maps reveal a priori evaluations of given places; Renaissance maps privilege the scale or ratio according to which we can locate these places. We tend to equate the Copernican revolution with the rise of a relational model of space.[13] Joan Gadol points out, however, that Alberti's work

[11]Leon Battista Alberti, *On Painting*, trans. John R. Spencer (New Haven: Yale University Press, 1956), 54–55.

[12]Joan Gadol, *Leon Battista Alberti: Universal Man of the Early Renaissance* (Chicago: University of Chicago Press, 1969), 69.

[13]For this shift in the conceptualization of space, see Erwin Panofsky, "Die

reveals the reliance of the Copernican model on the Ptolemaic renascence it supplanted.[14] Ptolemy maintains: "Geography looks at the position rather than the quality, noting the relation of distances everywhere." Because geography must "survey the whole, in its just proportions," it requires the study of "the exact position of any particular place, and the positions of the various countries, how they are situated in regard to one another, how situated as regards the whole." Ironically, Alberti may have found in Ptolemy's *Geography* the idea of applying proportional mapping to both painting and cartography: "as in an entire painting," Ptolemy writes, "we must first put in the larger features, and afterward those detailed features which portraits and pictures may require, giving them proportion in relation to one another so that their correct measure . . . can be seen by examining them."[15]

When Alberti arrived in Florence familiar with Ptolemy's *Geography*, he was able to appreciate the perspectival work of the painters Masaccio and Brunelleschi in terms set out by Toscanelli on geography and by Pelacani on optics.[16] Alberti's classic 1435 treatise *On*

Perspektive als 'Symbolische Form,' " *Vorträge der Bibliothek Warburg* (1924–25), 258–330; Panofsky, *Renaissance and Renascences* (1960; rpt. New York: Harper and Row, 1969); Ernst Cassirer, *The Individual and the Cosmos in Renaissance Philosophy*, trans. Mario Domandi (New York: Barnes and Noble, 1963), 183–201; Angus Armitage, *The World of Copernicus* (New York: New American Library, 1951); T. S. Kuhn, *The Copernican Revolution* (Cambridge: Harvard University Press, 1957); Stephen Toulmin and June Goodfield, *The Fabric of the Heavens* (New York: Harper and Row, 1961); Walter Ong, S.J., "System, Space, and Intellect in Renaissance Symbolism," in *The Barbarian Within and Other Fugitive Essays* (New York: Macmillan, 1962), 68–87; Rudolf Wittkower, *Architectural Principles in the Age of Humanism*, rev. ed. (London: Alec Tiranti, 1962); Heinrich Wölfflin, *Principles of Art History*, 7th ed., trans. M. D. Hottinger (New York: Dover Press, n.d.); and Wölfflin, *Die Klassische Kunst: The Art of the Italian Renaissance* (New York: Putnam's, 1928). For more specific work on perspectival space and painting, see William M. Ivins, Jr., *On the Rationalization of Sight* (New York: Metropolitan Museum of Art, 1938); Miriam Schild Bunim, *Space in Medieval Painting and the Forerunners of Perspective* (New York: Columbia University Press, 1940); and John White, *The Birth and Rebirth of Pictorial Space* (London: Faber and Faber, 1957), in addition to Joan Gadol's comprehensive study, *Alberti*.

[14]Gadol, *Alberti*, 70–75, 151–57, 195–200; I am indebted to Gadol's arguments concerning Alberti's reliance on Ptolemy's *Geography*.

[15]Claudius Ptolemy, *Geography*, trans. and ed. Edward Luther Stevenson (New York: New York Public Library, 1932), 25–26.

[16]For Brunelleschi's role in the development of painter's perspective see Rudolf Wittkower, "Brunelleschi and 'Proportion in Perspective,' " *Journal of the Warburg and*

Painting taught artists how to create the illusion of space and depth perception by drawing objects from a central, fixed vantage point. Adapting plane geometry to painting, Alberti demonstrates how the size of a given object varies in relation to its distance from the perceiver's eye. He advises painters to use the *velo*, or reticulated net, so as to treat things seen on a given plane "as if it were of transparent glass. Thus the visual pyramid could pass through it, placed at a definite distance with definite lights and a definite position of centre in space and in a definite place in respect to the observer."[17]

As if following the cool reason of Theseus, Alberti flatly warns us against using the art of perspective for the purposes of philosophical inquiry. "No one would deny that the painter has nothing to do with things that are not visible. The painter is concerned solely with representing what can be seen," writes Alberti confidently.[18] Living in the same town at the same time as Alberti, Nicholas of Cusa was similarly fascinated with the practical implications of models of measurement. Yet while Alberti was concerned with the practical manipulation of space, Cusa was more concerned with using geometrical optics to attain precise knowledge of our unknowingness. One reason for their apparent lack of mutual acknowledgment may have been Alberti's concern with limiting the application of perspective.[19]

Courtauld Institutes 16 (1953), 275–91; and Robert Klein, "Pomponius on Perspective," *Art Bulletin* 43 (1961), 211–30. Alberti dedicated *On Painting* to Brunelleschi, and the Renaissance biographer Giorgio Vasari maintained that Brunelleschi taught Masaccio the art of perspective. A close friend of both Brunelleschi and Alberti, the famous geographer Paolo Toscanelli (1397–1482) brought to Florence in 1424 a copy of Biagio Pelacani's *Quaestiones perspectivae*. This famous work, taught at the University of Padua in the 1390s, was influenced by writers such as John Peckham, if not by Roger Bacon and others. Yet all of these tracts were dependent on the classic texts on optics by Witelo and Alhazen. Alberti derived his theory of the pyramid of vision from the first European work on optics, Witelo's thirteenth-century *Perspectiva*. Witelo was in turn influenced by the Arab philosopher known in the West as al-Kwarhizan and later as Alhazen (965–1039). Since Alhazen's sources are still under examination, we can trace here the origins of Renaissance optics no further back than his *Book of Optics*, which was translated into Latin by Gerard of Cremona as *De aspectibus*.

[17]Alberti, *On Painting*, 51.

[18]Ibid., 43.

[19]Although we lack any concrete evidence of either correspondence or conference between Cusa and Alberti, scholars find it nearly impossible not to place the men together. "In the late 1450's," Gadol observes in *Leon Battista Alberti*, "Cusa's home in Rome was a gathering place for men of science like Peurbach, Regiomontanus, and Toscanelli; Alberti must have been a member of this group" (196). Both

Alberti neatly distinguishes *perspectiva artificialis*, his practical art of representing the structure of appearances, from *perspectiva naturalis*, the study of how we see. A. Mark Smith argues that "the ulterior concern of the perspectivists was epistemology and [so] . . . *perspectiva* should be understood as the science not of visual perception alone, but visual *cognition*."[20] If so, Alberti's distinctions seem designed to circumvent the mystical and metaphysical studies to which Cusa was committed.

Described by Cassirer as the first modern thinker, Cusa held that since we cannot know (God), we must explore *how* we cannot know as the only means of knowing (God).[21] Paradox, learned ignorance, and mathematical forms that confound reason were his constant study. Cusa's model of learned ignorance differs from the Socratic model upon which it draws in that Cusa figures erring and paradox as a form of truth, a mystical route to the divine. As the author of a doctrine of learned ignorance, Cusa maintains a radical pedagogy; his method requires that we accept our uncertainty about the object as the only means of knowing it. By working with, rather than against, the limitations of human knowledge, Cusa employs uncertainty as a way of knowing.

The first decisive step in Cusa's break with medieval scholastic theology is his argument that the mind, which works by comparison, cannot logically know God. Because "there is no comparative relation of the infinite to the finite," Cusa argues, "the measure and the measured—however equal they are—will always remain different. Therefore, it is not the case that by means of likeness a finite intellect can precisely attain the truth about things. . . . Whatever is not truth cannot measure truth precisely."[22] In *De mente*, the penultimate dialogue of *De idiota*, Cusa plays with etymology: "I

Cusa and Alberti were close friends of Paolo Toscanelli, with whom they shared a fascination with measurement. For Cusa's interest in measurement, see *De staticis experimentis* (*Concerning Experiments in Weight*), the final dialogue of Cusa's *De idiota*, translated in *Unity and Reform: Selected Writings of Nicholas de Cusa*, ed. John Patrick Dolan (Crawfordsville, Ind.: University of Notre Dame Press, 1962), 241–60.

[20]A. Mark Smith, "Getting the Big Picture in Perspectivist Optics," *Isis* 72 (1981), 569.

[21]Cassirer, *Individual and Cosmos*, 10.

[22]Cusa, *Nicholas of Cusa on Learned Ignorance: A Translation and an Appraisal of "De docta ignorantia,"* trans. Jasper Hopkins (Minneapolis: Arthur J. Banning, 1981), bk. 1, p. 52.

conjecture it is called *mens a mensurando*, the mind from measuring."
He describes the mind as a "living measure, measuring by it selfe, as
though a living paire of compasses, should measure by themselves,"
and concludes that "he who notes . . . that reasons are from the
minde, sees that no reason can reach to the measure of the minde.
Our minde therefore remaines unmeasurable, infinable, and interminable by any reason, which onely the uncreated minde measureth,
terminateth and boundeth, as the truth doth its living image, which is
of it, in it, and by it."[23]

Cusa never denies the possibility of knowing God; rather, he
maintains that our only recourse is to know our unknowingness
through learned ignorance, or *docta ignorantia*. The way in, he discovers, is through submission to a God who is beyond human
definition: "Accordingly I reject as a delusion any idea occurring to
me which seeketh to show Thee as comprehensible." Yet this apparent skepticism is in fact a search for ever more precise ways to figure
God as incomprehensible. Since "the wall beyond which I see Thee is
the end of all manner of signification in names,"[24] Cusa reasons, he
must find a language in which to figure that which escapes language:
"And this is our sufficiency which we have from God: knowing
unattainable precision cannot be reached except in a limited fashion
that partakes the manner of absolute precision."[25] For Cusa, the
answer to this quest for precision lies in geometrical optics. His work
reminds us that a concern with employing illusion as a means to
truth, and with employing perspective to figure cognitive paradoxes,
was a well-established tradition by Shakespeare's time.[26]

Cusa's work relies upon a distinction between the eye, which
sees, and the mind's eye, which sees that it can never see itself seeing.
If "God is the true Unlimited Sight," not "narrowed down to time
and place, to particular objects, and to other like conditions," we

[23]Cusa, *The Idiot in Four Books* (London: William Leake, 1650; rpt. San Fran-
cisco: California State Library, 1940), bk. 3 (*De mente*), pp. 55, 71, 27.

[24]Cusa, *The Vision of God*, trans. Emma Gurney Salter (1928; rpt. New York:
Frederick Ungar, 1960), 77–78, 58.

[25]Cusa, *De sapientia*, bk. 2, in *Unity and Reform*, ed. Dolan, 118.

[26]See Ronald Levao's *Renaissance Minds and Their Fictions: Cusanus, Sidney,
Shakespeare* (Berkeley: University of California Press, 1985), and Jackson Cope's
Theater and the Dream: From Metaphor to Form in Renaissance Drama (Baltimore: Johns
Hopkins University Press, 1973).

must see how we cannot see God.[27] In *De li non aliud*, Cusa suggests that although the hope of an undistorted reflection is dim, we must always remember to see as one who "sees snow through a red glass, sees the snow, and attributes the redness not to the snow, but to the glass."[28] In *De filiatione Dei*, Cusa describes our minds as different types of mirrors; in *De beryllo*, in terms of the concave and convex surfaces of a translucent stone. In *De ludo globi*, Cusa imagines the mind's quest for truth as spirals of a spinning ball marked with concave and convex surfaces; in *De possest*, he imagines it as a spinning top. In *De visione Dei*, Cusa employs a trick perspective portrait to show us how we can see that we cannot see God.

Seeking a *definite* form for the indefinite, Cusa both relies upon and subverts Alberti's model of right perspective. Since Cusa's God is the invisible source of the visible, Cusa reasons that not only must we see that we cannot see God, but we must see God as that which cannot be seen. And he employs trick perspectives to that end. Whereas most perspective paintings seek to hide their art, trick perspectives—an extension of the perspective system—foreground the illusions through which right perspective is constructed. One type of trick perspective, the anamorphic picture, reverses the traditional positions of right and erring spectatorship. The spectator must literally shape (*morphe*) again (*ana*) the image in order to see it correctly. Seen from straight on, the anamorph presents a blurred and distorted image; only when viewed from a specific oblique angle does the image become recognizable. In 1598, when the German traveler Hentzner saw the anamorphic portrait of Edward VI (figure 2) in Whitehall, he described it as follows: "A portrait of Edward VI King of England: at first sight a representation of some monstrosity; but if it be looked at straight through the hole in the lid or shutter, with which the picture is covered, it is seen in its proper proportions."[29] Holbein's *Ambassadors* (1533) may well be the best-known anamorphic picture, although only one section of it is really painted according to anamorphic principles. Seen from a certain angle, the

[27]Cusa, *The Vision of God*, 8.

[28]Cusa, *Nicholas of Cusa on God as Not-Other: A Translation and an Appraisal of "De li non aliud,"* trans. Jasper Hopkins (Minneapolis: University of Minnesota Press, 1979), 9.

[29]Hentzner quoted and translated by James B. Shaw, "The Perspective Picture: A Freak of German Sixteenth-Century Art," *Apollo* 6 (1927), 213.

Figure 2. William Scrots, anamorphic portrait of Edward VI (1546), oil on panel. Courtesy of the National Portrait Gallery, London.

streak at the bottom of the painting is revealed to be a death's head. Stephen Greenblatt explains: "It is only when one takes leave of this world—quite literally takes leave by walking away from the front of the canvas—that one can see the single alien object, the skull. The skull expresses the death that the viewer has, in effect, himself brought about by changing his perspective, by withdrawing his gaze from the figures of the painting."[30] The death's head therefore signals the death of a spectator consciousness, since we see the picture correctly only when we find ourselves as missing.

Enclosed with Cusa's *Vision of God* is a portrait whose eyes seem to follow the moving observer. This book, dedicated to the Benedictine monks at Tegernsee and composed for their spiritual meditation, includes directions for meditating upon the portrait as an icon. Its exercises require the monks to stand in different places in order to see how they are seen by the picture. In the act of observing themselves being observed, the monks may both acknowledge God's omnivoyence and imagine it. The icon provides us with a practical means of realizing that we, who can see from only a single point, can see that God sees us from all points. By instructing the brothers to see themselves being seen from a place where they cannot see themselves, Cusa enables them to see their own blindness.

Cusa's lessons may be broken down into a series of logical and not so logical steps. His first step is to acknowledge that our being is a function of God's sight: "I exist in that measure in which Thou art with me, and, since Thy look is Thy being, I am because Thou dost look at me, and if Thou didst turn Thy glance from me I should cease to be." Our visibility alone suggests to Cusa not self-consciousness but consciousness of God. Indeed, our visibility before God implies God's visibility as well. Our sight of God is no more than God seeing himself being seen: "In beholding me Thou givest Thyself to be seen of me, Thou who art a hidden God. None can see Thee save in so far as Thou grantest a sight of Thyself, nor is that sight aught else than Thy seeing him that seeth thee." As a mirror in which all is contained, God is the absolute eye that sees all things: "Thou art an Eye,

---

[30]Stephen Greenblatt, *Renaissance Self-Fashioning: From More to Shakespeare* (Chicago: University of Chicago Press, 1980), 20. See also Jacques Lacan, "Anamorphosis," *The Four Fundamental Concepts of Psycho-Analysis,* ed. Jacques-Alain Miller, trans. Alan Sheridan (New York: Norton, 1981), 88.

since with Thee having is being, wherefore in Thyself Thou dost observe all things." In contrast, the human eye is a limited mirror that can reflect only that to which it is turned: "If in me my seeing were an eye, as 'tis in Thee, my God, then in myself I should see all things, since the eye is like a mirror." We are human precisely because we cannot see as we are seen: "If I were to see as I am seen I should not be a creature." Yet God can see himself being seen: "And if Thou, God, didst not see as Thou art seen Thou wouldest not be God Almighty. Thou art to be seen of all creatures, and Thou seest all; in that Thou seest all, Thou art seen of all; for otherwise creatures could not exist, since they exist by Thy seeing. If they saw not Thee who seest them, they would not receive from Thee being; the being of the creature is Thy seeing and the being seen of Thee alike."[31]

Cusa often seems less concerned with the knowledge that God sees us than with the realization that we can see that we cannot see (God) in a precise manner. Shakespearean comedy similarly figures that which escapes both logic and vision in its games with right spectatorship. Like Cusa, Shakespeare stages both the eye that sees and the gaze that sees that the eye doesn't see. But in Shakespearean comedy it is the mind, rather than God, that sees itself seen as that which can never be seen. In Shakespearean comedy, the mind's eye is a mirror precisely because we can see ourselves both as actors and as audience to ourselves as actors. Shakespeare's characters derive place and position by referring to an unseen and inaccessible space within. Viola knows that she is not who she is. Hamlet not only delays, but knows he doesn't know why he delays. As Renaissance games with the gaze become more complex and more internalized, God as the all-seeing other is displaced by the community as other, which in turn is displaced by an internalized other—whether soul, social conscience, or unconscious—as that point with which we can never merge. Whether we desire to be seen from the imagined viewpoint of either God or the unconscious, we still posit a point outside of consciousness to figure the limitations of consciousness. The mind meditating upon its meditations provides the means for rethinking "right spectatorship."

[31]Cusa, *The Vision of God*, 16, 19–20, 37, 47.

III

The Renaissance fascination with the discovery and displacement of a spectator consciousness helps explain the revival of a tradition of learned ignorance. The pedagogical model attacked within Shakespeare's plays is based on a simple contrast between ignorance and knowledge, according to which knowledge is defined as the memorization of facts and teaching is defined as the art of discipline toward that end. Consider how the kindly but inept schoolteacher Master Evans questions William in his "accidence" (Latin grammar):

> Evans.   What is *lapis*, William?
> Will.   A stone.
> Evans.   And what is "a stone," William?
> Will.   A pebble.
> Evans.   No; it is *lapis*. I pray you remember in your prain.
> Will.   Lapis.
>
> (*The Merry Wives of Windsor*: 4.1.31–37)

The relieved mother concludes: "He is a better scholar than I thought he was," and Sir Hugh concurs: "He is a good sprag memory" (4.1.80–82). William may be less reliant on his book than Master Slender, but one obvious lesson of the play is that William indeed "profits nothing . . . at his book" (4.1.15), since generative learning is forbidden. The only pedagogical model upheld in Shakespeare's plays is demonstrated by clowns and fools, who employ paradox, humor, and double-binding interrogations to displace mastery and to generate learned ignorance.

The dramatic interplay between these two types of learning takes center stage in *The Taming of the Shrew*. The play within the play opens with a deferral of plans to return to the University of Padua— the home of the new learning, and alma mater of Toscanelli and Cusa. Lucentio, newly come to Padua to study at this famous university, decides to ditch the new learning in favor of love: "O this learning, what a thing it is!" (1.2.159). Ironically, Lucentio must pose as a schoolmaster to win Bianca's love, and the type of teacher he portrays explains his antipathy toward the university. A teacher of Greek, Latin, and other languages, Lucentio has as his chief duty to

21

train Bianca to construe her verbs with the use of Ovid's *Heroides* and *Metamorphoses*. As a schoolmaster of music and mathematics, Hortensio teaches the gamut, or diatonic scale, by the same method of rote learning.

However distasteful we find both Petruchio's teaching methods and his lessons, we cannot deny that his country house is indeed referred to as a school, that he is referred to as a schoolmaster, and that a recognizable teaching *style* is employed there. Petruchio's pedagogical style not only parodies the rote-learning method but anticipates the style of the various wise fools in the tragedies, comedies, and histories that follow. In response to Kate's question "Where did you study all this goodly speech?" Petruchio answers: "It is extempore, from my mother-wit" (2.1.262–63). His answer reflects a traditional Renaissance distinction between scholarly and natural education, or between the ignorantly learned and the learnedly ignorant. Although the comedies typically associate formal schooling with an unsuccessful pedagogical model, their wise fools' interrogative style is rooted in the rich scholastic tradition of the *disputatio*.[32] Petruchio's teaching is based on interrogations that result in paradox, humor, and "double binds"—the creation of what are termed "impossible" positions.[33] Petruchio is surely an authority figure who demands that others say as he says; at the same time, however, *what* he says is nonsense. In demanding obedience to ridiculous commands, he encourages Kate to adopt a stance that openly acknowledges its obedience to folly. He repeatedly commands his student to give the right answer only when no right answer is possible. Kate can no more answer whether the sun or the moon is shining than can the audience. By frustrating its readers with equally contradictory demands, *The Taming of the Shrew* encourages us to question how we derive and define knowledge.

The critique of a spectator consciousness in Shakespeare's come-

[32]See Joel B. Altman, *The Tudor Play of Mind: Rhetorical Inquiry and the Development of Elizabethan Drama* (Berkeley: University of California Press, 1978).

[33]See the development of Gregory Bateson's work on double binds in family system therapy as outlined in Paul Watzlawick, Janet Beavin Bavelas, and Don D. Jackson, *Pragmatics of Human Communication: A Study of Interactional Patterns, Pathologies, and Paradoxes* (New York: Norton, 1967); and Paul Watzlawick, John Weakland, and Richard Fisch, *Change: Principles of Problem Formation and Problem Resolution* (New York: Norton, 1974).

dies takes on added interest when read in the context of Cusa's optical experiments. For example, insofar as the title *The Taming of the Shrew* refers both to the play within the play and to its frame plot, we can never determine where the play proper begins or ends. Throughout this early comedy a position of spectatorship is contained by that which it observes: audiences are redefined as players, and players as audiences. Christopher Sly is both an onstage audience to the play *The Taming of the Shrew* and an unwitting actor trapped in a series of supposes; the beggar's reactions to being treated as a lord form yet another play, which frames the one he observes. Just as Sly is unaware that the lord is playing the role of his servant, so the actors who arrive to perform for the lord are unaware that Sly is not a lord. Unwittingly caught on stage, Sly is trapped when the lord views him as such, yet freed from this trap when he acknowledges his part and speedily recognizes his "madam wife." Similarly, at first Kate is an unwitting spectacle for the Paduans; Tranio dubs her appearance "some show to welcome us to town" (1.1.47). Later, Kate is forced to play audience to Petruchio's dramatic portrayal of her role as shrew. Her final submission speech is as paradoxical and as theatrical as the game she plays with Vincentio on the road back to Padua. Rather than dispute whether Kate is tamed or freed, I am concerned here with the cognitive paradox that renders such distinctions problematic. Kate has learned to be a spectator to herself as an actor, and so to conceive of herself as simultaneously inside and outside of the world of play.

We cannot settle precisely the relationship between technology and epistemology, but we can prove that Shakespeare's model of learned ignorance employs perspectival models to displace a spectator consciousness. At the level of plot, the comedies typically contrast the erring sight of folly with the right sight of reason only to confuse the two and so question their relationship. If the characters in *The Taming of the Shrew* appear to move away from erring vision and toward right vision as "right supremacy" (5.2.109), the play also concludes as a paradox that can't be deciphered; the "wonder" is that it is impossible to tell whether or not Kate is pretending to be tamed. At the beginning of *A Midsummer Night's Dream*, patriarchal perspective is openly equated with right sight and in turn contrasted with the erring sight of the infatuated lovers; at its close right and erring sight are successfully confused with each other. By the end of each of these comedies, right and erring vision have changed places so often that we are thoroughly confused about what does and should constitute right vision.

Rather than encourage us to adopt one viewpoint, Shakespeare's comedies play upon the relation of the knowable to the unknown as a changing constant that alone makes identity and proportion possible. *The Comedy of Errors*, for example, mocks right perspective through the development of contradictory perspectives on a single day's events. The limitations inherent in any single viewpoint within the play remind us of the problems inherent in discovering a correct perspective upon it. Ernest Gilman explains: "The very fullness and definition of perspective space implies the radical incompleteness of our vision, and the point of view becomes a drastic limitation, a set of blinders, as well as an epistemological privilege."[34] Right interpretation is presented as a virtual impossibility, requiring 360 degrees of viewing space and 120 minutes of absolute presence perfectly comprehended by one mind. Since individual viewpoint hampers rather than guarantees true sight, right interpretation is necessarily a communal activity. Yet even the group account pieced together at the conclusion of *The Comedy of Errors* is an ideal that can never be sustained. The play ultimately champions not objective truth but erring as truth, insofar as it traces the role of errors and repression in any stance of mastery. The denied usurping twin perspective with which one can never merge—be it unconscious, alterego, or demon; negation, disavowal, or repression—radically undermines any principle of identity. Truth is portrayed as that which wanders errantly and can never be pinned down.

From *The Comedy of Errors* to *Twelfth Night*, Shakespeare was developing perspectival plays that could never be seen correctly. The almost mathematical plotting of errors in Shakespeare's early comedies suggests a confident mastery of spatial relations both in terms of plot construction and play production. Perspective graphs help us to imagine the intricate relation among staging, perspective, and multiple plots. They also suggest why Shakespeare was likely to think of erring vision in terms of physical or psychological blind spots that yield positive, measurable knowledge. The early seventeenth-century graph by Jan Vredeman de Vries (figure 3), for example, calls to

---

[34]Gilman, *Curious Perspective*, 31.

Figure 3. Jan Vredeman de Vries, *Perspectiva* (Leiden, 1604–5). Reproduced courtesy of the Bancroft Library, University of California, Berkeley.

mind a dramatic narrative based on the precise intersection of multiple viewpoints. To enter the room is to become entangled in a complex set of intersecting gazes.

The Elizabethan theater in the round offered an unusually provocative physical site for the performance of plays fascinated with subverting the truth of any private, individual, or fixed vantage point. The multiple playing spaces of Shakespeare's theater encouraged him to play such spaces off against one another and to emphasize psychological blind spots with the use of physical blind spots. In *Hamlet*, Polonius is physically removed from view while spying on Hamlet, whereas Hamlet is unable to see himself in his quest for self-knowledge. Shakespearean drama recurrently plays upon distinctions between flat and round characters, naturalistic and illusionistic acting styles, two- and three-dimensional spaces, reciprocal and non-reciprocal viewing, and individual and multiple viewpoints to figure the representational paradoxes in which Western models of subjectivity are entangled. The dream of seeing oneself seeing oneself, whether in theater or psychoanalysis, is the fantasy of completed vision which Renaissance theater exposes as such.

Character would seem to provide the most obvious connection between perspective and the unseen space that we now term the unconscious. Yet only in Shakespeare's tragedies does the exploration of character reach a point of complexity in any way comparable to Freud's case histories. The more dispersed focus on general principles of psychological functioning in Shakespeare's comedies anticipates Freud's early work on the representation of unconscious processes. Given their focus on principles of idealization, negation, errors, humor, and dreams, the comedies may be said to work at the margins of representability. Shakespeare's early comedies focus on intersecting, erring perspectives generated by the plot; the later comedies gradually internalize the intersecting perspectives of the plot machinery within specific characters. Critics often complain that both plot and characters are unsatisfactorily integrated in *The Comedy of Errors* but ignore the play's exploration of the problem of integrating contradictory perspectives into a unified subject. As early as *The Merchant of Venice*, and certainly by *Twelfth Night*, however, Shakespeare's comic characters are both unified and split; they know that they are harboring thoughts hidden even to themselves. Round characters in this theater in the round are possible only insofar as the plays map out an interior place of unknowingness. By pointing to a certain absence within, these characters derive presence. In *The Merchant of Venice*, for example, perspective is no longer simply a function of physical space but a result of a split consciousness. Antonio complains:

> In sooth, I know not why I am so sad;
> It wearies me, you say it wearies you;
> But how I caught it, found it, or came by it,
> What stuff 'tis made of, whereof it is born,
> I am to learn;
> And such a want-wit sadness makes of me,
> That I have much ado to know myself.
>
> (1.1.1–7)

As early as *Richard II*, Shakespeare employs an anamorphic painting to figure the hidden spaces of the psyche. Richard's queen confides, "I know no cause / Why I should welcome such a guest as Grief" (2.2.6–7), and explains why:

> conceit is still deriv'd
> From some forefather grief; mine is not so,
> For nothing hath begot my something grief,
> Or something hath the nothing that I grieve—
> 'Tis in reversion that I do possess—
> But what it is that is not yet known what,
> I cannot name; 'tis nameless woe, I wot.
>
> (2.2.34–40)

With the help of trick perspectives, however, her nameless woe is given a local habitation and a name. In the course of dismissing the queen's grief as a result of "false sorrow's eye, / Which for things true weeps things imaginary" (2.2.26–27), Sir John Bushy puts her sorrow into perspective:

> Each substance of a grief hath twenty shadows,
> Which shows like grief itself, but is not so;
> For sorrow's eyes, glazed with blinding tears,
> Divides one thing entire to many objects,
> Like perspectives, which rightly gaz'd upon
> Show nothing but confusion; ey'd awry
> Distinguish form.
>
> (2.2.14–20)

Critics have disputed Shakespeare's model of perspective in this speech: "twenty shadows" suggests a perspective glass that multiplies images like a funhouse mirror; "eye'd awry," however, suggests an anamorph.[35]

Although Shakespeare's familiarity with the perspective tradi-

---

[35]See Gilman's reading of this speech in his chapter "*Richard II* and the Perspectives of History," ibid., 88–128.

tion is well established,[36] his conflation of various types of perspectives has been the occasion of some concern. Shakespeare's Sonnet 24 refers to perspective in Alberti's terms, as "painter's art":

> Mine eye hath play'd the painter and hath [stell'd]
> Thy beauty's form in table of my heart;
> My body is the frame wherein 'tis held,
> And perspective it is best painter's art.
> For through the painter must you see his skill,
> To find where your true image pictur'd lies,
> Which in my bosom's shop is hanging still,
> That hath his windows glazed with thine eyes.
>
> (1–8)

Yet Shakespeare also used the word *perspective* to refer to a perspective glass, which could make an object look larger or smaller, fragmented or doubled. In *Twelfth Night*, Orsino responds to the discovery of the twins by remarking: "One face, one voice, one habit, and two persons, / A natural perspective, that is and is not!" (5.1.216–17). In other plays, Shakespeare employs the term to refer to a trick portrait that presents different images from different points of view, as in Cleopatra's response to Antony's marriage: "Let him for ever go—let him not, Charmian— / Though he be painted one way like a Gorgon, / The other way's a Mars" (*Antony and Cleopatra*: 2.5.115–17). Ernest Gilman attributes this seemingly confused use of the term *perspective* to the fact that "in the visual arts England had barely felt the impact of the Renaissance before the end of the sixteenth century, and when it did the succession of continental styles were more or less simultaneously available as options."[37] Joan Gadol reminds us that trick perspectives are also perspectival works, for a perspective picture refers to a picture constructed according to a precise system of

[36]In *Shakespeare and the Arts of Design*, Fairchild argues that it is likely that Shakespeare visited the Steelyard and the winehouse there, and so had firsthand knowledge of Holbein's paintings, a number of which were on display in the guildhall before the German merchants were expelled (107). More specific proof of Shakespeare's familiarity with the perspective tradition may be found in Ernest Gilman's *Curious Perspective*, which offers a thorough account of Shakespeare's use of perspective, as does John Greenwood's *Shifting Perspectives and the Stylish Style*.

[37]Gilman, *Curious Perspective*, 52.

projection, regardless of the means by which that system is constructed.[38] Even though Shakespeare used the term *perspective* more loosely than we do today, he was clearly familiar with a variety of types of trick perspectives, and he employed them to figure hidden thoughts and emotions as the erring vision of the imagination.

Claudio Guillén describes how *Richard II* uses perspective to portray how "grief becomes accessible or visible to other men"—particularly through its "images presenting hollowness, emptiness, or the relationship between a contained thing and its container" and its stress on the relationship "between the empty crown, the bucket, and the suffering soul." Since the medieval system of symbolic correspondences between body and soul assured their unity, he reasons, "writers did not pretend, or feel the necessity, to portray inwardness independently from outer appearances." Yet by the sixteenth century, Guillén concludes, the correspondence between the physical and the spiritual is no longer assured: "The challenge which Shakespeare faces in this sense is the portrayal of the *homo interior* by means of visible action on the stage."[39] If this is indeed the challenge Shakespeare faced, trick perspectives helped him to dramatize if not to resolve that challenge. Much as Freud constructed a subject by reference to the unconscious, Shakespeare constructs self-conscious characters by having them refer to an unseen space within. By generating blind spots in a field of vision through trick perspectives, Shakespearean drama stages the unseen space of our being which Freud later rediscovers there.

IV

"The idea of perspective can be readily associated with a growing epistemological dualism," Guillén observes, "with a rigorous split between subject and object, as in the Cartesian distinction between mind and *res extensa*."[40] By the same logic, trick perspectives may be associated with a reaction against epistemological dualism. When

[38]Gadol, *Alberti*, 39.

[39]Claudio Guillén, "On the Concept and Metaphor of Perspective," in *Comparatists at Work: Studies in Comparative Literature*, ed. Stephen G. Nichols, Jr., and Richard B. Vowles (Waltham, Mass.: Blaisdell, 1968), 44–45.

[40]Ibid., 34.

Foucault draws our attention to the blind spot Velázquez concealed "under the painter's gaze" in *Las meninas*, he points us in the direction of emerging models of subjectivity: "We are observing ourselves being observed by the painter," he explains, "and made visible to his eyes by the same light that enables us to see him. And just as we are about to apprehend ourselves, transcribed by his hand as though in a mirror, we find that we can in fact apprehend nothing of that mirror but its lustreless back. The other side of a psyche."[41] Renaissance trick perspectives offered a means of studying the other side of the psyche by exploring how the spectator is never outside of that which she perceives. In this way they anticipated an epistemology based on the subversion of a spectator consciousness. "It is in Vignola and in Alberti that we find the progressive interrogation of the geometral laws of perspective," Lacan asserts, "and it is around research on perspective that is centred a privileged interest for the domain of vision—whose relation with the institution of the Cartesian subject, which is itself a sort of geometral point, a point of perspective, we cannot fail to see."[42]

Since Renaissance faculty psychology relied on the cognitive models offered by geometrical optics, Elizabethans were highly attuned to the play of delusion in their representations of the mind. Freud was the first to stress the importance of optics to psychoanalysis, and so to forge a connection between Renaissance and modern models of the mind: "We should picture the instrument which carries out our mental functions as resembling a compound microscope or a photographic apparatus, or something of the kind. On that basis, psychical locality will correspond to a point inside the apparatus at which one of the preliminary stages of an image comes into being. In the microscope and telescope, as we know, these occur in part at ideal points, regions in which no tangible component of the apparatus is situated."[43] Lacan follows suit by urging psychoanalysis to return to optics. The French rereading of Freud reminds us that the ego is a delusory centric point, always already in representation. And this return addresses the paradoxical models of self-representation we discover in Renaissance literature more directly than do the mod-

[41]Foucault, *Order of Things*, 6.
[42]Lacan, "Anamorphosis," 86.
[43]Freud, *Interpretation of Dreams*, SE, 5:536.

els currently offered by American ego psychology. In his introductory remarks to Jean Laplanche's *Life and Death in Psychoanalysis*, Jeffrey Mehlman argues that "whereas the 'American' (ego psychological) scheme thrives on its ignorance of the 'French' one, the latter mediates nothing so much as an elaborate theory of the inevitability of the error entailed by the former."[44] Ego psychology is problematic not because it fails to "apply" to Renaissance literature but because it fails to consider the first lesson of that branch of Renaissance psychology known as optics, which requires that we acknowledge the delusory play of the senses in the construction of images. Laplanche, a former student of Lacan's, explores how Freud's shifting definitions of the ego both expose and repress the ego's duplicity. In *The Ego and the Id*, Freud maintains that "the ego is first and foremost a bodily ego; it is not merely a surface entity, but is itself the projection of a surface." At another point in the same work, he declares that the ego's characteristic activities of representing and binding explain its ability to pass itself off as an intending subject: "When the ego assumes the features of the object, it is forcing itself, so to speak, upon the id as a love-object and is trying to make good the id's loss by saying: 'Look, you can love me too—I am so like the object.' "[45]

Since the ego substitutes itself for various love-objects, Laplanche reasons, "the ego is indeed an object, but a kind of relay object, capable of passing itself off, in a more or less deceptive and usurpatory manner, as a designing and wishing subject." But who is being deceived? According to Laplanche: "What is at stake here . . . is the *actually* ambiguous status of the ego: the ego, even though it is a reservoir of the libido cathecting it, can appear to be a *source*; it is not the subject of desire or wishes, nor even the site in which the drive originates . . . but it *can pass itself off as such*. A love object, the ego 'puts out' libido; it supplements and replaces love by positing itself as a loving subject." He concludes by warning us against "partaking in *a delusion which is not simply that of the advocates of 'ego psychology,' but of the ego itself.*"[46]

Lacan's mirror stage correlates these opposing ego functions by

---

[44]Jeffrey Mehlman, Translator's Introduction to Jean Laplanche, *Life and Death in Psychoanalysis* (Baltimore: Johns Hopkins University Press, 1976), x.

[45]Freud, *The Ego and the Id* (1923), *SE*, 19:26, 30.

[46]Laplanche, *Life and Death in Psychoanalysis*, 66, 74, 82.

figuring the ego as an *instance* of deceptive self-reference *initiated* by the recognition of an image of the unified body surface. Lacan posits a primary homeomorphic identification based on stimulation in an animal by another of its kind. But that unity is only provided by an external image assumed by the subject before full control over motor coordination is achieved. The visual stimulus of a gestalt of one's own species sets into play various psychic as well as physiological processes that in turn serve as the basis for later (secondary) identifications with others. According to Lacan, the mirror stage can "exhibit in an exemplary situation the symbolic matrix in which the *I* is precipitated in a primordial form, before it is objectified in the dialectic of identification with the other, and before language restores to it, in the universal, its function as subject." This spatial mapping thus "situates the agency of the ego, before its social determination, in a fictional direction."[47]

For Lacan, the ego is not a function of intentional consciousness but a delusory site of unity which always plays out its misrecognitions. Secondary identification with the culturally specific other, or the ideal reflection of the parental image, further decenters as it procures a reference point. The desire to be recognized by the other, so common to dramatic narrative, is evidence, finally, of the fundamental *misrecognition* through which subjectivity is procured. The assumption of the mirror image in the construction of the ego is the primary misrecognition, which in turn is rehearsed in our demand that others see us as we would see ourselves. The use of the other as a means of replaying this fantasy of wholeness is suggested by tragic and comic plots that play out this misrecognition in narrative form. Freud's various definitions of the ego—as a *projection* of the body surface, as a mechanism for identificatory processes, and as an object-turned-subject—are reread by Lacan as unfolding progressions in psychic functioning set into play by the spatial lure of the other's image. Since theatricality exposes the mask as a constitutive displacement and misrecognition, the tension between theatrical mask and dramatic narrative foregrounds the fiction of a spectator consciousness.

To figure primary and secondary identification, Lacan refers us

[47]Lacan, "The Mirror Stage," *Ecrits: A Selection*, trans. Alan Sheridan (New York: Norton, 1977), 2.

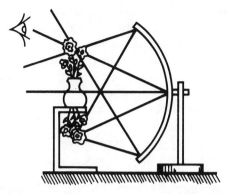

Figure 4. Lacan's diagram of primary identification, *The Seminar of Jacques Lacan,* bk. 1: *Freud's Papers on Technique, 1953–1954,* ed. Jacques-Alain Miller, trans. John Forrester, English translation © Cambridge University Press, 1988. First American edition (New York: W. W. Norton, 1988), 78. Used with the permission of W. W. Norton & Company, Inc.

to the famous optical experiment of the inverted bouquet in which a spherical mirror produces an upright image of an object that is placed both upside down and out of sight. For Lacan, this experiment functions as a heuristic model according to which "we can portray for ourselves the subject of the time before the birth of the ego, and the appearance of the latter." The experiment (see figure 4) works as follows: to the left of a spheric mirror sits a box whose open side faces the mirror and whose top reaches near its center. Within the box sits a bouquet of flowers; on top of the box is placed a vase. When we look into the mirror from the appropriate angle, the flowers appear right side up and contained by the vase. Lacan concludes: "the image of the body . . . is like the imaginary vase which contains the bouquet of real flowers."[48] But how?

For Lacan, the image of the vase functions as a container, much as the image of the body surface functions as a formative gestalt. During the mirror stage, the infant maps itself out spatially, introjecting and projecting a unified body surface or mirror image. These alternating mechanisms of expulsion and absorption, of projection and

[48]Lacan, *The Seminar of Jacques Lacan,* bk. 1: *Freud's Papers on Technique, 1953–1954,* ed. Jacques-Alain Miller, trans. John Forrester (New York: Norton, 1988), 79.

introjection, are based on the ability to visualize a containing and limiting function. Through this enabling image, visible and invisible, container and contained, a whole and its parts are structurally interrelated. The subject's relation to an inaccessible real (flowers) through the reflection of a containing body image (vase) enables it to structure its world, to set container and contained into an imaginary relationship. The gestalt of the containing image thus sets into motion processes of identification, projection, and introjection essential to the structuration of both fantasy and reality.

Lacan posits that we find ourselves not only through primary identification with the body surface but through secondary identification with the images of others. In order to figure secondary identification, he places an inverted vase inside the box, places the bouquet of flowers on top of that box, and directs the spectator to stand with her back to a spherical mirror that reverses the image of the vase (see figure 5). When the spectator looks into a plane mirror that reflects both the real flowers and the inverted reflection of the vase, the result is an image of a vase filled with flowers, as in the first instance, yet achieved in a more complex fashion. Since from one perspective we can see that these two images are constructed differently, and from another angle we cannot, the experiment offers an analogy of the means by which the ego displaces the love object and presents itself as a desiring subject. As in a love relationship, the relation between container and contained is twice removed, since the subject is doubly alienated from the source of its own image. Secondary identification re-covers the impossibility of owning the idealized image and so plays out a fundamental alienation that is expressed in relationships of desire, aggressivity, and rivalry. These optical experiments can therefore illustrate how the ego functions at various levels simultaneously—as container and thing contained, as subject and object, as a mechanism of spatial location and as a displaced and displacing actor trapped in its own identificatory mirages.

In comparison with these optical experiments, the paradoxes in Shakespearean comedy are easy to trace. The comedies corroborate Lacan's insight that "where the subject sees himself . . . it is not from there that he looks at himself."[49] One thinks of Kate's elusive metadramatic stance at the conclusion of *The Taming of the Shrew*, of Hal's

[49]Lacan, "Analysis and Truth," *Four Fundamental Concepts*, 144.

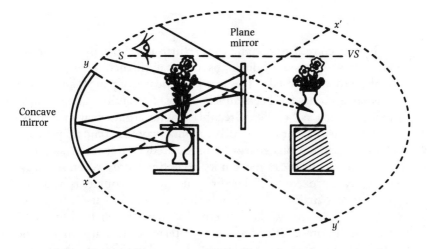

Figure 5. Lacan's diagram of secondary identification, *The Seminar of Jacques Lacan*, bk. 1: *Freud's Papers on Technique, 1953–1954*, ed. Jacques-Alain Miller, trans. John Forrester, English translation © Cambridge University Press, 1988. First American edition (New York: W. W. Norton, 1988), 139. Used with the permission of W. W. Norton & Company, Inc.

place both within and outside of the plot he supposedly stages in *1 Henry IV*, and of the rigorous distance that Viola seeks to maintain from her role in *Twelfth Night* as she announces: "I am not what I am" (3.1.141). These characters pronounce themselves to be images and laugh at those who would find in them a different kind of truth. Witness Olivia, invited by Cesario to remove one of a series of veils: "Look you, sir, such a one I was this present. Is't not well done?" (1.5.234–35). Juxtaposing I's in a flurry of flirtation, exchanging self for mask and other for self, Olivia stages the inevitability of self-usurpation. One thinks of Viola's question to Olivia: "Are you the lady of the house?" and Olivia's reply: "If I do not usurp myself, I am" (1.5.184–86). Yet Olivia must usurp herself in the very act of naming herself. That she is not in control of herself or her household, that she is not equivalent with herself, becomes increasingly evident even to her. By tracing such misrecognitions, Shakespearean comedy centers and decenters the subject as it circles about in fantasied appropriation of its mirror image, thereby staging the rivalry between ego and persona in the construction of subjectivity.

V

The French return to Freud thus returns psychoanalysis to optics and in turn suggests the value of psychoanalytic theory for the study of Shakespearean comedy. The attack on the use of psychoanalysis in Renaissance studies has been launched most forcefully of late by new historicists such as Stephen Greenblatt, who argues that in Renaissance literature "identity is conceived in a way that renders psychoanalytic interpretations marginal or belated." Greenblatt suggests that "psychoanalysis can redeem its belatedness only when it historicizes its own procedures." The first question, of course, is how one defines psychoanalytic theory, whether one equates it with "interpretation" or "identity," and whether one could ever read in a way that is not "belated." If one accepts the terms of this argument, one would have to agree that gender is conceived in the Renaissance in a way that necessarily renders feminist analyses belated, or that property is conceived of in a way that renders cultural-materialist studies "belated." Despite his admission that "the self as Freud depicts it is bound up not with secure possession but with instability and loss," Greenblatt asserts that "the intensity of Freud's vision of alienation would seem . . . to depend upon the dream of authentic possession, even if that possession is never realized and has never been securely established."[50] After duly observing that Freudian theory itself condemns this rhetoric of authenticity, he worries that Freudian theory nevertheless depends upon what it denies. Reasoning like Brutus on Caesar's death, Greenblatt envisions psychoanalysis as a serpent's egg that must be killed in the shell. Greenblatt is correct in urging psychoanalysis to historicize its procedures, but his own failure to do so is evident in his equation of psychoanalysis with American ego psychology and in his argument that psychoanalysis may be defined by the specific nature of its concerns—sexuality and aggression.

[50]Stephen Greenblatt, "Psychoanalysis and Renaissance Culture," in *Literary Theory and Renaissance Texts*, ed. Patricia Parker and David Quint (Baltimore: Johns Hopkins University Press, 1986), 221, 213. For the relation between contemporary psychoanalytic theory and Renaissance texts, see William Kerrigan, "The Articulation of the Ego in the English Renaissance," in *The Literary Freud: Mechanisms of Defense and the Poetic Will*, ed. Joseph Smith (New Haven: Yale University Press, 1980), 261–308.

Rather, psychoanalysis is better understood in the context of a tradition of learned ignorance and in terms of the strategies it employs for generating an awareness of blindness.

One can disarm the almost uncanny resistance that psychoanalysis is capable of generating by admitting the obvious: there has always been something *troubled* as well as *troubling* about psychoanalysis, and this *trouble* helps to explain both its power and its limitations. Not only do statistical studies question the therapeutic success of psychoanalysis, but cultural studies point to its gender and class bias.[51] The means by which power and knowledge are interrelated offers another road of attack; analyst François Roustang critiques analytic knowledge on the basis of its transmission through the transference and training of analysands.[52]

Putting to one side the issue of therapeutic value, let us assume that psychoanalysis is not a science and does not function like one. Rather than seek to secure a *place* for psychoanalysis, we might find value in its ability to *displace*. Since psychoanalytic theory studies that which by definition cannot be known (the unconscious), it holds philosophical interest as a self-subversive methodology in search of an object. As a critique of knowledge which subverts itself, psychoanalysis works through the problematics of the place of its own scene as a means of generating an awareness of blindness. Its distinctive merit and liability alike, as Stephen Melville explains, reside in its power to place itself in relation to what is unknown:

> Psychoanalysis finds its object in *ein anderer Schauplatz*. It is in the name of its privileged access to this other place that psychoanalysis moves into other disciplines and appropriates their objects to its own. But such a movement depends first of all on the ability of this presumed science to secure itself; its own place is not directly given but must be achieved. . . . Psychoanalysis has, in the very nature of its object, an interest in and

[51]Gilles Deleuze and Félix Guattari, *Anti-Oedipus: Capitalism and Schizophrenia*, trans. Robert Hurley, Mark Seem, and Helen R. Lane (Minneapolis: University of Minnesota Press, 1983). For an overview of feminist psychoanalytic criticism, see *The (M)other Tongue: Essays in Feminist Psychoanalytic Interpretation*, ed. Shirley Nelson Garner, Claire Kahane, Madelon Sprengnether (Ithaca: Cornell University Press, 1985).
[52]François Roustang, *Dire Mastery: Discipleship from Freud to Lacan*, trans. Ned Lukacher (Baltimore: Johns Hopkins University Press, 1982).

difficulty with the concept of place as well as an interest in and difficulty with the logic of place, topology.[53]

The troubled reception of psychoanalysis is partly due to its refusal to know itself as unknowing, to recognize its virtue as a science of unknowing. Its highly ambivalent self-presentation has fueled the ambivalence with which it has been received. Within the same work Freud describes psychoanalysis as a science of how to fill in the blank and as a science that proves the impossibility of so doing. Some critics emphasize Freud's statements on the undecidability of meaning at the expense of the more reductive pronouncements that surround them. But the most valuable recent studies of psychoanalytic theory refuse to choose—or choose instead to explore what these contradictions can teach us.[54] Shoshana Felman champions Freud's teaching as "unprecedented" "in that [it] . . . turns back upon itself so as to subvert itself."[55] And even Roustang claims: "The situation of analytic theory cannot be taken as a weakness or a failing that must be overcome, but as its nervous center, or its specific nature. No form of rationality can resist what the unconscious has to say, no rationality can account for the unconscious without misunderstanding it later on, and yet the unconscious cannot be recognized and cannot even be formulated as a hypothesis without an effort at rationality, without the goal of scientificity."[56]

As a critique of the Western *cogito*, psychoanalysis interrogates both traditional models of knowledge and pedagogical strategies based upon them. In fact, the term *analytic* refers to a philosophical model that problematizes its own approach in a peculiar way: "If a theory is analytic," Roustang explains, "it must be continuously refounded in response to its internal difficulties, the questions that arise from its practice, and the concepts it can borrow from other disciplines."[57] Rather than a traditional discourse of knowledge, psy-

[53]Stephen Melville, "Psychoanalysis and the Place of *Jouissance*," in "The Trial(s) of Psychoanalysis," ed. Françoise Meltzer, *Critical Inquiry* 13 (Winter 1987), 350.

[54]See Samuel Weber, *The Legend of Freud* (Minneapolis: University of Minnesota Press, 1982); and Weber, *Institution and Interpretation* (Minneapolis: University of Minnesota Press, 1987); as well as Stephen W. Melville, *Philosophy beside Itself: On Deconstruction and Modernism* (Minneapolis: University of Minnesota Press, 1986).

[55]Felman, *Jacques Lacan*, 90.

[56]Roustang, *Dire Mastery*, 66.

[57]Ibid.

choanalysis was always a critique of knowledge in search of itself. Its defensiveness, its defenselessness, its need to justify its drama, forms much of its appeal. A discourse on the run, psychoanalysis boasts a peculiar ability to work with the negation and generation of meaning, so that whatever attacks it proves it and whatever attempts to define it mistakes it. Like the authorial persona of Shakespeare's plays, psychoanalysis occupies the place of displacement, since whatever the unconscious is, *it is not that.*

Resistance to psychoanalysis may well stem from its identity as that which does not have a place and therefore finds one only through the interrogating displacement of another. In analysis, the one who is ready to be questioned is never the same as the one to whom the question is addressed. Analysis has begun when one prepares to meet in the analyst that which questions one's own resistance to what one knows. The analytic dialogue rehearses the relationship between that which knows that another does not know and the other's urgency to speak, or between the voice to which one will admit what has not been admitted and the voice that refuses to admit to knowing. "Psychoanalysis is a dialectic," states Lacan, "what Montaigne, in book III, chapter VIII, calls *an art of conversation.* The art of conversation of Socrates in the *Meno* is to teach the slave to give his own speech its true meaning."[58] The art of the interlocutor, like the art of the fool, requires that we know to whom we are speaking, and who is speaking us in turn.

Lacan takes Freud's notion of psychoanalysis as a talking cure seriously; he identifies the patient's speech as the sole medium of analysis, and he defines the analyst as the embodiment of the presence to whom that speech is addressed.[59] He reads the neurotic symptom as a chain of signifiers, a dislocated if not unspeakable discourse that is always alien to the subject who speaks it, and whose speaker and hearer must be rediscovered. Whether or not a literal idiolect is possible—a secret language invented for one by one—the aim of analysis is for that conversation to be heard and given resonance by the analyst. Accordingly, analysis works by resituating, through displacement, the place of speech or the place from which one is

[58]Lacan, "The Concept of Analysis," *Freud's Papers on Technique,* 278.
[59]Lacan, "The Function and Field of Speech and Language in Psychoanalysis," *Ecrits,* 30–113, esp. 40.

spoken. When the unspeakable conversation unfolds in the presence of a third party, it is no longer the same.

In the analytic dialogue, the interlocutor is never where she is expected, nor the speech of the analysand where it is expected. Serge Leclaire explains: "It is no longer surprising today to be faced by the extraordinary situation in which the interlocutor . . . seems to have as his only preoccupation that of never showing himself where one would expect him. From the beginning, the psychoanalyst is out of the patient's field of vision."[60] This subversive tactic may be traced back to Freud's experience with a lustful patient, after which he decided to move from a position directly facing the analysand to a position directly behind the analysand. The move was a felicitous one—so much so, in fact, that one might say that Freud finds his place as an analyst when he literally moves into a position of identification with the object under study, or with the unconscious as that which cannot be seen. Freud finds himself in identification with that which is definitely there (knowledge) but nonetheless hidden (repressed). His physical dislocation reminds us of his shift from a conception of knowledge as a substance that can be quantified to a conception of knowledge as a structural dynamic, and it reminds us of the pedagogical imperative that the interlocutor must play *at* and *with* the *boundaries* of the analysand's field of vision.

Whereas Lacan is careful to emphasize the problems in any attempt to "turn psychoanalysis into the extension of the Platonic dialogue,"[61] at the same time he equates psychoanalysis with a radical pedagogy aimed at displacing the subject supposed to know. His use of the terminology of learned ignorance is therefore hardly by chance:

> The analyst must not fail to recognise what I will call the dimension of ignorance's power of accession to being. . . . He doesn't have to guide

[60]Serge Leclaire, *Psychanalyser* (Paris: Minuit, 1968), 18.

[61]Lacan, "Knowledge, Truth, Opinion," *The Seminar of Jacques Lacan*, bk. 2: *The Ego in Freud's Theory and in the Technique of Psychoanalysis, 1954–55*, ed. Jacques-Alain Miller, trans. Sylvana Tomaselli (New York: Norton, 1988), 20. The participants in Lacan's seminar question this disavowal, as do a number of recent studies on the relation of Socratic dialogue to the psychoanalytic session. See Tullio Maranhão, *Therapeutic Discourse and Socratic Dialogue: A Cultural Critique* (Madison: University of Wisconsin Press, 1987).

the subject to a *Wissen*, to knowledge, but on to the paths by which access to this knowledge is gained. He must engage him in a dialectical operation, not say to him that he is wrong since he necessarily is in error, but show him that he speaks poorly, that is to say that he speaks without knowing, as one who is ignorant, because what counts are the paths of his error. . . . In other words, the position of the analyst must be that of an *ignorantia docta*, which does not mean knowing [*savante*], but formal, and what is capable of being formative for the subject. . . . If the psychoanalyst thinks he knows something . . . then that is already the beginning of his loss.[62]

VI

That psychoanalysis has borrowed from other disciplines or failed to record its debts is of less interest here than how those disciplines—theater, in particular—function within it as its repressed and uncanny other. Since Freud acknowledges that Sophocles and Shakespeare taught him about the unconscious, about transference, and about the use of dialogue to interrogate blindness, it is more than coincidental that literary works alien to modern notions of subjectivity can be used to illustrate key psychoanalytic principles. Felman reminds us that Sophocles' *Oedipus* functions as a tutor text on the nature of the psychoanalytic transference—the process whereby the analysand projects a major relationship onto the analyst.[63] Further, its dialogue openly sets forth a structuring dialectic that critiques a stance of mastery. Initially, we join both chorus and protagonist by casting Teiresias in the position of the subject supposed to know, according to his role as prophet. Yet Teiresias immediately disavows any access to truth: "Alas, how terrible is wisdom when it brings no profit to the man that's wise! This I knew well, but had forgotten it, else I would not have come here." If Teiresias knew this but forgot it, then it is his forgetting of what he knows about knowledge itself that is at issue. We not only forget, but what we forget it that we forget. In this sense, knowledge is not simply a fact to be remembered or

[62]Lacan, "The Concept of Analysis," 278.

[63]See Shoshana Felman, "Beyond Oedipus: The Specimen Story of Psychoanalysis," *Modern Language Notes* 98 (1983), 1021–53; and her reading of *Oedipus* in *Jacques Lacan*, 82–83.

forgotten but a fact regarding the nature of forgetting and remembering.

Despite this lesson, Oedipus still trusts in a model of knowledge as a transmittable commodity that need not entail subverting a position of mastery: "You'd rob us of this your gift of prophecy," he complains. But Teiresias stands firm: "I will not bring to the light of day my troubles, mine—rather than call them yours." At first Teiresias plays the ideal analyst in his adamant refusal to provide an answer: "Why is it you question me and waste your labour? I will tell you nothing." But soon Teiresias responds to Oedipus's request to speak by asking, "Did you not understand before or would you provoke me into speaking?" Finally, to the query "And who has taught you truth? Not your profession surely," Teiresias answers: "You have taught me, for you have made me speak against my will."[64] Since Teiresias now experiences the urgency to speak, and only at the prodding of Oedipus, their role reversal anticipates the analytic countertransference, according to which the analyst also projects a former relationship onto the analysand. Lacan explains that "as soon as the subject . . . supposed to know exists somewhere . . . there is transference."[65]

We may conclude that theatricality, psychoanalysis, and pedagogy alike provide a model for knowing ignorance through dialogue. Each is an interrogative performance art that stages knowledge as a structure rather than a substance; each is concerned with the structure of a recognition that reorganizes the relationship of ignorance to knowledge. Each has the goal of repositioning the desiring subject in relation to ignorance, knowledge, and a subject supposed to know. The subject supposed to know is a mirroring other—whether teacher to student, analyst to analysand, or antagonist to protagonist—who feeds back to the subject her own message from an asymmetrical standpoint. Typically, that feedback both deflects the subject's aim and renders the subject's position a fallacy. The transferential quality of this dialogic model results in the analysand's urgency to speech and her rehearing of her own idiolect, so that she occupies a different

[64]Sophocles, *Oedipus the King*, trans. David Grene (Chicago: University of Chicago Press, 1954), 23–25.

[65]Lacan, "Of the Subject Who Is Supposed to Know," *Four Fundamental Concepts*, 232.

position in relation to her resistances. By functioning as a mirror to an unseen space within the subject, one can stage and displace that otherness so that, for a brief moment, she can know her blindness.

Insofar as Shakespearean comedy works at the boundaries of reason, knowledge, and mastery and questions each in terms of a more radical model of learning as erring, we can use it to further our understanding of how we do not understand. To do so, however, is to privilege literature as a way of knowing. Felman asserts: "From a philosophical perspective, knowledge is mastery—that which masters its own meaning. Unlike Hegelian philosophy, which *believes it knows all that there is to know*; unlike Socratic (or contemporary post-Nietzschean) philosophy, which *believes it knows it does not know*—literature, for its part, *knows it knows but does not know the meaning of its knowledge*, does not know *what* it knows."[66] The following chapters examine texts that exemplify this peculiar form of awareness.

VII

If we discover ourselves in the Renaissance, we must also acknowledge the misrecognitions and distortions that make that recovery possible. All our readings are necessarily belated; we cannot help but seek our mirror images in the past. Hegel writes: "What is 'familiarly known' is not properly known, just for the reason that it is 'familiar.' When engaged in the process of knowing, it is the commonest form of self-deception."[67] Given the pivotal role of optical tricks in that peculiar moment of self-doubling and self-reference known as the Renaissance, the application of postmodern theory to Shakespearean drama is especially tempting. Despite the vast differences between them, both Renaissance and postmodern models of representation undermine the humanist impulse to "stand / As if a man were author of himself" (*Coriolanus* 5.3.35–36); both share a fascination with the entanglement of subjectivity in representation; and both employ representational paradoxes as a means of subverting ideals of human centrality and autonomy. But a dialogue between

[66]Felman, *Jacques Lacan*, 92.
[67]Georg Wilhelm Friedrich Hegel, *The Phenomenology of Mind*, trans. J. B. Baillie (New York: Harper, 1967), 92.

43

Figure 6. Erhard Schön, *Perspective* (1543), woodcut. Reproduced from Jurgis Baltrušaitis, *Anamorphoses* (Paris: Olivier Perrin, 1955), fig. 27.

these two models requires that we appreciate their differences as well as their similarities. Renaissance literature may *appear* to yield to postmodern paradigms because of its concern with figuring the paradoxical relationship of subjectivity to signification; yet our notions of subjectivity, signification, and paradox are quite different.

These differences are more easily conveyed in spatial terms. In the perspectival study by Erhard Schön, a student of Dürer's, human

44

Figure 7. Abraham Bosse, *Les perspecteurs* (1648), reproduced from Jurgis
Baltrušaitis, *Anamorphoses* (Paris: Olivier Perrin, 1955), fig. 14.

45

beings are tangled in a net of perspectives (figure 6). The block figures are nearly indistinguishable both from one another and from the landscape; being is a function of our construction by and submission to a divine law of perspective. As early as the 1648 sketch by Abraham Bosse, titled *Les perspecteurs* (figure 7), the group has been replaced by a triad of individuals who stand outside of the pictures they see. Still a different sense of the mind's blind spots is conveyed by M. C. Escher's work *The Print Gallery* (see figure 10, chapter 4), which depicts the individual as both separate from and entangled in the work he perceives. Compared with one another, these studies in perspective may be read to suggest the growing influence of perspective on the concept of the fully individuated human personality. Yet the prominent play of blind spots within these pictures is finally less important than the blind spots at work in the process of comparing them. Since modes of knowing are, at any time, multiple and contradictory, in question here is the process of ideological censorship that privileges one and represses another. The task of exploring how knowledge is organized differently in different cultures already partakes of the systems of exclusions and privileges that substitute homogeneity for heterogeneity.

By reading Shakespearean comedy through a postmodern lens, we both project our own desires upon it and rediscover the role of Renaissance concepts of projection and perspective in an emerging model of subjectivity. Since we can never read from a place where we are not, we can only read with an awareness of the play of distortions as we read. To attempt to eradicate our point of view is as foolish as to claim its objectivity. What Renaissance theorists suggest, instead, is that we acknowledge and work with these blind spots in our vision. Finally, our recuperation of the comedies can be no more than a study of the "accidents" in which we find them, in relation to the "accidents" in which we find ourselves.

2

A Fractured Gaze:
Theater, Cinema, Psychoanalysis

Mastering the unmasterable is the philosopher's wiliest game. No speculative trap is made better than the discourse that puts the unmasterable in the place of mastery. To construct it, however, one must stage a scene.

—Jean-Luc Nancy, *Le partage des voix*

I

Given the ease with which theatricality has been pressed into the service of a postmodern critique of presence, and given its long-standing contributions to the field of psychoanalysis, an inquiry into the forces that attract and bind this curious *ménage à trois* is long overdue. The appropriation by postmodern theorists of techniques of staging, framing, and mimicry is our first clue to the potential of theatricality both for and as theory. The reliance of psychoanalytic theory on oedipal narratives, acting out or psychodrama, and primal scenes further emphasizes the significance of this relationship. "If a drama could signify for Freud such crucial propositions of psychoanalytic thought," Cynthia Chase reasons, "then the signifying mode of drama warrants inquiry."[1] What warrants inquiry, however, is the signifying mode not of dramatic narrative but of theatricality itself. Why has theater moved from the stage per se to the stage of theory, and what function does it serve in critical theory today? We begin this inquiry with Jean-Luc Nancy's provocative

[1]Cynthia Chase, "Oedipal Textuality: Reading Freud's Reading of *Oedipus*," *Diacritics* 9 (March 1979), 54.

association of deconstructive philosophical practice with the technical process of staging a scene. Since psychoanalysis and deconstruction alike put the unmasterable in the place of mastery, are they necessarily theatrical? And if so, what scenes do they stage? Heidegger traces the etymology of both *theater* and *theory* back to the same Greek root:

> The word "theory" stems from the Greek verb *theōrein*. The noun belonging to it is *theōria*. Peculiar to these words is a lofty and mysterious meaning. The verb *theōrein* grew out of the coalescing of two root words, *thea* and *horaō*. *Thea* (cf. theater) is the outward look, the aspect, in which something shows itself, the outward appearance in which it offers itself. Plato marks this aspect in which what presences shows what it is, *eidos*. To have seen this aspect, *eidenai*, is to know [*wissen*]. The second root word in *theōrein*, *horaō*, means: to look at something attentively, to look it over, to view it closely. Thus it follows that *theōrein* is *thean horan*, to look attentively on the outward appearance wherein what presences becomes visible and, through such sight—seeing—to linger with it.[2]

The question posed by Heidegger's argument is how that which presences can ever show itself without displacing itself.

Theater has long been celebrated as a stronghold of presence, embodiment, and reciprocity—particularly by those working outside or at the margins of the discipline. Film theorists such as Christian Metz, for example, repeat a popular sentiment when they defend theater as one of the last remaining art forms to celebrate a pure moment of presence. Challenging this point of view is the argument by contemporary art critics that theater displaces presence and must be devalued for precisely this reason. Michael Fried, for example, describes theater as a medium more concerned with the act of showing than with what, in fact, is shown and on that basis proclaims it the enemy of art. To those working within theater, however, these viewpoints offer less a problem than an illusion of alternatives, and both viewpoints falter in their nostalgia for presence. To either celebrate or condemn theater on the basis of its equation with either presence or absence, substance or show, is to deny the complex play

[2]Martin Heidegger, "Science and Reflection," in *The Question Concerning Technology and Other Essays*, trans. William Lovitt (New York: Harper & Row, 1977), 163.

of presence and absence that we term *theatricality*. Rather than choose one position over the other, we might best understand what it is that theater shows by bringing these two arguments into dialogue.

Metz opens his study of psychoanalysis and cinema with the observation that reality in theater "is physically present, in the same space as the spectator. The cinema only gives it in effigy, inaccessible from the outset, in a primordial *elsewhere*." Desire in cinema thus depends upon the absence of a physical other: "During the screening of the film, the audience is present, and aware of the actor, but the actor is absent, and unaware of the audience; and during the shooting, when the actor was present, it was the audience which was absent. . . . The exchange of seeing and being-seen will be fractured in its centre, and its two disjointed halves allocated to different moments in time; another split. I never see my partner, but only his photograph."[3] For Metz, identification in the cinematic experience is *either* with the voyeur *or* with the exhibitionist; he therefore concludes that the cinematic denies the reciprocity between voyeurism and exhibitionism which theater openly acknowledges.

Following Metz, film theorists have convincingly argued that a certain play with an unreal space of articulation is intrinsic to the cinematic use of symbolic form. The question theater critics must ask is whether cinema has a monopoly on this notorious shell game. Metz ignores the fact not only that "all that is on the stage is a sign,"[4] as the Prague school would have it, but that we are never offstage and so never outside of writing and representation. He never explores how the present physical body is "always already" written, or how the actor's mask functions like the "I" to locate the speaking subject. In his concern with the physical absence or presence of either actors or audiences, Metz fails to consider the complex relay of looks within theater and cinema alike. These problems surface once Metz begins to distinguish between the sense of reality in both mediums. He finally settles for a description of theater as "a set of real pieces of behaviour actively directed at the evocation of something unreal, whereas cinematic fiction is experienced rather as the quasi-real pres-

[3]Christian Metz, *The Imaginary Signifier: Psychoanalysis and the Cinema*, trans. Celia Britton et al. (Bloomington: Indiana University Press, 1982), 61, 95.

[4]Jiří Veltruský, "Man and Object in the Theater," collected in *A Prague School Reader on Esthetics, Literary Structure, and Style*, ed. and trans. Paul L. Garvin (Washington, D.C.: Georgetown University Press, 1964), 84.

ence of that unreal itself."[5] Since the terms *real, unreal,* and *quasi-real* threaten to lose all meaning here, we might rethink this insight more simply. Whereas the cinematic evokes the illusion of a present "somewhere," theater's energies are committed to the display of an "elsewhere." Indeed, we might argue that theater is precisely that mode of inquiry or analysis devoted to the question of what "a set of real pieces of behaviour" might be. Rather than define theater as an unchanging identifiable object in the real, we might rethink it as a culturally conditioned mode of staging the construction of the real. Rather than trace the physical presence or absence of either actors or audience, we can rethink voyeurism and exhibition in terms of an absence inscribed in the scopic and invocatory drives.[6] Finally, we might stage theater as a display that constructs presence by displacing it.

Ironically, those critics who maintain that theatricality is more concerned with displacement than with presence attack theater on precisely these grounds. *Theatricality* is still used today as a pejorative term to refer to behavior that is false or inauthentic to the extent that its concern with being seen takes precedence over, and in fact distorts, what it shows. In his famous manifesto against the theatricality of minimalist art, Michael Fried proclaims: "*Art degenerates as it approaches the condition of theatre.*" Further, he claims that the challenge artists face today is the avoidance of theatricality: "*The success, even the survival, of the arts has come increasingly to depend on their ability to defeat theatre.*" The "presence of literalist art," he continues, ". . . is basically a theatrical effect or quality—a kind of *stage* presence. It is a function, not just of the obtrusiveness and, often, even aggressiveness of literalist work, but of the special complicity that that work extorts from the beholder," which is "simply in being *aware* of it and, so to speak, in acting accordingly."[7] Fried's thesis encourages us to

[5]Metz, *Imaginary Signifier,* 67.

[6]In *Sexuality in the Field of Vision* (London: Verso, 1986), Jacqueline Rose explains that "the scopic and invocatory drives . . . simply reveal the absence of the object which underpins the drive *per se,* rather than being characterised by an absence which can be equated with the physical absence of the object from the cinematic screen" (195). She adds that Metz's "stress on the absence of the object seen has as its corollary a notion of a full non-imaginary relation to the object, and the assigning of the invocatory and scopic drives to the realm of the imaginary *because of* the distance which underpins their relation to the object" (195).

[7]Michael Fried, "Art and Objecthood" may be found in *Minimal Art: A Critical Anthology,* ed. Gregory Battock (New York: E. P. Dutton, 1968), 141, 139, 127–28.

question what a theory of theater would be like which had no recourse to such terms as *the real*, *the essential*, or *the authentic*. But to raise that question is not to be trapped within the terms of an argument that distinguishes between works whose value is inherent and "theatrical" works whose nature and value depend upon the particular circumstances in which a spectator experiences a work. Rethinking the shifting category of the real would involve a very different project, one that might take as its starting point the culturally determined constructions of the image and the real as set out in Jean Baudrillard's "Precession of Simulacra."[8] Since theater operates as a critique of boundaries, the project of containing it requires a more complex schema.

Clearly Fried has another agenda in mind. No sooner does he safely enclose the deconstructive critique of a metaphysics of presence within the neat category of theatricality than he defines theatricality as the enemy of the visual arts and finally of art itself. His plan is to assure the pure objecthood or presence of the aesthetic work through a return to the same modernist tropes upon which Metz relies. The problems here are evident: just as questionable as the wish that we can return to modernism at all is the idea that we can effect that return by denying the constitutive role of the excluded in the formation of identity, or that we can deny rather than rethink the objections advanced by contemporary theory. Fried's conclusion that minimalist art is symptomatic of an age more concerned with showing than with seeing may be true. But is theatricality more concerned with the act of showing than with the inherent quality of what, in fact, is shown? Or is theatricality precisely the challenge to try to separate the two?

Let us concede Fried's major point—that art is now moving in a direction of theatricality to an extent that is indeed unprecedented—and put to one side for the moment any value judgment about this development. Let us assume that theatricality calls into question inherent value or "objecthood" and thereby threatens aesthetics as we know it. We can even concede that *"what lies* between *the arts is*

<hr/>

See also Fried, *Absorption and Theatricality: Painting and Beholder in the Age of Diderot* (Berkeley: University of California Press, 1980).

[8]Jean Baudrillard, "The Precession of Simulacra," in *Art after Modernism: Rethinking Representation*, ed. Brian Wallis (New York: New Museum of Contemporary Art, 1984), 253–81. This essay also appears in Baudrillard's *Simulations*, trans. Paul Foss and Paul Patton (New York: Semiotext(e), 1983).

theatre,"[9] since theater refers both to a framed product and to the acts of framing and staging. In question, finally, is not whether there is any value in revealing product as inseparable from process but whether this critique of a spectator consciousness can be avoided. If theatricality is a showing and if showing is a staging or displacement, then what one shows can never be that which is. In this sense, theatricality can only display the problematic of display itself, can only rehearse the paradox implicit in a spectator consciousness; it is that which constantly proclaims that what is seen is never where it is. If theatricality mocks the desire for any secure position of spectatorship, if it threatens the traditional concepts of objecthood and observer alike, then its strategies are not only useful but essential to the critique of representation. Before we return to the fractured gaze that Metz developed and rethink its implications for theater, we must acknowledge that the gaze as defined by psychoanalytic theory is no less than a critique of a spectator consciousness. Accordingly, we forgo the advantage of siding with either Metz or Fried and bring in a third party to complicate our schema—Lacan.

II

Lacan's 1932 essay "The Mirror Stage" exemplifies the reliance of psychoanalysis on theatrical terms and techniques. In the mirror stage, the infant misidentifies with an image of bodily coherence and stability prior to the achievement of full motor coordination. Lacan explains: "We have only to understand the mirror stage *as an identification*, in the full sense that analysis gives to the term: namely, the transformation that takes place in the subject when he assumes an image." The "*mirror stage* is a drama . . . which manufactures for the subject, caught up in the lure of spatial identification, the succession of phantasies that extends from a fragmented body-image to a form of its totality . . . and, lastly, to the assumption of the armour of an alienating identity."[10] Since Lacan's mirror stage relies upon an innate intuition of the outline of the human form, critics rightly argue that it

[9]Fried, "Art and Objecthood," 142.
[10]Lacan, "The Mirror Stage," *Ecrits: A Selection*, trans. Alan Sheridan (New York: Norton, 1977), 2, 4.

cannot be situated temporally except as a deferred vision or *après coup*. And yet the theatrical terms Lacan employs suggest that he is less concerned with developmental stages than with the *stage* of the psychic apparatus, upon which are played out various ego identifications. Accordingly, we can rethink this early essay in terms of Lacan's more complex theory of the gaze.

Méconnaissance is Lacan's term for the misrecognitions through which the ego is constructed and the illusory identifications, whether of gender or ideology, through which it is sustained. The term reminds us that Lacan's mirror stage has broader implications, especially because the mirror stage need not rely on a physical mirror per se: "the idea of the mirror should be understood as an object which reflects—not just the visible, but also what is heard, touched and willed by the child."[11] Yet why is the infant's identification with the human image, voice, or touch a misidentification? For Lacan, self-identification is based on a representation that alienates as it procures: "Man becomes aware of this reflection from the point of view of the other; he is an other for himself."[12] Following Freud's work on negation, Lacan argues that self-reference is procured only through an expulsion and repression of a part of our being.[13] When the subject takes its reflection as object it finds a place at the cost of misrecognition. Jacqueline Rose observes that "the constitution of the subject in the moment of its splitting . . . [is] a moment which we can already discern in the fiction of self-representation," since "the subject sees itself as a whole only by being placed *elsewhere*."[14]

Desire and aggressivity mark the distance between the subject and its ideal image, termed *ideal* because it can never be fully assimilated. The ego's reliance on the negation of its construction therefore places it on an imaginary axis. Narcissistic self-identification in turn

[11]Lacan, "Cure psychanalytique à l'aide de la poupée fleur," *Revue française de la psychanalyse* 4 (October–December 1949), 567, as quoted in Jacqueline Rose, Introduction—2 to *Feminine Sexuality: Jacques Lacan and the Ecole Freudienne*, ed. Juliet Mitchell and Jacqueline Rose, trans. Jacqueline Rose (New York: Norton, 1985), 30.

[12]Lacan, *Séminaire*, bk. 2 (Paris: Seuil, 1954–55), 138, as translated by Ellie Ragland-Sullivan in *Jacques Lacan and the Philosophy of Psychoanalysis* (Urbana: University of Illinois Press, 1986), 93.

[13]This aspect of Lacan's work draws upon Freud's "On Narcissism: An Introduction" (1914), *SE*, 14:67–102; "Negation" (1925), *SE*, 19:235–39; and "Splitting of the Ego in the Process of Defence" (1940 [1938]), *SE*, 23:271–78.

[14]Rose, *Sexuality in the Field of Vision*, 183.

plagues later object relations; the lack that is played out in our relations with others is not based simply on the absence of a physical other but on a lack in being as a result of our construction through a reflected image. Formed in the subject's assumption of its mirror image and sutured in its identification with the "I" of language, the ego is also and always reminding us that the "I" is an other. The quest for recognition, the desire for another to mirror us as we would see ourselves, is grounded for Lacan in the impossibility of joining the *je* and *moi*, the speaking subject and the subject of speech. Paradoxes of self-reference play upon the splits occasioned by the structure of language and subjectivity. In the mask of drama as in paradoxical games of self-reference, the ego's masquerade as origin is played out. Lacan concludes: "The statement, 'I'm a man,' . . . at most can mean no more than, 'I'm like he whom I recognize to be a man, and so recognize myself as being such.' In the last resort, these various formulas are to be understood only in reference to the truth of 'I is an other,' an observation that is less astonishing to the intuition of the poet than obvious to the gaze of the psychoanalyst."[15]

Following Freud, Lacan proclaims that poets alone know the "truth" of the unconscious. But Lacan's work is less concerned with using psychoanalysis to understand poetry than with using poetry to prove the truth of psychoanalysis. Lacan paid little attention to aesthetics, or to Freud's classification of the uncanny as a branch of aesthetics. However, the uncanny offers a strangely Lacanian understanding of the pleasure we derive from our games with symbolic form. For Lacan as for Freud, the uncanny refers to a perception of familiar unfamiliarity and so signals a return of the repressed.[16] Yet for Lacan, what have been repressed are not simply sexual wishes but the loss or negation that speaks our translation into symbolic form. The repressed is the price we pay for entry into a world of images and words that then stand in for us. The uncanny therefore always points to a repressed signified, but that signified is itself a signifier of our inscription in symbolic form.

Jacques-Alain Miller developed a theory of suture to explain the relevance of the structuring function of the lack to Lacanian theory. For Miller, suture implies not only a stitching together of a subject

---

[15]Lacan, "Aggressivity in Psychoanalysis," *Ecrits*, 23.
[16]Freud, "The 'Uncanny'" (1919), *SE*, 17:217–56.

position but a displacement of a lack in that construction. He defines suture as a "logic of the signifier" which "names the relation of the subject to the chain of its discourse." It both "figures there as the element which is lacking, in the form of a stand-in" and refers to "the general relation of lack to the structure of which it is an element, inasmuch as it implies the position of a taking-the-place of."[17] Miller's work depends upon an analogy between the subject's relation to signification and the zero's relation to the progression of numbers; he compares the subject as lack and as sutured with the zero as lack and as number. What is excluded from the numerable is that which is not identical with itself. Similarly, the subject is both excluded from language, to which it is alien, and yet inscribed within it through such placeholders as the pronoun "I." The "I," like the zero number, traces both an absence and its suturing as presence. The subject is sutured by language into the signifying chain, much as the zero number sutures the absence of the zero lack. The moment of suture, of access to the "I," is a point of pseudo-identification based on the assumption of a delusory mirror image. Language both negates and procures, both displaces and places the subject. As we hit signification we are divided by it and exceed it; subjectivity is that intersection of being and language which is not fully recuperable, yet which reverberates in our play with symbolic form.

In our fetishization of sound, word, and image as they trace this early misrecognition are the seeds of an aesthetic theory. Our play with the mirror image of theater exposes our sense of loss and disjunction in relation to the forms in which we exist. Being in language results in a fascination with words as that other in which we are lacking and in which we find ourselves as not our own. Poetry speaks the splitting of the ego as an effect of being in words, recalling the apprehension of the alienating anchoring of the word. Our fascinated play with sounds and figures rehearses our earlier attempts to integrate the echoes and images of the mirror stage. In all these forms

---

[17]Jacques-Alain Miller, "Suture (Elements of the Logic of the Signifier)," *Screen* 18 (Winter 1977–78), 25–26 (first published in French in 1966). Lacan originally used the word *suture* to refer to a "pseudo-identification that exists between . . . the time of terminal arrest of the gesture and what, in another dialectic that I called the dialectic of identificatory haste, I put as the first time, namely, the moment of seeing," in "What Is a Picture?" *The Four Fundamental Concepts of Psycho-Analysis*, ed. Jacques-Alain Miller, trans. Alan Sheridan (New York: Norton, 1981), 117.

we replay our sense of the uncanny and compelling force of the reflections in which we find ourselves as lost.

Freud's thesis that the ego is a projection of the body's surface is central to the understanding of a variety of mediums, as is the shell game that Metz equates with cinema alone. The ego's basis in the assumption of a projected image helps to explain the aggressive rivalry common to drama and the narcissistic voyeurism characteristic of cinema. Both mediums bear witness to our fascination with the spatial lure of the human form. The appeal of theater thus depends upon an uncanny awareness of a fundamental loss in relation to the mirror image through which subjectivity is procured. Our apprehension of the loss and desire inscribed in theater's alternating play with presence and absence, repression and representation, points to the value of theater as a way of knowing.

III

Film theorists quickly appropriated Lacan's mirror stage and Miller's theory of suture to explain the mechanisms by which the subject is inserted or sutured into the cinematic fiction. Arguing that cinematic discourse, like all discourse, constructs a subject through its displacement and its passage as lack, Jean-Pierre Oudart applies Miller's suture theory to film analysis.[18] Oudart's theory relies upon an intriguing parallel between the shot/reverse shot formation and the equally coercive syntactical relations in the linguistic order. These comparisons hold promise for theater theory, yet need to be rethought in light of more recent critiques of Lacan's schemas, including Lacan's own revision of his earlier work.

The shot/reverse shot is a camera technique in which a disowned look is followed by a reverse shot of the character whose point of view articulates that look. As Kaja Silverman successfully demonstrates, many Hitchcock films begin with a freedom of specularity unconstrained by such conventions of physical reality as point of

[18]Jean-Pierre Oudart, "Cinema and Suture," *Screen* 18 (Winter 1977–78), 35–47, originally published in French in 1969. In *Questions of Cinema* (Bloomington: Indiana University Press, 1981), Stephen Heath has convincingly argued that we need not accept the one-to-one equation of suture with the shot/reverse shot formation (96–98).

view.[19] Unanchored, our look ranges freely through keyholes, windows, and walls; as the angles become more impossible, however, they also become more threatening. The viewer's discomfort is relieved only at the price of identification with a character who then possesses the look and directs it in a relay of looks that in turn construct the cinematic narrative. We are sutured, then, not only when we identify with a point of view in language or in the symbolic order, but when we move from identification to identification in a series of filmic shots.

In Max Ophuls's *Lola Montes*, for example, one shot is a disowned view of Lola in the circus arena. The questions that are posed to her by the crowd are all variants of the question "What does woman want?" and are all equally barbaric. Yet the following shot of the crowd answers the question "Who is looking?" by drawing us away from this uneasy stance and into the fictional narrative. The shot encourages us to suture the absence of point of view by identifying with the static subject positions offered by the characters within the narrative. Rather than admit our status as voyeurs who sadistically pelt Lola with questions and looks, rather than admit what the impresario is doing by placing a caged woman in a circus arena and selling her favors, we enter—or are sutured into—the world of the fiction. The desire of the look propels us to the next look; the shot is acknowledged and denied as the fiction takes hold. The reverse shot covers over the emptiness perceived in the 180-degree shot that Oudart terms "The Absent One" and that he employs to refer to the place where the look is actually enunciated—the camera itself. The reverse shot sutures this lack by encouraging us to identify with a point of view, and so inscribes us within the relay of looks through which the film narrative is constructed.

Following Oudart, Daniel Dayan describes the action of the shot/reverse shot in precisely sequenced steps based on Lacan's early descriptions of the mirror stage:

When the viewer discovers the frame—the first step in reading the film—the triumph of his former *possession* of the image fades out. The

---

[19]I am indebted here to Kaja Silverman's discussion in *The Subject of Semiotics* (Oxford: Oxford University Press, 1983), 194–236, of how suture functions in Alfred Hitchcock's *Birds* and *Psycho* and in Max Ophuls's *Lola Montes*.

viewer discovers that the camera is hiding things, and therefore dis-
trusts it and the frame itself, which he now understands to be arbitrary.
He wonders why the frame is what it is. This radically transforms his
mode of participation—the unreal space between characters and/or
objects is no longer perceived as pleasurable. It is now the space which
separates the camera from the characters. The latter have lost their
quality of presence. . . . The spectator discovers that his possession of
space was only partial, illusory. He feels dispossessed of what he is
prevented from seeing. He discovers that he is only authorized to see
what happens to be in the axis of the glance of another spectator, who is
ghostly or absent.[20]

Our initial perception of the fullness of the image contrasts sharply
with the actual limitations that construct perspective and that mark
our entry into the symbolic. The imagined plenitude of the idealized
mirror image and the loss that is realized and then repressed through
identification with the point of view delineated by the symbolic
order thus recalls the neatly sequenced developmental stages of
Lacan's early model of the mirror stage.

Dayan carefully traces the spectator's movement away from the
joy of an idealized plenitude or presence, through a concern with the
question of who controls the gaze, and finally on to a relieved
acceptance of an answer in the fictional identification of suture. This
application of suture theory, while enormously useful to the study of
film, poses problems when reexamined in terms of Lacan's increasingly critical stance toward his earlier attempts to posit an initial
unity which is first split and later sutured. According to the accounts
offered by film theory, our anticipation of bodily unity in the idealized mirror image is unrelated to desire; when desire and aggressivity infiltrate the mirror, the question of who controls the gaze
becomes paramount. The *jouissance* of pure seeing, in which the
image is experienced as an imaginary plenitude unbounded by any
gaze, is the first false step, for there is pleasure as well as pain

[20]Daniel Dayan, "The Tutor-Code of Classical Cinema," *Film Quarterly* 28 (Fall
1974), reprinted in *Movies and Methods*, ed. Bill Nichols (Berkeley: University of
California Press, 1976), 448. Dayan explains how suture serves a variety of ideological functions and describes it as a coercive system that forces us to identify not only
with particular subject positions but with certain formations of power and with
values that support them.

associated with *jouissance*. The first glance is always infiltrated by the threat of reversal; the "I see" is accompanied by the "I am seen," or by the double as usurping image. Even the earliest moments of the mirror stage, Lacan later cautions, are infiltrated by a play of desire and aggression which subverts any ideal unity: "For the Other, the place of discourse, always latent to the triangulation that consecrates that distance, is not yet so long as it has not spread right into the specular relation in its purest moment: in the gesture with which the child in front of the mirror, turning to the one who is holding it, appeals with its look to the witness who decants, verifying it, the recognition of the image, of the jubilant assumption, where indeed *it already was.*"[21]

In order to rethink a model based on the concept of a privileged origin, Lacan turns once again to Freud. And in Freud's numerous rereadings of his grandson's game of lost and found in *Beyond the Pleasure Principle* Lacan finds a reading of the relation of loss to representation that suits his purposes.[22] Without denying Freud's argument that we desire a lost object, Lacan emphasizes the ways in which we find ourselves in language only as that which can be lost. The simplest game of lost and found requires a subject who is capable of desiring an object. What we seek in our games of lost and found, Lacan concludes, is not only a return to unity with a maternal object or a mirror image; rather, through such games we also play out our awareness of the procuring displacement that is signification, and so we retrace the means by which we are both lost and found in language. The demand directed to the other of discourse is not simply a desire to master loss but a process of finding oneself as that which can be both lost and found. Precisely because this demand results from the child's own identification with itself as absent, this desire can never be fulfilled.

Jacqueline Rose thus charges film theorists with failing to take into account this development in Lacan's thought: "The movement away from a stress on illusory totality and identity, to identity as a function of repeated difference can thus be seen as representing a shift in Lacan's emphasis from the Imaginary, to the structure of linguistic

[21]Lacan, "Remarque sur le rapport de Daniel Lagache: 'Psychanalyse et structure de la personnalité,'" *Ecrits* (Paris: Seuil, 1966), 678, as quoted in Rose, *Sexuality in the Field of Vision*, 186.

[22]Freud, *Beyond the Pleasure Principle* (1920), *SE*, 18:3–64; for Lacan see Chap. 6.

insistence as already underpinning moments prior to its intervening symbolisation." She explains: "At the point where language ceases to be a potentially full speech and is seen as a structure or set of differences based on a primary absence, there can no longer be a simple progression from the Imaginary (mis-recognition) to the Symbolic (mediation, recognition), since the emphasis is now on the 'splitting' which is constitutive of language itself."[23]

Film theorists have been reluctant to abandon a model that so clearly distinguishes between the specular and the linguistic, the imaginary and the symbolic, the preoedipal and the oedipal registers. Yet such distinctions result in a mistaken understanding of the imaginary as somehow free of the play of aggressivity and desire, and so ignore how the gaze functions as a part-object of desire. If we must equate the imaginary with identifications marked by duality—ambivalence, doubling, reversal, paranoia—and equate the symbolic with linguistic identifications marked by difference, we must also acknowledge that neither register is really separate from the other. The imaginary always already pervades the symbolic, reminding us of its mythic status, much as the symbolic necessarily pervades all constructions of the imaginary, thus accounting for its decided cultural and ideological bias.

Once Lacan acknowledges the impossibility of separating these registers, it becomes clear that the plenitude of the image cannot be posited as somehow outside the play of supplementarity and temporality. If the movement from imaginary to symbolic in the construction of the look challenges any linear ordering based on progression or development, if language is a structure of differences in which we only find ourselves as split, if identity in language is a function of repeated difference rather than an illusory plenitude, then the syntax of cinematic discourse, or suture, must be rethought. And it must be rethought not along the lines of the shot/reverse shot, not as the privileged activity of cinematic pleasure that moves from plenitude to lack to recovery, but rather as that which elides any clear distinction between shot and reverse shot, or between eye and gaze. The fractured reciprocity inherent in the process of self-reference can only be captured in the deferred action whereby that which resists representation appears within it.

[23]Rose, *Sexuality in the Field of Vision*, 185, 176.

IV

Lacan attacks Western thought as a "philosophical tradition represented by plenitude encountered by the subject in the mode of contemplation." He pointedly asks whether we cannot "also grasp that which has been eluded, namely, the function of the gaze? I mean, and Maurice Merleau-Ponty points this out, that we are beings who are looked at, in the spectacle of the world. That which makes us consciousness institutes us by the same token as *speculum mundi*. Is there no satisfaction in being under that gaze of which, following Merleau-Ponty, I spoke just now, that gaze that circumscribes us, and which in the first instance makes us beings who are looked at, but without showing this?"[24] In a study of Descartes's treatise *La dioptrique*, Merleau-Ponty directs our attention to an illustration designed to trace the path of rays of light from a given object to the eye that sees it (figure 8). But what is the function of the man who stands at the bottom of this diagram? Or as Merleau-Ponty asks: "*Who* will see the image painted in the eyes or in the brain? . . . Descartes already sees that we always put a little man in man, that our objectifying view of our own body always obliges us to seek *still further inside* that *seeing man* we thought we had under our eyes. But what he does not see is that the primordial vision that one must indeed come to cannot be the *thought of seeing*."[25] Lacan's theory of the gaze is designed to explain why.

The Cartesian *cogito* denies "that which governs the gaze most secretly and that which always escapes from the grasp of that form of vision that is satisfied with itself in imagining itself as consciousness," explains Lacan. "That in which the consciousness may turn back upon itself—grasp itself . . . *as seeing oneself seeing oneself*—represents mere sleight of hand. An avoidance of the function of the gaze is at work there." Conversely, the gaze may be correlated with

[24]Lacan, "The Split between the Eye and the Gaze," *Four Fundamental Concepts*, 74–75.

[25]Maurice Merleau-Ponty, Working Notes, 1959, *The Visible and the Invisible, Followed by Working Notes*, ed. Claude Lefort, trans. Alphonso Lingis (Evanston, Ill.: Northwestern University Press, 1968), 210. See also René Descartes, *La dioptrique*, vol. 6 of *Oeuvres de Descartes*, ed. C. Adam and P. Tannery (Paris: Vrin, 1965), 79–228; and N. K. Smith's English translation, *Descartes: Philosophical Writings* (New York: Random House, 1958), especially the chapter "Descartes' Theory of Vision as Expounded in his *Dioptric*," 145–59.

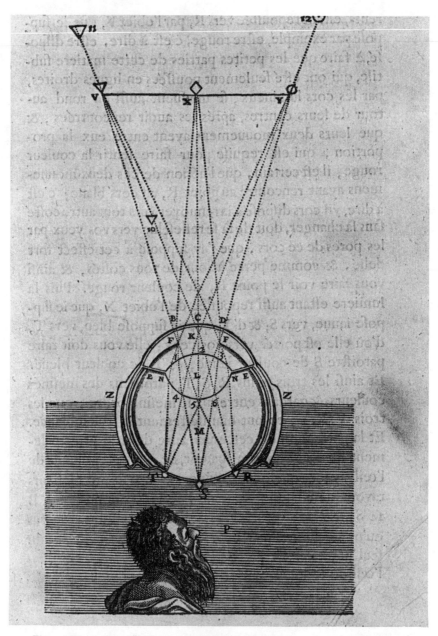

Figure 8. From René Descartes, *La dioptrique* (Leiden, 1637). Reproduced courtesy of the Bancroft Library, University of California, Berkeley.

the awareness that we can never see ourselves seeing. "In our relation to things," Lacan suggests, "in so far as this relation is constituted by the way of vision, and ordered in the figures of representation, something slips, passes, is transmitted, from stage to stage, and is always to some degree eluded in it—that is what we call the gaze."[26] "For my part," he announces, "I set out from the fact that there is something that establishes a fracture, a bi-partition, a splitting of the being to which the being accommodates itself, even in the natural world." He adds: "What determines me, at the most profound level, in the visible, is that gaze that is outside" since "in the scopic field, the gaze is outside, I am looked at, that is to say, I am a picture."[27] Following Lacan, Merleau-Ponty describes the moment when the child recognizes that *"there can be a viewpoint taken on him"* as that which "makes possible a contemplation of self."[28] Yet can I ever see the picture that is me? The gaze comes into play when we realize that we are seen from a point within as well as from without with which we can never merge. The realization that we are seen organizes both the field of our vision and a blind spot in that field. As in Mark Strand's "In a field / I am the absence / of field," the "I" becomes the blind spot that must move to keep things whole.[29]

The objectification of the self by an alien viewpoint enables, as it undermines, self-consciousness by calling into play an unconscious look. Ellie Ragland-Sullivan observes that "the limitations of consciousness may be witnessed in what Lacan has described as a *scotoma* (Greek, obscuration of part of the field of vision). . . . The *regard* is not simply a glance cast from the eye, nor a glance from reflective consciousness," she explains, "because the *regard* has the power to activate within consciousness an awareness of unconscious motivation and intentionality." "Authentic analytic consciousness . . . resides in seeing oneself being seen (*se voir se voir*) in the Other (A)," Ragland-Sullivan explains, adding that "in privileged moments such as these, the gaze functions as the reverse side of consciousness and

[26]Lacan, "Split between the Eye and the Gaze," 74, 73.

[27]Lacan, "What Is a Picture?" 106.

[28]Maurice Merleau-Ponty, *The Primacy of Perception and Other Essays on Phenomenological Psychology, the Philosophy of Art, History, and Politics,* ed. James M. Edie (Evanston, Ill.: Northwestern University Press, 1964), 136.

[29]Mark Strand, "Keeping Things Whole," *Reasons for Moving: Poems* (New York: Atheneum, 1968), 40.

elides itself."[30] Analytic consciousness, then, both acknowledges the desire to own the place of one's look and accepts its impossibility, insofar as one is always already seen from a place where one is not.

How, then, do we approach the problem of desire in theater? Where is the spectator's desire and how is it played out? Lacan's complicated and seemingly contradictory treatment of the *objet petit a* seems designed to account for the look as an elusive object of desire, something far less tangible than the theory of transitional objects developed by D. W. Winnicott. Both cinema and theater play upon the relation between the desiring eye and the gaze as *objet petit a*—the carefully undefined Lacanian term for the part-object of desire itself. Since the look is also a drive, the look is both desiring and desired. An anonymous author writes in *Scilicet*: "The look, as a partial object *a*, is deeply hidden and unattainable to the same extent as I am unable to see myself from the place where the Other is looking at me."[31] It appears that Lacan's schema depends on tracing within the structuration of the look that aspect of the look that resists structuration—the gaze. Ragland-Sullivan explains how seeing is not only an object of desire in Lacanian theory but that which structures desire:

> The gaze is one of the first structuring mechanisms of the human subject. It was introjected as a part-object in the pre–mirror stage before the eye acquired its function of seeing and representing the subject and, consequently, before there was any sense of alterity. In the mirror stage the gaze is the dialectical bridge to self-recognition; perceptually speaking, the prespecular objects of Desire become permanently enmeshed in a network of inner vision.[32]

Since theater privileges the gaze over the look, it privileges the return look that acknowledges how we are embedded in a network of signifiers that are also objects of desire. "Generally speaking, the relation between the gaze and what one wishes to see involves a lure," Lacan continues. "The subject is presented as other than he is, and what one shows him is not what he wishes to see. It is in this way that the eye may function as *objet a*, that is to say, at the level of the

[30]Ragland-Sullivan, *Jacques Lacan*, 94.
[31]"Le clivage du sujet et son identification," *Scilicet* 2–3 (1970), 120, translated in Rose, *Sexuality in the Field of Vision*, 167.
[32]Ragland-Sullivan, *Jacques Lacan*, 94–95.

lack." Since we can never see ourselves from the point from which we view others, Lacan observes that *"what I look at is never what I wish to see."*[33] If what the voyeur looks for is what the exhibitionist shows, what the exhibitionist shows is that which cannot be seen insofar as the desire for self-presence can never be fulfilled. Theater plays upon the desire for presence, but, as Derrida reminds us, "this desire carries in itself the destiny of its non-satisfaction."[34]

How can the theory of the gaze be employed by theater theory? Merleau-Ponty's rejection of "panoramic thinking" led him to advance instead "the idea of *chiasm*, that is: every relation with being is *simultaneously* a taking and a being taken, the hold is held, it is *inscribed* and inscribed in the same being that it takes hold of."[35] "There is dialectic only in that type of being in which a junction of subjects occurs," he reasons, "being which is not only a spectacle that each subject presents to itself for its own benefit but which is rather their common residence, the place of their exchange and of their reciprocal interpretation [sic]."[36] In place of a Sartrean look, Merleau-Ponty posits Paul Valéry's model of the interchange of looks: "Once gazes interlock, there are no longer *quite* two persons and it's hard for either to remain *alone*. This exchange . . . effects . . . a transposition, a metathesis or intercrossing of two 'lifelines,' two viewpoints. You take my appearance, my image, and I take yours. You are not I, since you see me and I don't see myself. What is missing for me is this 'I' whom you can see. And what *you* miss is the 'you' I see."[37] We are not so very far away here from Metz's description of the fractured look. And despite Lacan's differences with Merleau-Ponty, we are not very far away from Lacan's work on the gaze, as evidenced in

[33]Lacan, "Line and Light," *Four Fundamental Concepts*, 104, 103.

[34]Jacques Derrida, " '. . . *That Dangerous Supplement* . . . ,' " *Of Grammatology*, trans. Gayatri Chakravorty Spivak (Baltimore: Johns Hopkins University Press, 1976), 143.

[35]Merleau-Ponty, Working Notes 1960, *The Visible and the Invisible*, 266.

[36]Merleau-Ponty, *Adventures of the Dialectic*, trans. Joseph Bien (Evanston, Ill.: Northwestern University Press, 1973), 204; the French is *"insertion."*

[37]Paul Valéry, *Analects*, trans. Stuart Gilbert, vol. 14 of *The Collected Works of Paul Valéry*, ed. Jackson Mathews (Princeton: Princeton University Press, 1970), 26. Merleau-Ponty quotes this passage in *Signs*, trans. Richard C. McCleary (Evanston, Ill.: Northwestern University Press, 1964), 231; and in *Themes from the Lectures at the Collège de France, 1952–60*, trans. John O'Neill (Evanston, Ill.: Northwestern University Press, 1970), 14.

Lacan's statement: "When, in love, I solicit a look, what is profoundly unsatisfying and always missing is that—*You never look at me from the place from which I see you.*"[38]

We may recall that Metz's phrase for cinema was a simple "I never see my beloved, but only his photograph." Shakespeare's phrase for theater might be Brutus's "The eye sees not itself / But by reflection, by some other things" (*Julius Caesar:* 1.2.52–53). In both cases a circuitous and mediated route prevents recognition. On the side of neither presence nor absence, theater stages a continual posing and reposing of the interplay of regards and so plays out the desire to fix position in relationship. In Shakespearean drama the desire to close up the place of one's look is figured not only in Brutus's response to Cassius's query but in dramatic plots of comic and tragic misrecognition alike. Similarly, for Valéry the intercrossing of regards is a "simultaneous, reciprocal limitation" which effects a "decentering."[39] This strategic decentering challenges the distinction between observer and observed, eye and gaze, and so suggests the power of theater as theory.

V

In a strategic move, Metz proposes that cinema pretends not to know that it is being seen and so plays out a dual, essentially paranoid fantasy: (1) the actor's fantasy of being watched without knowing who is watching; and (2) the spectator's fantasy of watching people who are unaware that they are being seen. In cinema, he maintains, "'seeing' is no longer a matter of sending something back, but of catching something unawares." This "catching unawares" is characteristic of story, cinema, and dream alike, insofar as each denies its source of articulation, pretends not to know what it is doing, and so hides its control of the spectator. Metz reads the difference between the cinematic and the theatrical in terms of the popular distinction between story and discourse.[40] Story tells us without telling us that it

[38]Lacan, "Line and Light," 103. For Lacan's critique of Merleau-Ponty, see "Maurice Merleau-Ponty," *Les temps modernes*, nos. 184–85 (1961), 245–54.

[39]Valéry, *Analects*, 26.

[40]Metz, *Imaginary Signifier*, 95. See also "Story/Discourse (A Note on Two Kinds of Voyeurism)," ibid., 91–97. Metz's use of the terms *histoire* and *discours* follows Emile Benveniste.

is telling; it denies, whereas discourse acknowledges, the role of the enunciative apparatus in its construction and reception. Whereas this characterization merely repeats, and so complicates, the distinction between traditional narrative cinema and avant-garde cinema, it also suggests that cinema necessarily relies upon theatrical strategies in order to be avant-garde.[41]

The implications of voyeurism and paranoia for film theory have been extensively studied, but we have yet to rethink theater in these terms as well.[42] Theatrical discourse is not only ambivalent—given the agon, the moment of indecision, the multiplication of possibilities and points of view—but paranoid, given its fascination with a persecuted or threatened identity, its controlled exhibitionism, its staring down of the spectator, and its displacement of self-displacement onto an audience. The paranoid's fear is based upon a fantasy of being the object of a regard which he can never reflect back, and in this sense may well be linked to the voyeuristic pleasure of cinema. In contrast, theater suggests a more reactive desire: it plays out the fantasy of reflecting a look in such a way as to stare it down. Theatrical behavior is an active response to the sense that one is seen; it transforms the paranoid's fear of not being able to reflect a look into pleasure through the form of defense known as identification with the aggressor. The desire in theater is a desire for the subversion of the look, even if the look that is finally subverted is one's own.

Film theorists typically attribute to cinema a privileged relationship to the imaginary order. They defend this argument by pointing to theater's close ties with the symbolic, its firm grounding in an identifiable stage and body, and its reliance on character identifications that can be reversed but never subverted. However useful the distinction, this traditional association is itself subject to reversal. In cinema, we are sutured into identification with the camera and with the story. In theater, however, the processes of seeing and being seen are inseparable from each other and from the recognition of a fracture at their core. Because of the cinematic fiction's reliance on a series of cuts that continually shift our focus, the rule of spectatorship in

---

[41]For a useful discussion of this distinction see Peter Wollen, "Godard and Counter-Cinema: *Vent d'Est,*" in *Narrative, Apparatus, Ideology: A Film Theory Reader,* ed. Philip Rosen (New York: Columbia University Press, 1986), 120–29.

[42]See Jacqueline Rose, "Paranoia and the Film System," *Screen* 17 (1976–77), 85–104.

cinema is to seek closure at any cost. When we go to see a film, we have no choice but to allow the camera to position us *somewhere*. Yet theater forces us to acknowledge that we are displaced from any sure position and indeed *constituted* by this fracture between showing and seeing. Whereas cinema encourages a more direct perceptual identification with the seeing eye of the camera, theater divides and disperses the possibilities of identification, in the process problematizing both identification and point of view. The cinematic foregrounds a moment in which the subject is clearly identified as the object of another's regard. Yet theater addresses the process of self-identification and its consequences, whether in the mask, the agon, narrative plots of misrecognition, or in the display of a look that cannot be returned.

If we posit that the experience of cinema provides a model for the subject's insertion into its world, we must acknowledge that the camera is an external and alien piece of machinery. A camera may regard us, theatricalize itself, or even attack itself, but it remains the space of the Absent One, a perspective we can never share. Freed from a fetishized apparatus and its limitations, freed from a prosthesis that encourages a vocabulary of fetishes, castration, and lacks, theatricality speaks the impossibility of closure and replacement. Whereas the cinematic apparatus projects a stability of place that can only be fetishized, theatricality points to itself and reveals the place of one's look as always already in motion.

If we follow Metz's lead in seeking to clarify certain distinctions between the cinematic and the theatrical, we do so only to consider their future development in terms of each other. Recent work on identification and misrecognition in film which explores the cinematic construction of voice and body suggests a productive route for theater theory.[43] Theater theorists might profitably examine how

[43]See, for example, Mary Ann Doane, "Misrecognition and Identity," *Ciné-Tracts* 3 (1980), 25–32; "Woman's Stake: Filming the Female Body," *October* 17 (1981), 23–36; and "The Voice in the Cinema: The Articulation of Body and Space," *Yale French Studies*, no. 60 (1980), 33–50. See also Silverman, *The Subject of Semiotics*; and Silverman, *The Acoustic Mirror: The Female Voice in Psychoanalysis and Cinema* (Bloomington: Indiana University Press, 1988); Teresa de Lauretis, *Alice Doesn't: Feminism, Semiotics, and Cinema* (Bloomington: Indiana University Press, 1984); and de Lauretis, *Technologies of Gender: Essays on Theory, Film, and Fiction* (Bloomington: Indiana University Press, 1987); as well as Jacqueline Rose, *Sexuality in the Field of Vision*.

various aspects of the cinematic machinery—the voiceover, the shot-to-shot formation—are fulfilled differently in theater to construct or subvert presence. More precisely, these studies might explore how the relationship of the cinematic to the theatrical is always already inscribed in a repetition of looks which holds within itself the possibility of a reversal of these terms.

Paul Willemen's work points in this direction. He appropriates Lacan's theory of the gaze for a theory of the fourth look in cinema, whereby the viewer is surprised by an imagined look from the camera.[44] Willemen's fourth look relies upon the three already posited by Laura Mulvey: the look of the camera that records the event, the look of the audience at the film, and the look of the characters within the film at each other.[45] The fourth look is an imagined look experienced by the audience as a sense that it is seen in the process of seeing. Stephen Dwoskin's *Girl*, a film based on a single take of an embarrassed naked young woman, offers one example of the fourth look; the films of Yvonne Rainer offer another, since the filmic characters repeatedly pose for the camera and so openly remind us that we are seen seeing. Since Willemen's theory is essentially theatrical, we may simplify and yet extend his argument to suggest that certain films are theatrical (that is, exhibit a fourth look) insofar as as they *show that they know that they are showing.*

Metz may well be correct in maintaining that traditional Western narrative cinema seeks to deny its theatricality insofar as it plays upon fantasies of seeing *or* being seen, of seeing *without* being seen. Conversely, theater not only foregrounds this fracture but entangles us within its paradoxes. And in this sense theater displays a fractured gaze, or *shows that it knows that it is showing* (that which can never be seen). Lacan observes expansively: "The world is all-seeing, but it is not exhibitionistic—it does not provoke our gaze. When it begins to provoke it, the feeling of strangeness begins too. What does this mean, if not that, in the so-called waking state, there is an elision of the gaze, and an elision of the fact that not only does it look, *it* also *shows*. In the field of the dream, on the other hand, what characterizes

[44]Paul Willemen, "Voyeurism, the Look, and Dwoskin," in *Narrative, Apparatus, Ideology*, ed. Rosen, 210–18.

[45]Laura Mulvey, "Visual Pleasure and Narrative Cinema," *Screen* 16 (1975), 6–18, rpt. in *Narrative, Apparatus, Ideology*, 198–209.

69

the images is that *it shows*."[46] What differentiates theatricality from the cinematic is its *display of display*, which returns us to an all-showing state. *Theatricality shows that it knows that it shows*, and so turns itself inside out in a series of frames framed by their contents. The cinematic, on the other hand, seeks, as in dreams, to *deny that it knows that it shows*. Whereas cinema encourages us to suture at all costs, theater plays out this unbridgeable gap, thereby forcing us to locate ourselves within a fractured gaze.

The pejorative use of the term *theatricality* as mere surface or show thus fails to take into account the more strategic use of show as an interactive trap. Lacan maintains that only psychoanalysis explains how the human being reveals its capture in a symbolic dimension. Yet theater also displays, stages, and so displaces our sense of being caught out by a look. Widely acknowledged to be one of the most theatrical of theorists on the postmodern scene, Lacan appears to have confined his interest in theater to his style of presentation. When he writes about *Hamlet*, for example, he employs the play as a vehicle to further the aims of psychoanalytic theory.[47] When he writes on the gaze, his references are invariably to painting, rather than theater. In discussing animal mimicry, Lacan maintains that it "is no doubt the equivalent of the function which, in man, is exercised in painting"[48]—without pausing to consider the more obvious role of mimicry in theater. We are like other animals, Lacan contends, in that we are "mapped socially"; the key difference resides in our play with the mask and the mirror: "Only the subject—the human subject, the subject of the desire that is the essence of man—is not, unlike the animal, entirely caught up in this imaginary capture. He maps himself in it. How? In so far as he isolates the function of the screen and plays with it. Man, in effect, knows how to play with the mask as that beyond which there is the gaze. The screen is here the locus of mediation."[49]

[46]Lacan, "Split between the Eye and the Gaze," 75.

[47]See Lacan, "Desire and the Interpretation of Desire in *Hamlet*," *Yale French Studies* 55/56 (1977), rpt. in *Literature and Psychoanalysis: The Question of Reading: Otherwise*, ed. Shoshana Felman (Baltimore: Johns Hopkins University Press, 1982), 11–52. Since a number of Lacan's seminars remain unpublished, it is too soon to refer with any certainty to the topics that Lacan fails to address. I refer, therefore, only to his published writings.

[48]Lacan, "What Is a Picture?" 109.

[49]Ibid., 107.

Lacan concedes that in acts of sex and aggression, we employ the mask as a lure to entrap the other: "In both situations, the being breaks up . . . between its being and its semblance, between itself and that paper tiger it shows to the other." He explains that "the being gives of himself, or receives from the other, something that is like a mask, a double, an envelope, a thrown-off skin, thrown off in order to cover the frame of a shield." Finally, he employs the mask of gender as an example: "It is no doubt through the mediation of masks that the masculine and the feminine meet in the most acute, most intense way."[50] Yet in theater as well as in sex and aggression, the mask functions as a lure that traps the other by displaying the loss that derives from our represented status. Our symbolic play with the screen and the mask finds its most direct equivalent in theatricality, which displays and so displaces our captivation by a look.

When we say that something or someone is theatrical, we refer not only to a show but to a showing of a mask, not only to a display but to a display of displacement. The lure of theater is the mask that shows itself as such. Theater's masks announce that the "I" is another; its characters assure us of their displacement, by announcing "I am already taken" as in "this seat is taken" (for a performance) or as in "that was no lady, that was my wife" (mother). What fascinates us in theater is a look that teasingly submits to our look only to trap us in the process. The actor calls the spectator's desire into play by exhibiting an image to trap our restless eyes—by showing one's sex, one's mask, one's persona as already taken. The actor's mask discloses that it has always already been presented to our eyes, and so is designed to be taken up by them. Yet we no sooner stake our claim to a resting space in this field of vision than we are stared down by a look that challenges our own and reveals it as defined by another.

If the audience seeks to offend with its eyes by seeing what must not be seen, the actor's pleasure lies in satisfying the impulse to show and to shock, so that the audience is exposed as well. The striptease is theatrical in that its stage is a virtual battlefield of the look. Will the stripper maintain his status as the purloined object of the look, so as to preserve the female spectator's bearing of that look? Or will he look back in a way that displaces her look in return? The actor succeeds only by disorganizing the audience's field of perception,

[50]Ibid.

71

showing it something other than what it wants to see. The actor can only subvert his objectification by displacing and so controlling the audience's displacing gaze. He calls the game, offends the offender, knowing the offense is but an offense of the eye.

Theater's games with the mask and the mirror thus play upon and play out our sense of being captured in a symbolic dimension. Whereas cinema need merely play upon the desire of the look, theater appeals to the desire to expose and reverse the displacement effected by the gaze. Theater is designed to entangle the other's look with one's purloined image in order to reverse the process, and so to expose the other's look as already purloined as well. If theater presents the human body alive and breathing before us, it is also and always speaking to us of the place where we are not. Like the shield held up to view Medusa, theater offers a perspective glass by means of which our look is revealed as always already reflected, defined by the exchange of signifiers that displace as they place us in the symbolic. By means of such curious games of projection and transference, both psychoanalysis and theater stage the circuitous routes through which we find ourselves as lost as the only viable form of self-knowledge.

VI

What we are recording here is a paradigm shift only beginning to be registered in theater studies: a shift away from a model based on presence and toward an intertextual model based on *différance*. The new theoretical directions marked out by this approach follow the simple turn *away* from the Cartesian "I think therefore I am," and *toward* Lacan's "I am not wherever I am the plaything of my thought; I think of what I am where I do not think to think."[51] When the sanctioned identities of author, play, and discipline are redefined as texts, which are then revealed to be intertextual and so not stable, continuous, or self-present, we are adopting a theatrical paradigm. Intertexuality is a richly theatrical concept, as evidenced in Mikhail Bakhtin's discussion of dialogic texts and in Roland Barthes's defini-

[51]Lacan, "The Agency of the Letter in the Unconscious, or Reason since Freud," *Ecrits*, 166.

tion of the text as a space "made of multiple writings, drawn from many cultures and entering into mutual relations of dialogue, parody, and contestation."[52] Using techniques of appropriation and mimicry, collage and quotation, postmodern theory unravels the fiction of textual integrity and so displays work as text and text as performance.

Postmodernism is usually described as a turn away from, if not against, Western narratives of mastery.[53] But postmodern theory also relies upon a subversion of explanatory narratives at the level of style. And theatricality explains this style. In a perceptive overview of the critical scene, Mária Minich Brewer observes: "Theatre allows philosophical discourse to shift from thought as seeing and knowing, originating in the subject alone, to the many decentered processes of framing and staging that representation requires but dissimulates."[54] Why the word *dissimulates* if not that the acts of framing and staging themselves depend upon the fiction of the objective observer, of the object itself, and of the boundary that separates the two? Attacking the ideal of a transcendental signified outside of the play of meaning and representation, Derrida argues that signifying structures inevitably depend upon a process of supplementarity: "One could say . . . that this movement of play, permitted by the lack or absence of a center or origin, is the movement of *supplementarity*. One cannot determine the center and exhaust totalization because the sign which replaces the center, which supplements it, taking the center's place in its absence—this sign is added, occurs as a surplus, as a *supplement*."[55] Lacan similarly describes the play of the supplement when he explains how the ego is constructed through a play of regards and then sets itself up as the origin at the source. The misrecognition of the ego as a transcendental signified outside of language and representation

[52]M. M. Bakhtin, *The Dialogic Imagination: Four Essays*, ed. Michael Holquist, trans. Caryl Emerson and Holquist (Austin: University of Texas Press, 1981). See his use of such terms as *heteroglossia, polyphony*, and *carnivalization*; Roland Barthes, "The Death of the Author," *Image/Music/Text*, trans. Stephen Heath (New York: Hill and Wang, 1977), 148.

[53]Jean-François Lyotard, *The Postmodern Condition: A Report on Knowledge*, trans. Geoff Bennington and Brian Massumi (Minneapolis: University of Minnesota Press, 1984).

[54]Mária Minich Brewer, "Performing Theory," *Theatre Journal* 37 (March 1985), 16.

[55]Derrida, "Structure, Sign, and Play," *Writing and Difference*, trans. Alan Bass (Chicago: University of Chicago Press, 1978), 289.

results in a false presumption of autonomy and mastery. The play of the supplement in Lacan's theory of the ego similarly employs theatrics to undermine a fixed perspective.

From this standpoint it makes sense to characterize postmodernism as a move from narrative to theater, from a spectator consciousness to a displaced and displacing performer consciousness, from the structure of story to the infinite play and display of discourse. Psychoanalysis and postmodernism alike employ theater to deny the possibility of an objective observer, a static object, or a stable process of viewing. Both employ theatrical devices to subvert the observer's stable position, and so result in a continuous play of partial viewpoints—none of them stable, secure, or complete. Both work with, rather than against, blind spots in our field of vision, displacing a spectator consciousness by foregrounding its construction in terms of a relay of a lack. Both are fascinated with displaying and so displacing presence, with staging their own staging, with framing contents framing their containers. Like the theatrical mask, the postmodern reading necessarily points to itself as already taken and, in turn, necessarily subverts whatever look would comfortably rest there. Ironically, then, a theatrics of reading requires the radical subversion of the metaphysics of presence in which theater is traditionally implicated, and heralds the use of theater not merely as an object of analysis but as a process.

VII

We may conclude that theatricality depends less upon a disparity between representer and represented than upon a constitutive displacement based on this disparity. For example, Freud's work on anxiety as fear experienced in the absence of a causative factor does not lead directly to a theory of the theatrical, nor does T. S. Eliot's theory that Hamlet's emotions lack an objective correlative. Rather, theatricality requires that we enact this disparity, point to a present absence, and stage a perspectivally generated blind spot as the object of (in)attention. What psychoanalysis has learned from theater is a condition of knowing unknowingness which finds its expression in the exhibition of blindness as a form of insight.

Theater roots self-consciousness in an awareness that one is seen, and finally seen as unseeing. When Cassius offers to mirror Brutus, he sets himself up as the source of Brutus's ideal reflection: "I, your glass, / Will modestly discover to yourself / That of yourself which you yet know not of" (1.2.68–70). Western dramas of recognition and misrecognition still pivot upon the fiction that the disparity introduced by the mask can be closed up through dialogue or action, that the double can once again be single without loss of self-consciousness. Both tragedy and comedy play upon this display of another's blindness. In the tragic we identify with the one seen as unseeing; in the comic with the one who sees another as unseeing. In Sophocles' *Ajax* both perspectives merge when Athena's divine laughter is replaced by sympathetic identification with Ajax instead. When a character parades a lack without knowing that he is doing so—and Ajax in *Troilus and Cressida* certainly offers an example—the lack parades as substance without knowing itself as such. More self-aware characters such as Viola or Feste in *Twelfth Night* acknowledge this lack as their own. They openly proclaim that they are not who they are, and look on with bemused detachment as the other characters seek to deny what they do not understand. Both comic and tragic plots may turn upon the protagonist's awareness that this lack merely serves as a trap for others, a screen upon which they will project their fantasies. Hamlet's "I have that within which passes show" (1.2.85) is a taunt or dare, an invitation that tempts the reader to "find / Where truth is hid" (*Hamlet*: 2.2.157–58). By staging the hermeneutic code of questions and answers, by staging the enigmas that structure dramatic narratives as precisely that which is not at issue, such plots manage to upstage not only the efforts of the characters to find where truth is hid, but the efforts of the readers as well. When this search for meaning is revealed as a pose and staged as that which is not the object of attention, theater suggests a different way of knowing.

And in such moments a kind of absence speaks. "What is at stake," William Richardson writes of Heidegger's work, "is a conception of Being as the process of disclosure that includes an absence intrinsic to its presencing."[56] By staging the subversion of self-reference, theatricality suggests the forced exhibition of something

[56] William J. Richardson, "Psychoanalysis and the Being-Question," in *Interpreting Lacan*, ed. Joseph H. Smith and William Kerrigan (New Haven: Yale University Press, 1983), 144. See also his *Heidegger: Through Phenomenology to Thought* (The Hague: Nijhoff, 1963).

that we do not equate with consciousness, something that insists on showing itself as that which cannot be staged. Theatricality is foregrounded in the simple moment of pointing to an absence, as in the mask that points to itself as it advances. In this moment the itness of the I shows itself as what it is not in the act of self-reference. Jean Hyppolite explains:

> "I am going to tell you what I am not; pay attention, that is exactly what I am." That is how Freud engages with the function of negation and, in order to do this, he uses . . . the word *Aufhebung*. . . . It is Hegel's dialectical word, which means simultaneously to deny, to suppress and to conserve, and fundamentally to raise up. . . . Presenting one's being in the mode of not being it, that is truly what is at issue in this *Aufhebung* of the repression, which isn't an acceptance of what is repressed. The person speaking says: "This is what I am not." It would no longer be repressed, if repressed signified unconsciousness, since it is conscious. But in its essentials, the repression persists, in the form of non-acceptance.[57]

The phrase "But didn't you know that you didn't know?" is quintessentially theatrical, as are the narratives of "The Emperor's New Clothes," "The Purloined Letter," and any number of works by Henry James. The erotics of knowledge depends upon revealing this nothing, staging or exhibiting an absence as a way of commenting on the double of presence.

We conclude with a question that opens up many more. At the end of Lacan's seminar "The Split between the Eye and the Gaze," X. Audouard asks: "*To what extent is it necessary, in analysis, to let the subject know that one is looking at him, that is to say, that one is situated as the person who is observing in the subject the process of looking at oneself?*"[58] Freud prided himself on his particular positioning in the analytic setting—"seeing . . . but not seen myself."[59] Yet wasn't Freud fooling himself here, and wasn't this the delusion that Lacan uncovered?

[57]Jean Hyppolite, "A Spoken Commentary on Freud's *Verneinung*," Appendix to Lacan, *Freud's Papers on Technique*, bk. 1 of *The Seminar of Jacques Lacan*, ed. Jacques-Alain Miller, trans. John Forrester (New York: Norton, 1988), 291.

[58]Lacan, "Split between the Eye and the Gaze," 77.

[59]Sigmund Freud, *An Autobiographical Study*, trans. James Strachey (New York: Norton, 1963), 47.

Lacan answers Audouard defensively, belittling him by pretending to read him literally: "We do not say to the patient, at every end and turn, *Now, now! What a face you're making!*, or *The top button of your waistcoat is undone.* It is not, after all, for nothing that analysis is not carried out face to face."[60] The exasperated tone may not be excusable, but it does suggest how the analyst's presence evokes or provokes the analysand's unconscious self-regard. The presence of the analyst elicits and disrupts the gaze; the patient knows she is being watched, and so watches and hears herself differently; the second mirror is in place, mirroring the first, thereby placing and displacing body, voice, and gaze.

[60]Lacan, "Split between the Eye and the Gaze," 78.

77

3

Reading Errantly:
Misrecognition and the Uncanny
in *The Comedy of Errors*

> What in fact is the phenomenon of delusional belief? It is, I insist,
> failure to recognize, with all that this term contains of an essential
> antinomy. For to fail to recognize presupposes a recognition, as is
> manifested in a systematic failure to recognize, where it must
> obviously be admitted that what is denied is in some fashion recog-
> nized. . . . It seems clear to me that in his feelings of influence and
> automatism, the subject does not recognize his productions as his
> own. It is in this respect that we all agree that a madman is a
> madman. But isn't the remarkable thing rather that he should have
> to take cognizance of it? And isn't the question rather to discover
> what he knows about himself in these productions without recog-
> nizing himself in them?
>
> —Lacan, "Propos sur la causalité psychique"

I

The Comedy of Errors stages denied connections on a variety
of levels of imaginative experience. The play is ostensibly
about mistaken recognitions and mistaken timing: despite the presence of identical twins within the same town, the two brothers never
meet up with each other and so never discover the cause of their
confusion. Since these misrecognitions are merely physical, situa-
tional errors, they at first seem to bolster our sense of superiority; we
know who everyone really is and why these misunderstandings
occur. But as the mood darkens, as it oscillates ever more rapidly

78

between comic terror and romance, nightmare and wish fulfillment, we come to identify with the experiences of these erring creatures. We partake in an uncanny fantasy that we recognize at some level but fail to understand.

The Comedy of Errors dramatizes a nightmare vision in comic form—a truly terrifying fantasy of a sudden, inexplicable disjunction between personal and communal accounts of one's identity. Those who are most familiar proclaim one a total stranger, and strangers evince a mysteriously gained familiarity. A recent production of the play emphasized this sense of the uncanny. Egeon's pathetic query— "Not know my voice! O time's extremity, / Hast thou so crack'd and splitted my poor tongue / In seven short years, that here my only son / Knows not my feeble key of untun'd cares?" (5.1.308–11)— was delivered to a winking, snickering crowd onstage, and at each piteous lament the uncomprehending townspeople laughed the louder.

The term *uncanny* aptly describes the mood of *The Comedy of Errors*, since the conflation of the familiar and the unknown is operative at a number of levels of this many-leveled play. Freud maintains that "the uncanny [*unheimlich*] is something which is secretly familiar [*heimlich-heimisch*], which has undergone repression and then returned from it." For this reason, "linguistic usage has extended *das Heimliche* ['homely'] into its opposite, *das Unheimliche*; for this uncanny is in reality nothing new or alien, but something which is familiar and old-established in the mind and which has become alienated from it only through the process of repression."[1]

But *The Comedy of Errors* operates at the level of the uncanny for its critics as well, for as we read the play we continually sense connections that we cannot understand. This comedy insists on its own meaninglessness and yet tantalizes us with the possibility of coherent meaning. The play exhibits a remarkable drive toward closure through a romance plot of the separation and reunion of members of a family, an extensive chain of imagery, an allegorical structure, a morality-based plot, and a permanent stage set. At the same time the play undermines the possibility of closure through a disjunctive double plot that develops only through errors, chance, and miracle. The convoluted logic of this illogical plot progresses

[1]Freud, "The 'Uncanny'" (1919), *SE*, 17:245, 241.

from Egeon's mysterious crime and meaningless debt, through his sons' punishment for failure to pay mistaken debts, and finally on to Egeon's miraculous redemption and forgiveness. The patterns of crime-punishment-forgiveness and debt-payment-redemption assert narrative logic; the use of mystery, mistakes, miracle, and a disjunctive double plot deny that logic. Connections that might unite main plot and frame plot, join the father's mysterious crime to the children's mistaken punishment, and relate the twins' payment of mistaken debts to Egeon's miraculous forgiveness are at once forged and denied. The interplay of logic and absurdity, transgression and innocence, punishment and nonsense, may help to explain why a work with such elaborately wrought chains of meaning has been received for centuries as meaningless farce.

Since we have been unable to find a means of uniting these plots—and yet we sense their connection—our own readings display this sense of uncanny connections anticipated and yet denied. Rather than deny this problem we can study the awareness of erring at work in our attempts to deny it, and rethink the reading process itself in terms of erring awareness. The project of reading *The Comedy of Errors* reveals how the identity of the literary work, like the identity of the subject, is uncanny *precisely because of its awareness of its failure to capture awareness*. The value of Shakespeare's comedies may be enfolded within this problem. Given that they repeat within themselves the properties of mind they describe, the comedies are truly *riddled* with meaning. These structural disjunctions suggest ambivalence toward making connections both at the level of interpersonal relations and at the level of meaning. Accordingly, *The Comedy of Errors* is as much "about" its own construction of meaning as it is about the construction or reconstruction of the family. A full articulation of the play's levels of self-awareness is impossible—and this may well be the point. Yet insofar as the play comprehends repression on a variety of levels at once, it functions as an example of the thing it "represents," and so "countenances" its own blindness. And insofar as the play claims to do no more than to articulate splits in subjectivity as a response to the problem of meaning, it frees itself as well as us of the burden of full awareness. What the play "means," then, is as impossible to contain as who we are; the same principle of meaning applies equally to play and player, and the assumption of self-identity in either case no longer applies. *The Comedy of Errors* stages identity as that place where issues of representation and repression, structuration and subjectivity intersect. Identity is treated as a form of knowledge, knowledge as a subset of meaning, and meaning as a process in which repression and recognition vie for mastery.

II

Critics who pose such questions as who is reading or where reading takes place will find *The Comedy of Errors* a convenient vehicle for staging these dilemmas, and for raising many more. When is an uncanny text a canny text? How do we determine a play's level of awareness? Is there any way of speaking about this problem that avoids the pretense that the text is a psyche, split between conscious and unconscious, and so always repressing its own meanings? If we term this text *uncanny*, how do we determine its awareness of its levels of awareness?

The Comedy of Errors is widely considered Shakespeare's most insignificant, unselfconscious, and disjointed play. The degree of critical consensus here would be comforting were it not for the various hints that the play's construction of the knowing subject is a ruse. *The Comedy of Errors* is the only Shakespearean play that turns entirely upon certain knowledge possessed by the audience from the beginning and revealed to the characters only at the conclusion. We know everything; the text knows nothing—*or so we think*. One major critic informs us that this play is "two-dimensional only, unsubstantial, not intended to be taken seriously."[2] Another assures us that "everything which Shakespeare meant by *The Comedy of Errors* is immediately perceptible. . . . All we have to do is grasp the broadly absurd situation, and follow the ingenious fugue of the plot. To get the point, nothing beyond mental alertness of an easy kind is required."[3] The editor of the Pelican Shakespeare edition complains that "there is left over nothing really to think about—except, if one wishes, the tremendously puzzling question of what so grips and

[2]Berners A. W. Jackson, Introduction to *The Two Gentlemen of Verona*, in the Pelican Shakespeare (Baltimore: Penguin, 1969), 116.

[3]Francis Fergusson, "*The Comedy of Errors* and *Much Ado about Nothing*," *Sewanee Review* 62 (1954), 37, 28.

amuses an audience during a play which has so little thought in it."[4]
Critics encourage us to value *The Comedy of Errors* as an "assimilation
and extension of Plautine comedy," to marvel at its "symmetry and
near-flawlessness of plot," and to plumb its rich "harmonic structure" for interrelated themes and patterns of imagery, but warn us to
forgo the search for "deeper" meanings.[5]

Scholars frequently regard both the inception and the conclusion
of the main plot, derived from Plautus's *Menaechmi* and *Amphitruo*, as
arbitrary. According to Paul Jorgensen, the farce of misrecognitions
records nothing more than a random "rearranging of human pup-
pets" in an essentially static situation.[6] Harold Jenkins maintains that
"the confusion of the twins . . . [is] little more than an adroit device to
bring about a happy ending"; it "is really the result of accidental
circumstances and is as accidentally cleared up."[7] And Francis Fergusson muses that "the arabesques of absurdity in *The Comedy of
Errors* might continue indefinitely."[8] Although critics acknowledge,
following G. R. Elliott, that each character confronts the horror of
mistaken identity, they also maintain, with Jorgensen, that "no one
learns more about himself or his neighbor as a result of the errors."[9]
Since, as Jorgensen complains, "in no other play . . . is the purpose
of the confusion less apparent," he and other critics conclude that the
farcical mixup conveys what Larry Champion assesses as "no more
and no less than the sheer merriment of controlled confusion."[10]

[4]Paul A. Jorgensen, Introduction to *The Comedy of Errors*, in *The Pelican Shakespeare*, 55.

[5]Harry Levin, Introduction to *The Comedy of Errors*, in the Signet Classic
Shakespeare (New York: New American Library, 1965), xxiii; Jorgensen, Introduction, 56; Harold Brooks, "Themes and Structure in *The Comedy of Errors*," in *Early
Shakespeare*, ed. John Russell Brown and Bernard Harris (London: Edward Arnold,
1961), 70–71.

[6]Jorgensen, Introduction, 55.

[7]Harold Jenkins, "Shakespeare's *Twelfth Night*," in *Shakespeare: The Comedies: A
Collection of Critical Essays*, ed. Kenneth Muir (Englewood Cliffs, N.J.: Prentice-Hall,
1965), 73.

[8]Fergusson, "*Comedy of Errors* and *Much Ado*," 27.

[9]Jorgensen, Introduction, 57. See also Fergusson, "*Comedy of Errors* and *Much
Ado*," 34. This view is strongly expressed by Larry S. Champion, *The Evolution of
Shakespeare's Comedy: A Study in Dramatic Perspective* (Cambridge: Harvard University Press, 1970), 13, 19, 61; opposed in D. A. Traversi's *Approach to Shakespeare*, 3d
ed., rev., vol. I (New York: Doubleday-Anchor, 1969), 64, 68. In "Weirdness in *The
Comedy of Errors*," *University of Toronto Quarterly* 9 (1939), 95–106, G. R. Elliott
persuasively connects the horror of mistaken identity to the play's strange mood of
nightmare.

[10]Jorgensen, Introduction, 57; Champion, *Evolution of Shakespeare's Comedy*, 17.

Directors of this play are less disturbed by these farcical discon-
nections than by the notorious practical difficulties posed by the
frame plot: an illogical situation, an unexpected mood of pathos,
seemingly interminable speeches recounting past events, and easily
forgettable characters who fail to reappear until the last scene of the
play. Scholars generally agree that the frame plot, adapted from
Apollonius of Tyre, is both poorly integrated into the rest of the play
and incompatible with its mood.[11] And yet some critics claim that
the frame plot both "humanizes" the farce and adds "emotional
tension . . . to what would otherwise have remained a two-dimensional drama."[12] Despite elaborate New Critical studies of complex
themes and patterns of imagery in this play, these problems remain
unresolved.[13]

But should they be resolved? And what are the consequences of
accepting rather than denying fragmentation and disjunction? One
consequence is a recognition of how much we have in common with
the characters in the play, since neither characters nor audience seems
willing or able to accept disjunction. Our failed attempts to unify *The
Comedy of Errors* suggest the unflattering position of the Dromio
servants, whose well-meaning attempts to mediate between characters result in disaster. Accordingly, our desire to integrate the plots is
far more interesting than any discovery of a means whereby they
could be joined. C. L. Barber proposes that one reason for merging
the two plots is "that the bonds of marriage, broken in [the parents']
case by romantic accident, are also very much at issue in the intervening scenes."[14] This hypothesis comes closest to offering a unifying

[11]See Arthur Quiller-Couch, Introduction to *The Comedy of Errors*, in the New
Cambridge Shakespeare (1922; rpt. Cambridge: Cambridge University Press, 1962);
Champion, *Evolution of Shakespeare's Comedy*; Elliott, "Weirdness in *The Comedy of
Errors*"; and H. B. Charlton, *Shakespearian Comedy* (London: Methuen, 1938).

[12]Elliott, "Weirdness in *The Comedy of Errors*," 97; and see Levin, Introduction,
xxix.

[13]See especially Brooks, "Themes and Structure in *The Comedy of Errors*"; R. A.
Foakes, Introduction to *The Comedy of Errors*, in the Arden Shakespeare (London:
Methuen, 1962); William Babula, "'If I Dream Not': Unity in *The Comedy of Errors*,"
South Atlantic Bulletin 38 (1973), 26–33; Vincent F. Petronella, "Structure and Theme
through Separation and Union in Shakespeare's *The Comedy of Errors*," *Modern
Language Review* 69 (1974), 481–88; and Barbara Freedman, "Egeon's Debt: Self-
Division and Self-Redemption in *The Comedy of Errors*," *English Literary Renaissance*
10 (1980), 360–83.

[14]C. L. Barber, "Shakespearian Comedy in *The Comedy of Errors*," *College
English* 25 (1976), 497.

principle for the play; yet Barber wisely resists attempting to impose coherence on the fractured plot. And so the characters' plight in attempting to unify their experiences forces us to question our role as readers. Do we need to prove the frame plot intrinsic to the play or the main plot purposive? Must our reading reassemble the text so that what seems out of place has a place—and if so, when does this process properly end?

The Comedy of Errors raises a host of questions concerning levels of awareness in both the text and the reader. In terms of imaginative logic, what is being worked through in this play? At the same time, why, in whom, and on what stage is it denied and repeated, resisted and reenacted? As we trace the play's plotted course, we can explore how the reading process is implicated in the principles of identity and repression we examine. If we cannot fix the identity of the play, we can follow our misreadings to explore how meaning, repression, and recognition intersect. At best, we can hope to identify various levels of awareness at work in our reading and to catch them in moments of interrupting, caricaturing, containing, and escaping one another. Since the etymology of *errors* suggests not only mistakes but wandering, we will move with this play and seek to catch our errors as we make them. The significant misrecognitions are not, finally, those that take place between the characters in the play, but those that occur because of the play of character itself. The telling misprisions include our unquestioning identification with such phantom figures as the omniscient reader of this text or the unified ego of so many other texts. To read *The Comedy of Errors* in this way is to acknowledge the sway of the uncanny in our lives. It is to acknowledge that, insofar as we cannot avoid the principle of errors the play articulates, we can never hope to read the play correctly.

III

For the purpose of engaging critical debate, let us take the play's bait and try on the different reading styles offered by the major characters. To understand Antipholus of Ephesus, for example, is to join him as a reader, to under-stand a point of view from which understanding is not problematic. Like Malvolio after him (and Oedipus before), he loudly asserts that he knows who he is. And he defines himself through boundaries, hierarchies, repression, and exclusion—through what he owns, and through the servants and women whom he owns. Luciana's set speech affirms this principle of identity: "There's nothing situate under heaven's eye / But hath his bound in earth, in sea, in sky. / The beasts, the fishes, and the winged fowls / Are their males' subjects and at their controls: / Man, more divine, the master of all these, / Lord of the wide world and wild wat'ry seas, / . . . Are masters to their females, and their lords" (2.1.16–21, 24).

Almost a caricature of the worst of the New Critics, the Ephesian master is blind to the other readings of events advanced throughout the play. His view of the world is not unlike the chain of command described in Luciana's set speech; he inhabits a closed interpretive universe with a limited number of signifiers and signifieds. Meaning is simply a matter of joining them up according to a principle of right relationship. The sign remains stable, binary oppositions still hold, man is at the center of the universe, and all is right with the world. And the play upholds this mode of reading in its concern with bringing together father and sons, husband and wife, brother and brother into "right relationship"; and in encouraging us to locate meaning that, like the prodigal son, once was lost and at last is found. These strategies suggest a comforting and stable world order which sanctions a reading of the organic unity of both self and text.

The Comedy of Errors also undermines this viewpoint, however, by upholding an opposing reading of identity and meaning. For example, if identity is simply a matter of whom we can dominate, then Antipholus of Ephesus is not himself, for he is neither master in his own home nor his own master. That he is not is demonstrated by his long-lost twin brother, the doppelganger, or denied other within the self, whose actions suggest the phenomenon that Freud termed "the return of the repressed." The prototypical romantic, this twin seeks his identity in whatever he encounters and lacks the boundaries we associate with ego stability. He emerges from the sea only to threaten to drown those ashore; he lends himself to a protean principle of meaning and identity and so takes the shape or place of whatever he encounters. He is all too willing to embrace the other, or the other's point of view, or the other's wife, to the point that madness and chaos finally threaten his existence. Almost a caricature of the worst of the deconstructive critics, this twin champions a principle of the infinite commutability of the signified and celebrates the limitless exchange and transformation of meaning. Insofar as meaning and identity are based not only on privileging some meanings but on repressing the possibility of other meanings that surface in time, this return of the repressed threatens all fictions of closure. By inadvertently challenging the principles of property and repression upon which Western identity is based, this twin adds to a farce of displacement by one's double a fantasy of the endless display and displacement of meaning.

And the play can also be shown to bear out this style of reading. At the level of character, *The Comedy of Errors* keeps multiplying subjects and points of view: it splits its main characters into identical twins, and it splits the male subject into husband and bachelor, homebody and traveler, businessman and poet, sinner and exorcist, servant and master. Further, it splits the female subject into the two holy trinities—angel, devil, nun; and mother, wife, courtesan. At the same time the play proliferates contradictory meanings through games of wit and wordplay and through a dispersal of levels of awareness that haunts any text that would presume to contain this play. That there is no outside to this or any other text is graphically illustrated by the way its multiple levels of awareness imply an infinite regress that in turn rebounds upon itself to collapse those levels. We no sooner consider ourselves superior in awareness to the twin Antipholi than we recall that these "masters" imagine themselves superior to their wives, who in turn enjoy superiority over their servants, who in turn feel superior to "their" women. Yet at any one level, superiority over another is accompanied by a limitation in awareness implied by the level above it. As a result, superiority and inferiority, mastery and bondage, knowledge and errors occupy the same site. The idea of under-standing *Errors* is itself called into question by these games with a supposedly omniscient reader.

Even to pose a choice between these two styles of reading is to imply that we can stand outside of them. To attempt to fix or contain the meanings of the play is to deny the principles of repression and representation through which identity and meaning necessarily function. The play contains us in its comedy of errors and encourages us to share the very assumptions it undermines. We contradict ourselves if we assert that the play exhibits ambivalence toward closure, for we thereby imply that we can fix the play's meanings. If we argue that

86

the twin subjects embody authorial intention, we must add that they embody it as that which escapes representational closure. Meaning is staged as subject to a potentially infinite process of splitting and repression. The conflict between repression and representation is enacted both on the stage of the play and within any discourse that would fix the play, close its meanings, and restore its unity.

Before we proclaim Antipholus of Syracuse the master reader, however, we need to consider the limits of his reading style. The traveler's mode of reading all too easily denies the cultural context of any reading and so disowns responsibility for its point of view. It relies upon an unspoken fantasy that we can avoid being displaced by other readings as long as we continually redefine the nature of reading. It suggests that we can remove reading from a context of mastery and truth and innocently envision it as the infinite play of the supplement. Antipholus of Syracuse offers a useful cautionary principle for readers, insofar as his reading style denies that it takes a place. Whereas it calls into question the boundaries between dream and reality, self and other, past and present, order and disorder, it can account for neither these binary oppositions nor the principle of repression they imply.

Where, then, do we stand or wander in this debate? Can we privilege one style of reading over the other? The conclusion of the play at first appears to offer a ridiculously simple solution to this complicated problem. By equating the twin sons with opposing principles of identity and change and then uniting these brothers at its conclusion, the play implies that identity and change are no longer mutually exclusive concepts. As with most of the so-called solutions to Shakespeare's comedies, however, this ending blatantly ignores the complexity of the problems we have been encouraged to entertain. There is no Heraclitean sophistication here, no complex definition of the human animal as that which changes. Since Emilia and Egeon have done nothing to correct the error of over twenty years of separation, the compatibility of these two changed creatures may well strain their imaginations as much as our own.

The concluding nonverbal cues openly interrogate the narrative drive toward closure, as the twin Dromios try to carry out their promise of forevermore going "hand in hand, not one before another" (5.1.426). Are they not comically inept here, as elsewhere, in carrying out their good intentions? Can they always enter every door at precisely the same time? The Dromio servants' recognition that one must go before the other recalls Luciana's sense that identity depends upon a law of priority and place. The exits of the other characters have hardly followed democratic practice, after all. The Dromios have had to wait their turn. They have not been invited to exit at the same time as their masters, nor did the masters exit with "their" ladies, who presumably left the stage before them. Following the comedies' discursive doublespeak, this conclusion underscores the relation between identity and repression.

The limits of both reading styles, as well as the impossibility of either choosing between them or joining them, are graphically portrayed by the Dromio servants. In their clownish efforts to mediate between the twins, the Dromios offer us a mirror image of our own frustrated attempts to unite this play. The funniest moments in *The Comedy of Errors* are the beatings of the Dromio servants. The Dromios never know the cause of their motion and never question the angry beatings they receive upon delivering their messages. Well-meaning but thickheaded, they are the true butts of farce—doomed to err, doomed to disobey their masters' commands, doomed to be beaten but never to know why: "When I am cold, he heats me with beating; when I am warm, he cools me with beating. I am wak'd with it when I sleep, rais'd with it when I sit, driven out of doors with it when I go from home, welcom'd home with it when I return; nay, I bear it on my shoulders, as a beggar wont her brat; and I think when he hath lam'd me, I shall beg with it from door to door" (4.4.32–39).

The function of these perplexed messengers is to act as potential mediators between disjunctive worlds—whether past and present, single and marital personae—with unfailingly disastrous results. These clownish servants convey the sense of helplessness that accompanies the futile attempt to live in mutually exclusive worlds and to meet their contradictory demands. Try as they may to understand a given message and to carry it with all due speed to its proper destination, the Dromios are unable to keep up with the changing worlds of the play. As they automatically give the right message to the wrong person, they offer an image of the self unable to cope with or adapt to the demands of a changing environment. Not only do they remind us of the reader's foolish attempts to join up the play's fragmented parts, they also suggest the binding and purposive ego functions caught in the grasp of an automatic and dysfunctional repetition. Like the ego functions, the Dromios' function is to bring disjunctive selves and worlds together. Continually frustrated in their attempts—beaten, mocked, and scorned by all parties—they graphically depict a situation in which the ego is not master in its own house. If we cannot yet give up our dreams of a unified ego, if we cannot avoid the desire to piece together this play, we must accept that in so doing we are not only playing into the hands of a plot that would prove these efforts impossible, but playing the role of fools.

IV

As persistent messengers, we continue to follow the spirit of the uncanny and to work at the relation of the strange and the familiar. Some of the best treatments of *The Comedy of Errors* have focused on its exploration of the relationship of temporality and identity. Gāmini Salgādo explores "the tricks [*Errors*] plays, in form, language, and action, with what we take to be a normal temporal sequence," and concludes: "If a developed sense of time and a sense of individuality are virtually two aspects of the same thing, this may account for the uncanny and more-than-farcical resonance of the play."[15] When Egeon isn't recognized by his son, he blames "time's deformed hand" (5.1.299) for the misrecognition. Since the play's humor works through a disruption of "order," and since its wit and wordplay center around the problem of recovering—and denying the recovery of—something lost in time, we might take this fantasy more seriously.

This time, however, we will read from Adriana's point of view. Not surprisingly, the speech that appears to piece everything together is offered by the excluded, discredited voice of a woman. In Act 2, Adriana equates her husband's neglect of marital duties with his own self-estrangement and self-division: "How comes it now, my husband, O, how comes it, / That thou art then estranged from thyself? / Thyself I call it, being strange to me, / That, undividable

[15]Gāmini Salgādo, "'Time's Deformed Hand': Sequence, Consequence, and Inconsequence in *The Comedy of Errors,*" *Shakespeare Survey* 25 (1972), 81, 82. For an extended treatment of this problem, see J. Dennis Huston's exciting chapter on *The Comedy of Errors* in *Shakespeare's Comedies of Play* (New York: Columbia University Press, 1981).

incorporate, / Am better than thy dear self's better part. / Ah, do not tear away thyself from me" (2.2.119–24). Adriana's reasoning is at least consistent: separation from one's spouse results in a division of the personality into contradictory marital ("thou," "me") and single ("thyself") personae. This elaborate system has the distinction of positing a unified, coherent ideal self, and so holds out the promise of unifying self and text, identity and meaning. Its irrelevance to the situation at hand, however, suggests that we are laboring under another illusion.

The terms of Adriana's equation fail to apply to the man she addresses as her husband, since Antipholus of Syracuse is a bachelor. Nor do they apply to the intended recipient of this speech since, despite Adriana's jealousy, the couple is not yet estranged. The situation does apply to Egeon, however, who has been separated from his spouse, and so from a part of himself, for well over twenty years. As in so many plots based on the usurping double, the sense of closure that we associate with individual identity is eroded, and we experience the phenomenon described as "the second self in time."[16] By reading Egeon's plight as one in which disowned or split-off parts of the self are still recognized by others, we can unite this disjointed plot. But as we take the play's bait, we must remember who and what is being caught.

If Egeon is estranged not only from his wife but from his marital identity, divided into single and marital personae, his twin sons graphically suggest his divided state. The birth of the twins occurs only after Egeon's first separation from his wife, and when his wife comes to see him in Epidamnum. In Adriana's terms, duality is conceived only when Egeon's single identity ("thyself") and marital identity ("thou") confront each other. The twins' symbolic function is further suggested by the correspondence of their opposing characteristics to Egeon's accounts of his marital and postmarital, past and present, unified and divided identities. Antipholus of Ephesus is literally that "part" of Egeon which has remained lost with his wife since the storm first separated the couple. Antipholus of Syracuse is that "part" of Egeon that has remained with him. Like the former

---

[16]C. F. Keppler coined this term in *The Literature of the Second Self* (Tucson: University of Arizona Press, 1972) but failed to note its relevance to this play.

Egeon, the Ephesian twin is the settled, respectable citizen; his denied counterpart is drawn in the likeness of the present image of his father—an unhappy sojourner. The Ephesian twin is firmly ensconced in a familial situation; the Syracusan is a wandering bachelor, seeking the domestic stability Egeon has lost. The Ephesian is a businessman, recalled in Egeon's description of his former life to Duke Solinus (1.1.39–40); his brother is an impractical romantic who hazards all in an apparently bootless journey, much like his "hopeless and helpless" father.

Despite some confusion about the order of the twins' births, the married brother is twice referred to and commonly accepted as the elder; this precedence further encourages us to associate him with Egeon's past and his single brother with Egeon's present situation. The Ephesian has no knowledge of his brother; as Egeon's pre-tempest persona, he cannot anticipate future self-division. The Syracusan, as representative of Egeon's present identity, is aware of his divided condition and seeks to remedy it. Antipholus of Syracuse is further associated with Egeon's divided state when he is advised by a friend to deny his birthplace and to call his home Epidamnum, thereby recalling Egeon's separation from his birthplace, wife, and past when he left for Epidamnum. The Syracusan twin lodges at the Centaur, sign of a divided state; the Ephesian brother who must be recovered lives at the Phoenix, sign of rebirth.

The allegorical schema of the "second self in time" neatly ties together the fragmented plots. It relates the mixup of the twins' identities to Egeon's problem and its resolution in the frame plot. And it suggests that the play enacts a fantasy of confronting and integrating split-off parts of the "self" in time. The tempest that divided Egeon from his wife literally divided his past and present, marital and single identities as well, represented by Egeon's separated twin sons. Antipholus of Ephesus is the stable, secure marital identity of Egeon's youth; Antipholus of Syracuse is Egeon's fragile present persona, the single traveler seeking to recover his other half, to integrate himself, to be reborn: "So I, to find a mother and a brother, / In quest of them (unhappy), ah, lose myself" (1.2.39–40). Egeon's search for a past identity is suggested by his physical separation from Emilia in the frame plot and by Antipholus of Syracuse's search for his long-lost married brother in the main plot. By dividing the personality up neatly into halves, *The Comedy of Errors* holds out the possibility of self-presence. As thematic imagery forges one chain between the fractured plots, the allegorical framework of the second self in time forges an even more stable link, implying that self-redemption can indeed be final and complete.

Were we to stop here, we could conclude that *The Comedy of Errors* is not simply about the physical division and reunion of a family but about the psychic division and integration of the personality. In fact, once this allegorical schema is brought to our attention, hidden "connections" seem everywhere, encouraging us to tie together the play's religious references, its Gray's Inn Christmas performance, its puns on debts and redemption, its emendation of the twins' age from twenty-five to thirty-three, and much more. Yet this reading does not "clinch" the play or supersede other readings. To credit this master narrative, we would have to explain why no one has uncovered it for well over three hundred years. Rather than applaud our own efforts as detectives, we might detect the humor directed at any such stance of mastery. Wasn't C. L. Barber right to stop short of reading the twins as representatives of their father's divided state, since such a reading denies that this is a play about denial? "I deny it not" (5.1.379) is a phrase that we hear and yet deny throughout this curious work. Of more significance than our recovery of a hidden plot is our acknowledgment of its problematic status. Since the play strenuously denies that Egeon was guilty for leaving his wife, any reading of his guilt as something that is worked out or paid for by his sons is simply unwarranted. As we continue to read this play, it is essential that we preserve at the level of meaning the sense of duality and ambivalence which is visually emphasized in the image of identical twins. The uncanny implies a familiar unfamiliarity in relation to time and so both does and undoes the work of repression. Since the uncanny implies a return of the repressed, it offers a comforting sense that what is lost can always be found; since it also points to the inevitability of future repression, it implies that identity and meaning can never be stable. As we continue to err in the direction of allegory, we need to attend to the ways in which the play's ambivalence toward representation and repression troubles any reading.

92

V

Adriana's desire to pin blame, the twins' desire to punish their servants, Egeon's innocent crime—all betray a curious ambivalence toward guilt and indebtedness. Since the twins are always confused with each other in a way that forces each to mistakenly identify with the other's debts,[17] their indebtedness both evokes Egeon's debt and denies any meaningful relationship to it. Obsessive fantasies of being unable to repay a debt typically suggest guilt regarding an inability to fulfill one's obligations. In this case, the broken marriage bond functions as the debt whose payment alone can retrieve a denied marital persona. But insofar as the play never fully owns up to this debt, the sense of guilt moves symptomatically through the text like a signifier cut loose from its signified—as if by splitting and duplication it could avoid knowing what it knows. In this sense, *The Comedy of Errors* is not only about repression, or even about the return of the repressed, but about the repression of this return. The result is a series of ever more contradictory stories that prevent us from taking any single viewpoint upon them. These elaborate displacements of a situation of indebtedness typify this play's obsessive mode of ordering, fragmenting, and then reordering a highly intricate plot in such a way that it no longer conveys the same meanings at all.

For example, *The Comedy of Errors* actually records two different transgressions: Egeon's violation of Ephesian law in the frame plot and his sons' run-ins with domestic law in the main plot. Not only does the dual status of culprit and crime wonderfully confuse the issue, but the fact that both transgressions are invalidated—whether by ignorance of the law or by mistaken identification of the culprit—renders the punishment either perversely arbitrary or comically absurd. Egeon's debt is actual, obscure, and monetary; his sons' debts are mistaken, meaningful, and marital. On one hand this play is obsessed with confronting, punishing, and forgiving debts; that action follows a logical pattern and is accompanied by significant

[17]Harold Brooks appears to have been the first to recognize that all the mistaken identifications center around debts; see his "Themes and Structure in *The Comedy of Errors*."

93

emotional reaction. On the other hand, the play either invalidates those debts or obscures their content, thereby denying their significance. The question is not what unifies the two debts—for the marital debt does so quite nicely—but at what level of awareness this text is operating in relation to these denials.

We could attribute these contradictions to a functional displacement of meaning and argue that the punishment of unpaid debts is made acceptable by their disguise and denial. But by whom and for whom are these debts and their punishment "made acceptable"? That the play compulsively repeats a situation of indebtedness—adding marital to monetary debts, mistaken debts to actual debts, sons' debts to a father's debt—is undeniable. So is the pattern whereby Egeon's monetary debt is associated with his son's potential monetary debt, equated through replacement with a mistaken marital debt, and so promptly discharged. As the Syracusan twin turns from fear of actual monetary debt to payment for a mistaken marital debt, so his brother turns from fear of an actual marital debt to payment for a mistaken monetary debt. Given such an intricate pattern, as well as the means by which this farcical confrontation of debts results in Egeon's redemption, it would appear that some sort of debt is being repeated and "worked through."

Adriana's copious complaints of marital neglect, coupled with the kitchen maid Nell's equally relentless marital demands, strongly argue for the existence of a valid marital debt—or an odd disjunction between accounts of what constitutes marital obligations in Ephesus. Adriana rightly believes her husband guilty of not returning home that day, and he admits that wrong in considering the jeweler's work on the gold chain to be an excuse for his absence (3.1.1–5). The highlight of Egeon's story is also a failure to return home, regardless of whether this is due to "cruel fate," to business obligations (1.1.41–43), or to personal preference (1.1.58–60).

Since Egeon allows eighteen years to elapse before searching for anyone—and his search is motivated by the loss of his sons—one is tempted to associate the action of "cruel fate" with denied dreams of independence. To do so, however, is to repeat the characters' errors in their attempts to pin blame. By assuming misrecognition as a principle of meaning, the play renders comical any attempt to recognize its meaning from one point of view. Its performance of the subject as erring and divided forces any critical discourse that would master it to confront its own errors—its propensity to locate and unify a given character, author, or the text "itself." As our attempt to pin blame on one character or to thematize the play in terms of a controlling idea fails, as the tendency to speak of the play's author, action, or awareness becomes increasingly less viable, the very terms of critical discourse begin to fragment and turn against themselves.

Psychoanalytic critics have been notoriously guilty of the quest for hidden or denied meanings that would make sense of this play. They have argued loudly and senselessly over whether or not Egeon "meant" to flee his marriage and over whether or not the wish to escape one's wife is the unacceptable, repressed fantasy that the play obsessively repeats in disguised form. Theories that Egeon's punishment is due to his ambivalence toward domesticity, his lust for money, or his repressed oedipal wishes are equally unconvincing.[18] Can a fictional storm punish a fictional character for his disguised wishes?

If *The Comedy of Errors* is taken at face value, Egeon is clearly absolved of any guilt. He was no more aware of the feud between Ephesus and Syracuse than he was in a position to halt the tempest. Although we can "uncover" Freudian slips throughout his copious protests of innocence, the challenge we face as readers is to consider how our readings are implicated in the very process of uncovering

---

[18]G. G. Gervinus maintains that the family's errors are internal or psychological and stem from a conflict of domestic love and a love of wandering. As proof of ambivalence toward domesticity in this play he cites Egeon's interest in straying from home, Emilia's willful if not jealous plans to follow Egeon, and that the couple's plan to return home was made against Egeon's wishes. See "*The Comedy of Errors* and *The Taming of the Shrew*," *Shakespeare Commentaries*, trans. F. E. Bunnett (London: Smith, Elder, 1863). In "Some Notes on Love and Money in *The Comedy of Errors*," in *Critical Dimensions: English, German, and Comparative Literature Essays in Honor of Aurelio Zanco*, ed. Mario Currelli and Alberto Martino (Cuneo, Italy: Saste, 1978), 107–16, Charles Haines argues that Egeon is guilty of leaving a pregnant wife to attend to business: "To this compelling interest in commerce may be traced all the subsequent accidents in his life and in the lives of his family. All of the breakdowns in human relationship in *Errors* flow from this early evidence of the tyranny of money" (114). In "Shakespeare's Early Errors," *International Journal of Psycho-Analysis* 36 (1955), 114–33, A. Bronson Feldman reads this play as "an apology for Shakespeare's errors in matrimony" (116). Ambivalence toward matrimony is supposedly demonstrated in the fantasy of receiving sexual pleasure without paying for it; in the split figures of the wife; and in an oedipal fantasy that explains the sons' desire for reunion with their mother, Egeon's punishment as a father figure and intruder, and Egeon's release from punishment when the sons regain their mother.

and covering up which we would analyze. The challenge we face is neither to pin blame nor to close up the play's meanings but to acknowledge that which resists these efforts. From one standpoint, Egeon's story suggests guilt regarding both the denial of a marital bond and a wish for previous marital separations, and so provides the "missing link" that changes an arbitrary farce plot into a meaningfully directed fantasy. Yet Egeon repeatedly denies any ill will that would affirm this core fantasy, and his resistance is fitting, given a play that never stands in one place regarding innocence or guilt.

Errors resists as it encourages our efforts to fix any of its characters—Antipholus of Ephesus or Syracuse, Dromio of Ephesus or Syracuse, Adriana or Luciana, Luce or Nell—in any final identity. And this resistance forces us to remember that Egeon is not a person and that he has no sons who can re-present him. Egeon is merely a stand-in, in a series of stand-ins, for a sense of guilt that can neither be internalized nor integrated. To argue that the twins re-present Egeon's divided state is therefore as problematic as to maintain that Egeon's disguised wishes motivate the plot, or that the twins are a "part" of Egeon. There is no culprit here, only scapegoats; no crime, only errors. Since this sense of loss and sin lacks a subject in which to ground it, it is passed back and forth within the play, only to find a predictable resting spot in the representation of woman. Guilt drifts almost magically away from Egeon, away from his twin sons, away from the Dromio servants, away from some exorcised fiend, and when all else fails, onto Adriana—guilty, sinful woman. The process of scapegoating follows a typical Shakespearean pattern as guilt gets passed from father to son, from master to servant, and from husband to wife. The play attributes its sense of impending doom to the simple fact that, as one character puts it, "I am due to a woman: one that claims me, one that haunts me, one that will have me" (3.2.81–83). But we can no more accept this fantasy of blame than we can accept any fantasy of an absolute origin.

VI

The theatrical history of *The Comedy of Errors* offers another context for understanding the play's interest in juxtaposing the discourses of court and church, debts and redemption. The first recorded performance took place during the customary Christmas revels at Gray's Inn, and both recorded performances of the play during Shakespeare's lifetime occurred on Holy Innocents Day, which commemorates Herod's slaughter of innocent children in his attempt to destroy the Christ child. The superimposition of a religious narrative of Christian redemption on a simple Plautine farce of physical mishaps works to contain the splits and repressions incurred by debts and so to limit rather than disseminate meanings. The thematics of redemption functions to resolve ambivalence toward indebtedness by suggesting that what was lost can be found and that debts can be successfully redeemed.

Perhaps the easiest way to read *The Comedy of Errors* is as an exploration of various definitions of the term *redemption*. The simplest meaning of *redeem*, according to the *Oxford English Dictionary*, is to regain or recover something lost—an obvious and constant subject of this play's learned wit. Antipholus of Syracuse would teach his Dromio that "there's a time for all things" (2.2.65). Dromio would disprove this adage by proving that there is "no time to recover hair lost by nature" (2.2.102–3) and so "there is no time to recover" (2.2.105) anything at all. Dromio of Syracuse complains that "time is a very bankrout" (4.2.58) and "a thief" (4.2.59), since "time comes stealing on by night and day" (4.2.60). But he admits that sometimes time can "turn back an hour in a day" (4.2.62) and then, as Adriana also acknowledges, "the hours come back" (4.2.55)—"as if Time were in debt!" (4.2.57).

The peril associated with time's movement in this play calls to mind the famous moment in Harold Lloyd's *Safety Last* (see figure 9). Lloyd portrays a man who stays alive by just barely holding on to the hands of a giant clock—as if to make time stand still. The many references to time standing still in *The Comedy of Errors* suggest that the problem of redeeming time is a key source of the play's near paralysis in the form of a senseless repetition of farcical mishaps. Egeon has also been attempting to recover something lost in time but is conveniently interrupted when faced with an insurmountable debt in attempting to cross into Ephesus. The warring towns of Ephesus and Syracuse find their only correlation in this text in the characters of Antipholus of Ephesus and Antipholus of Syracuse. Since the characters are not enemies, the war has meaning only insofar as the twins represent Egeon's contradictory personae. The forbidden

Figure 9. Harold Lloyd in *Safety Last*, film still (Pathé, 1923). Courtesy of the Museum of Modern Art Film Stills Archive.

boundary between the two towns and the penalty for crossing it suggests the precariousness of a split identity: if the Syracusan and Ephesian twins meet, one or the other must be destroyed. A way out of this dilemma is provided by payment of "a thousand marks . . . / To quit the penalty and to ransom him" (1.1.21–22). This debt reminds us that *to redeem* literally means "to buy back," to recover only "by payment of the amount due, or by fulfilling some obligation" (*OED*). The curious financial arrangement implies that Egeon can recover his marital identity only on the condition that he pay neglected marital debts. This also explains why Antipholus of Syracuse enters Ephesus, is apprehended by Adriana for neglected marital obligations, and dutifully returns home with her. The misidentification of the twins through a series of debts thus serves as a path through which the ideal of self-continuity is forged.

Adriana pays her husband's debt, thereby symbolically freeing him of marital debt. But the play refuses to let him off this easily: he is released by Adriana only to be bound by an exorcist who will purge him of his sins. With the entry of Pinch, the exorcist, the punitive plot threatens to run amok. Only when Antipholus of Ephesus escapes from his bonds and revenges himself upon this pinching, punishing parasite does the play move toward a sense of release and forgiveness. Redemption in the sense of a deliverance from sin takes over the plot when the Syracusan twin escapes into the priory and is offered full protection both from the law and from the scorn of a jealous wife. The movement from father to son, law to mercy, bondage to freedom, separation to reunion, and death to rebirth joins the play's events to its Christmastime occasion: Egeon's sons are freed from bondage, his separated family is reunited, Egeon is released from the penalty of death, and his death is replaced by his sons' symbolic rebirth.

This reading is further strengthened by the change in the twins' age, earlier listed as twenty-five, to thirty-three—the sacred number of the years of Christ's life.[19] Abbess Emilia concludes: "Thirty-three years have I but gone in travail / Of you, my sons, and till this present hour / My heavy burthen [ne'er] delivered" (5.1.401–3). Similarly, the apostle Paul witnesses: "We know that the whole creation has been groaning in travail together until now; and not only the creation, but we ourselves, who have the first fruits of the Spirit, groan

[19]For examples of the symbolic use of the number "thirty-three," see Ernst Curtius, *European Literature and the Latin Middle Ages*, trans. Willard R. Trask (Princeton: Princeton University Press, 1953), 505. We may follow Lewis Theobald in presuming that the twins' age is twenty-five, for Antipholus of Syracuse "at eighteen years became inquisitive / After his brother" (1.1.125–26) and presumably then set out in search of him, and Egeon twice refers at the conclusion to the seven years that have elapsed since he and Antipholus of Syracuse parted (5.1.310, 321). Theobald's decision to emend Adriana's "thirty-three years" to "twenty-five," however, destroys what appears to be an intentional symbolic reference inserted, perhaps, in honor of the Christmas occasion of the Gray's Inn performance.

inwardly as we wait for adoption as sons, the redemption of our bodies. For in this hope we were saved" (Romans 8:22–24). Still another meaning of *redeem*—"to restore or bring into a condition or state"(*OED*)—prevails when the sons are freed, united, and adopted by their father. *The Comedy of Errors* can therefore be read as a play with and upon redemption: it demonstrates how one redeems (re-covers) oneself by redeeming (making payment for) one's debts as one redeems (goes in exchange for) one's alter ego, and how one is thereby redeemed (released) from bondage only to share in the fruits of redemption (as rebirth).

Since this way of thinking about self-division was common to the Elizabethan morality play, which in turned influenced much Renaissance drama, less scholarly audiences than the lawyers at Gray's Inn would be apt to discover some such allegory at work.[20] The grim opening of *The Comedy of Errors* reveals a common man in bondage for sin, facing death, and despairing of mercy, thereby signaling the conventional portrait of natural unredeemed man in the morality plays. Its conclusion also follows a conventional morality-patterned action: Egeon's wife emerges from the priory in time to save him, Egeon is released from bondage, and his sins are forgiven by a merciful judge. The journey of the self toward redemption is figured in the twins' confrontations with the temptation and re-generation offered by the contrasting figures of vice (the courtesan) and of virtue (Luciana). The Ephesian brother's worldly interest in material and physical pleasure is contrasted with the piety of his brother to suggest the warring earthly and heavenly elements in Everyman's nature. The neglected marital identity is portrayed as in need of redemption; the single identity is associated with a spiritual agent willing to undergo penance to redeem its fallen counterpart.

An Elizabethan audience would probably understand the twins on a variety of levels: as long-lost brothers in a family, as dissociated parts of the self, or as warring earthly and heavenly elements in the nature of Everyman. They could read the plot in terms of a romantic comedy formula—as it moves from separation, through bewilder-ment, to reunion and harmony of family members or lovers; in terms of a psychological formula—as it progresses from repression through

[20]Sylvia D. Feldman, *The Morality-Patterned Comedy of the Renaissance* (The Hague: Mouton, 1970).

confrontation to integration of parts of the self; and in terms of a morality-patterned formula—which charts a development from self-division and bondage through penance to redemption.

Paul's letter to the Ephesians, long accepted as a major source for this play, has never been studied in the context of the second self in time. Scholars have observed that this letter includes such elements as years of wandering, a shipwreck, the Aegean (Egeon) and Adriatic (Adriana) seas, Syracuse, Corinth, Ephesus and its demonic magic, revenge taken upon evil exorcists, and a conflict between law and mercy, bondage and redemption.[21] But its message, for which Paul is being held prisoner at the time, is the union of two hostile nations, Gentiles and Jews, in the body of Christ: "For he is our peace, who has made us both one, and has broken down the dividing wall of hostility, by abolishing in his flesh the law of commandments and ordinances, that he might create in himself one new man in place of the two, so making peace, and might reconcile us both to God in one body through the cross, thereby bringing the hostility to an end" (Ephesians 2:14–3:1). Paul's imagery of the creation of "one new man in place of the two," of one body in which two hostile people are joined in harmony, suggests the problem of joining two hostile identities within one psyche. The two hostile nations are figured in Syracuse and Ephesus and are joined in the body of their common father, Egeon.

It should not be sacrilegious to observe that these gestures of closure are themselves bound to fail, not unlike the characters' attempts to bind themselves to each other or the reader's attempts to bind together various meanings discovered within the play. The problem the play poses is not whether time can turn back but whether we can keep up with the losses we incur as time moves forward— whether we can ever be synonymous with ourselves, pay our debts, or be "redeemed." Our need to unify texts and selves is doomed to err, to travel, to wander, and to fail. Since experience in time creates further splits and fissures in the newly integrated self, how can we believe that Egeon, or the author, or the play, is ever whole? How can

[21]See R. A. Foakes, Appendices to the Arden edition of *The Comedy of Errors*, 113–15; Geoffrey Bullough, Introduction to *The Comedy of Errors*, in *Narrative and Dramatic Sources of Shakespeare* (New York: Columbia University Press, 1966), 1:9–10; Richmond Noble, *Shakespeare's Biblical Knowledge and Use of the Book of Common Prayer as Exemplified in the Plays of the First Folio* (New York: Macmillan, 1935).

we believe that even the most unifying of readings closes discussion of the play, permanently represses all potential readings, is final or complete?

The conclusion of *The Comedy of Errors* offers two interpretations of identity only to mediate between them in a provisional compromise. Adriana defines identity as a composite of internalized relationships with others which is fixed and irreversible: "For know, my love, as easy mayst thou fall / A drop of water in the breaking gulf, / And take unmingled thence that drop again, / Without addition or diminishing, / As take from me thyself and not me too" (2.2.125–29). But Egeon's identity is not simply the sum of his past identifications with others. The Syracusan son is also an essential part of Egeon, born in his denial of his past, nurtured and sustained apart from home and wife. If Egeon is willing to hazard this persona to retrieve his former self, he is unwilling to abandon it completely. Egeon's identity is not found through the actual restoration or the denial of his past relationships with others. Egeon has never set out in search of his beloved Emilia, his "bliss," nor does he mention ever experiencing the desire to do so, despite the twenty-five years they have spent in apparently needless separation. When Emilia finally makes her appearance at the conclusion of the play, Egeon's first words to her are a request for his son. It is not his wife but Antipholus of Ephesus that Egeon "labored of a love to see" (1.1.130); it is only himself (Antipholus of Ephesus) for whom Egeon "hazarded" himself (Antipholus of Syracuse) (1.1.131). Were Egeon to find himself in the renewal of past relationships, this would be tantamount to resolving the identity crisis through the destruction of his present Syracusan identity, rather than through the relation of his present to his past.

The play offers a neat solution to this crisis in its definition of identity as the perception of self-continuity or as the identification and integration of various self-concepts in a time continuum. Of course, the marital reunion celebrated at the conclusion is neither looked for nor, according to some critics, really effected—but this is irrelevant at the end of a comedy.[22] This return of the repressed threatens a return to the repressive, and so is not as stable as critics

[22]In "*The Comedy of Errors*: A Different Kind of Comedy," *New Literary History* 9 (1978), W. Thomas MacCary notes that the "entire argument prepares us not for the union of man and wife—its view of marriage is especially pessimistic—but for the reunion of twins with each other and with their parents" (525). He argues that the play was written under indirect influence from the pre-Menandrine tradition and con-

suppose—but this is not pertinent to the ego's fictions of triumph. That this solution is a virtual impossibility, that it denies the inevitability of future self-division, is only hinted at by the strange doubling onstage. The use of twins undermines the possibility of self-presence by suggesting that identity is a matter of two who can never be one; being is a function of splitting and attempting to recuperate that loss in further splits. Identity is re-presented as grounded in yet prevented by repression and always haunted by the inevitability of a return of the repressed.

VII

Psychoanalytic readings of the comic tend to confirm these narratives of closure. The ostensible goal of the traditional psychoanalytic reading is to reconstruct the denied wish or fantasy at the "core" of the joke or dream. For example, were *The Comedy of Errors* to clarify the connection between father and sons, it is likely that the mistakes of identity and the punishment ensuing from them would fail to be humorous. Instead, these connections are carefully disguised, at once asserted and denied in a way that we associate with the uncanny, so that we sense a significance we never fully understand. This play's sensibility thus exemplifies Eric Bentley's hypothesis that in farce "there is an acknowledgment of absurdity—and . . . a counterclaim to a kind of sense."[23] Neither, as Bentley notes, ever wins out; meaning and madness battle for priority.

Since farce, like dreams, couples a functional denial of significance with often disturbing and highly significant content, one can read illogic, contradiction, omission, and mistakes as signifiers of a functional dislocation of meaning.[24] Accordingly, one could argue

---

cludes that *Errors* is not romantic comedy but narcissistic, egocentric preoedipal comedy. See his discussion of the preoedipal, narcissistic object-choices in Shakespearean comedy in *Friends and Lovers: The Phenomenology of Desire in Shakespearean Comedy* (New York: Columbia University Press, 1985). Here MacCary more fully explores why the play concludes with no definite marriage plans for Antipholus of Syracuse and Luciana and why the marriage of Adriana and Antipholus of Ephesus is left unreconstructed.

[23]Eric Bentley, *The Life of the Drama* (New York: Atheneum, 1964), 245.

[24]Barbara Freedman, "Errors in Comedy: A Psychoanalytic Theory of Farce," in *Shakespearean Comedy*, ed. Maurice Charney (New York: New York Literary Forum, 1980), 233–43.

that the aggression directed against the Dromios and their masters displaces aggression "intended" for Egeon, and so the plot is punishing the crime of neglected marital obligations. The punishment of the two Dromios, for example, is never openly associated with any transgression on their part. The play includes but denies Egeon's transgression, focusing instead on random acts of punishment which miraculously result in his redemption. The marital debt is both denied and displaced; only the mistake, the unexpected confusion of the twins' identities, is blamed for all the aggression in the play. The effect of that aggression is similarly denied: Dromio may complain of his beatings or the Ephesian twin of his treatment by Dr. Pinch, but these actions are senselessly delivered and senselessly received. The fast pace, complexity, and extraordinary subject matter of the plot further contribute to this general distortion of the sense of reality, and so are equally vital to our humorous acceptance of this fantasy.

Yet even if we uncover a fantasy behind the play's comic punishment, we cannot say whose it is, what hides it, or how to privilege it. Whether we are analyzing dreams or jokes, the analytic model of fantasy is itself problematic, since it depends upon the illusion of an unchanging reader who works through a single ahistorical fantasy by reading a potentially unified and stable text. We are thus forced to question how aware this play is of the role of denial in the success of its own humor. Since comedy is capable of interrupting and addressing its own production, and since this comedy, in particular, explores the role of the unconscious in the production of meaning, what kind of discourse can under-stand and re-present this? How can we forge a theory of representation in Shakespearean comedy as well as in that comedy of errors known as literary criticism?

More compelling than a reading of the displacement of meaning in farce is the way in which farce subverts meaning, displaces any stable reading, and forces us to rethink such basic terms as *author*, *play*, *meaning*, and *fantasy*. *The Comedy of Errors* suggests less a displaced core fantasy than the impossibility of discovering any single core or fantasy that "governs" a text. Perhaps the best gloss on the play is the definition of the primal scene offered by Jean Laplanche and J.-B. Pontalis: "The original fantasy is first and foremost fantasy: it lies beyond the history of the subject but nevertheless in history: a kind of language and symbolic sequence, but loaded with elements of imagination; a structure, but activated by [certain] contingent elements. As such it is characterized by certain traits which make it difficult to assimilate to a purely transcendental schema, even if it provides the possibility of experience."[25] We can easily analyze the farce play as symptom and uncover hidden transgressions being punished in disguised form. But what is most interesting about farce—of which *The Comedy of Errors* is a variety—is not its repetition of a familiar pattern of wish and defense, but its subversion of that model. What is peculiar about farce and the uncanny alike is not the disguise of a core fantasy but the *recognition* of that disguise.

In farce, plot is more disturbing than content; there is something manic and uncontrolled about the way that the plot unfolds. Bentley explains that although we commonly enjoy illicit fantasies in farce, there is always a disturbing sense of nightmare associated with their fulfillment; we sense that we are driven "from bedroom to bedroom by demons," or we experience a loss of free will and control to something that "bristles with menace," something that in turn threatens to lose control. The more that characters lose control in farce, the more tightly the plot is wound up; the more that characters seek gratification, the more severely the plot punishes them for it. "Melodrama and farce are both arts of escape," argues Bentley, "and what they are running away from is not only social problems but all other forms of moral responsibility. They are running away from the conscience and all its creations."[26] Yet if farce involves running away from the conscience, it appears to reenact that chase with the conscience in the starring role. The characteristic sense of anxiety and menace in a highly elaborate, paranoid plot; the celebrated chase, the hallmark of farce; the series of blows mistakenly delivered—all are signs of a comedy of the superego.

Whereas comedy is concerned with unity, adaptation, purposiveness, and harmony, farce is committed to the discontinuous and the dysfunctional. Its aggression and regression are not in the service of the ego but directly opposed to ego mastery. Accommodation to the reality principle, subservience to the ego—these aims and activities are antithetical to the subversive, rather than festive, spirit of farce. Farce is just the opposite of a neatly disguised fantasy of wish

[25]Jean Laplanche and J.-B. Pontalis, "Fantasy and the Origins of Sexuality," *International Journal of Psychoanalysis* 49 (1968), 10.
[26]Bentley, *Life of the Drama*, 247–48, 255.

fulfillment and in this sense opposes the adaptive functions of both dream and comedy. As discontinuous, dysfunctional, and demonic form gone wild, farce swings between the extremes of chaotic anti-form and compulsively elaborate plots.

Like nightmares, farce suggests an awareness and interruption of unconscious content. Albert Bermel explains:

> The pace and insanity of farce in turn create an atmosphere onstage that approximates the conditions of a dream world or, rather, of a night-mare: the terrors of humiliation—of being, say, unable to remember the simple answer to a leading question; of being found in a stranger's bedroom without pants on; of being taken for a notorious criminal or a lunatic with not a scrap of evidence to support one's identity—such typical dream fears are familiar to audiences. As they recognize them, consciously or unconsciously, they laugh; they are relieved witnesses of somebody else's nightmare.[27]

What is peculiar about farce is not the content of its fantasies but its *recognition of fantasy*. Farce shares with nightmares the ability to stage the *interruption* of representation itself. The interruption of wishes, the recognition of wishes, the horror of wishes—all imply what we might term a failure of the ego functions.

In this sense, farce is closer to that form of anxiety dream known as the punishment dream. In all dreams, Charles Brenner explains,

> the ego anticipates guilt, that is, superego condemnation, if the part of the latent content which derives from the repressed should find too direct an expression in the manifest dream. Consequently the ego's defenses oppose the emergence of this part of the latent content, which is again no different from what goes on in most other dreams. How-ever, the result in the so-called punishment dreams is that the manifest dream, instead of expressing a more or less disguised fantasy of the fulfillment of a repressed wish, expresses a more or less disguised fantasy of punishment for the wish in question, certainly a most ex-traordinary "compromise" among ego, id, and superego.[28]

---

[27] Albert Bermel, "Farce," *The Reader's Encyclopedia of World Drama*, ed. John Gassner and Edward Quinn (New York: Thomas Y. Crowell, 1969), 264–65.

[28] Charles Brenner, *An Elementary Textbook of Psychoanalysis* (1955; rpt. Garden City, N.Y.: Doubleday-Anchor, 1957), 184.

More significant than any fantasy content here is the element of "compromise" in the staging of the interruption of staging itself. Like the nightmare and the anxiety dream, the punishment dream suggests a complex reciprocal awareness between levels of psychic functioning that can anticipate, interrupt, represent, and even caricature one another. In farce, as in the punishment dream, the superego not only anticipates and interrupts the representation of wishes by enacting a drama of seemingly absurd punishment but also interrupts, interprets, and recapitulates the representational process. What is terrifying, automatic, and malevolent about plot in farce is an uncanny awareness of the automatic nature of unconscious representation; a quality of the anxiety of the ego under siege spills over onto the representational screen itself, and form becomes both manic and superego-ridden.

Farce not only resists our attempts to fix its meanings but resists meaning itself, as well as a single representational model that could stage it. It caricatures the dream as the "well-made play" and mocks the ego's interest in representations that suggest unity, purposiveness, and integrity. The genre easily accommodates itself to surreal forms, sliding quickly and almost uncontrollably from erotic dream to nightmare. It structures events in a way that implies a caricature of the well-made play; its plots are both controlled and uncontrolled in a way that suggests unconscious processes at work. Michel Foucault comes close to describing this manic tempo when he observes how, in psychological disorders involving temporality, "time is rendered instantaneous by fragmentation; and, lacking any opening on to the past and future, it spins round upon its axis, proceeding either by leaps or by repetitions."[29] If that which is senselessly repeated is that which cannot be remembered, then the uncanny, automatic, and senseless action of farce suggests less a form of mastery than a masterless form. Jean Baudrillard explains this compulsive tempo of repetition: "Affect or representation, every repetitive figure of sense is a figure of death. Only senseless recurrence unleashes pleasure, that which proceeds neither from a conscious order nor an unconscious disorder, but which is a reversion and reiteration of pure form, taking

---

[29]Michel Foucault, *Mental Illness and Psychology*, trans. Alan Sheridan (New York: Harper and Row, 1976), 51.

the form of increasing the stakes and challenging the law of contents and their accumulation."[30]

Susanne Langer maintains that "the pure sense of life is the underlying feeling of comedy." She describes this sensibility as that which "sets organic nature apart from inorganic: self-preservation, self-restoration, functional tendency, purpose. Life is teleological, the rest of nature is, apparently, mechanical; to maintain the pattern of vitality in a non-living universe is the most elementary instinctual purpose."[31] But Henri Bergson comes closer to describing the mood and action of *The Comedy of Errors* when he attributes the comic to "something mechanical encrusted upon the living" or to "that side of a person which reveals his likeness to a thing, that aspect of human events which, through its peculiar inelasticity, conveys the impression of pure mechanism, of automatism, of movement without life."[32] If we read these two definitions against each other, they lead to the hypothesis that farce suggests something closer to a death drive than to the "pure sense of life" celebrated by Western narrative comedy. Unlike comedy, farce shows human beings unable to cope with or adapt to their environments. Instincts that are designed to help us survive are not only dependable but often rigidly mechanical. When these "purposive vital functions" are perceived as dysfunctional, automatic, irrational, and perilously inflexible, then the farcical vision comes into focus. That farce should take the ego as its object, just as objects were once taken for the ego, makes eminent sense from this excentric standpoint.

VIII

The difficulty we experience in reading *The Comedy of Errors* may be attributed in part to the influence of ego psychology on literary theory. The more we try to unify the play according to a model of stability and continuity, the more these attempts fail. Rather than

[30]Jean Baudrillard, *De la séduction* (Paris: Galilée, 1979), 78.

[31]Susanne Langer, "The Comic Rhythm," *Feeling and Form* (New York: Scribner's, 1953), 326–50, rpt. in *Comedy: Meaning and Form*, 2d ed., ed. Robert Corrigan (New York: Harper and Row, 1981), 68.

[32]Henri Bergson, "Laughter" (1900), in *Comedy: Meaning and Form*, 331, 332.

apply psychoanalysis to *The Comedy of Errors*, we might rethink psychoanalytic theory from its fractured standpoint. The Dromios' efforts to bind meaning call to mind Freud's descriptions of the ego as substitute and as flunky, as scapegoat and as body surface.[33] Since these messengers are necessarily substitutes, they suggest a principle of supplementarity that reinterprets identity in terms of the binding and supplementary activity of the ego functions. The ego is best understood as neither present nor unified but as a series of traces seeking to bind or a signifying process of deferral and recuperative activity which works in the spaces between past and future. Like Freud's ego, the Dromios are servile messengers caught between two worlds, accepted in neither, and attempting to control both.

Theater offers an explanation of the ego as the usurping double, as a projection or representation of the body surface. As a screen image that purloins presence, the ego is a gestalt mechanism that passes itself off for those discrete elements it combines and upon which it traces its signature. Theater has always been staging this battle of presence and representation, which explains why Artaud "uncovered" the importance of the figure of the double for theater: "It is the history of the body / which *pursued* (and did not follow) mine / and which, in order to go first and be born, / projected itself across my body / and / was born / through the disemboweling of my body / of which he kept a piece / in order to / pass himself off / as me."[34]

What are the implications for psychoanalytic theory of a play that questions the possibility of a stance of mastery outside of it, that takes the ego itself as an object of scorn? What would it mean to implement the play of the ego as supplement in the reading process except to split our reading and explore where it is not our own? At least one lesson we gain from reading psychoanalysis through *The Comedy of Errors* is a paradoxical theory of knowledge based on the *inevitability* of errors and exclusion. *Errors* foregrounds errors, traces levels of misrecognition in its own construction, and in the process represents its own conflicts with repression. The discovery and representation of the unconscious may subvert a static and unified position, but it

[33]Freud, *The Ego and the Id* (1923), *SE*, 19:26, n.1.

[34]Antonin Artaud, as quoted by Jacques Derrida in "La parole soufflée," *Writing and Difference*, trans. Alan Bass (Chicago: University of Chicago Press, 1978), 181.

also makes position possible. The denial of self-presence doesn't negate presence but redefines it as a distancing or spacing we always seek but fail to close. To acknowledge the play of the unconscious is not to deny that we are in a process of dialogue with ourselves and with others, with our splits as we split. Yet it does requires a more dynamic and dramatic model of reading based on the progression of the subject in relation to its discourse—a model of reading based on decentering and positionality, on splitting and attempting to recuperate that loss.

The Comedy of Errors suggests a model of reading based neither on presence nor on absence, neither certainty nor uncertainty. Rather, it requires a model based on *staging misrecognition* and on *staging as misrecognition*—on the inevitability of a repetition that distends and extends being in a splitting that can never be reversed or recovered. Shakespeare's comedies enact the impossibility of self-presence, yet derive identity from this awareness. "I am not what I am" is an assertion of identity through an assumption of misrecognition—in *Oedipus* as in *Errors*, *Twelfth Night* as in *King Lear*. Shakespeare's comedies display this misrecognition, own up to and affirm it, and derive position from the place where we are not. Lacan claims: "It was in fact the so-called Copernican revolution to which Freud himself compared his discovery, emphasizing that it was once again a question of the place man assigns to himself at the centre of a universe. Is the place that I occupy as the subject of a signifier concentric or excentric, in relation to the place I occupy as subject of the signified?—that is the question."[35] Theater derives position from displacement and misrecognition, which is why we think of *Hamlet* here as well as *The Comedy of Errors* and why even Laszlo Versényi's discussion of *Oedipus* sounds a bit Lacanian: "Not knowing what he is, man cannot be what he is; knowing what he is, man cannot bear to exist. Life is *hamartia*, an erring, for to live is to be out of balance, and every effort of the knower to right this balance merely tips the scale toward his doom."[36]

The Lacanian model differs, of course, but similarly posits misrecognition as a condition of subjectivity. Lacan maintains: "It is not

[35]Lacan, "The Agency of the Letter in the Unconscious, or Reason since Freud," *Ecrits: A Selection*, trans. Alan Sheridan (New York: Norton, 1977), 165.
[36]Laszlo Versényi, "The Flaw of Oedipus," in *Oedipus Tyrannus*, trans. and ed. Luci Berkowitz and Theodore F. Brunner (New York: Norton, 1970), 206.

simply that the subject is, in a static way, lacking, in error. It is that, in a moving way, in his discourse, he is essentially situated in the dimension of the *making a mistake (se tromper)*."[37] Being is thus a process of dispersal and failed recuperation, a psychic tail-chasing of sorts. Lacan describes the splitting of the ego in the analytic session as similar to the flight of Zeno's arrow: "Half of the subject's *ego* passes over to the other side of the wall that separates the analysand from the analyst, then half of that half, and so on, in an asymptotic procession that will never succeed."[38] In short, Lacan posits a double bind in which the subject confronts language, being confronts meaning, and either option makes the other impossible. Yet out of this double bind, from this recuperative effort, Lacan derives symbolic form.

Inasmuch as psychoanalysis attempts, according to Leo Bersani, to give "a theoretical account of precisely those forces which obstruct, undermine, play havoc with theoretical accounts themselves,"[39] it would appear to be in trouble, and yet it is in less trouble than those discourses that attempt to deny this paradox. *The Comedy of Errors*, for example, encourages us to consider its construction as well as our own on a variety of levels, particularly those levels we either cannot or choose not to consider. Its structure offers a model of how the mind and so how meaning works: we no sooner assert the unity of identity than unconscious splits proliferate and doubles appear; we no sooner loosen ego boundaries and open ourselves up to different points of view than the mind organizes, privileges, represses. What *The Comedy of Errors* finally puts on stage are such basic principles of psychological functioning as splitting, projection, denial, and repression as they haunt our quest for meaning. Since subjectivity is implicated in and predicated upon otherness, identity is itself a product of projection, transference, repression, and internalization. Neither self nor text is ever stable, continuous, or self-present.

To identify where the play finally stands on identity or on any

---

[37]Lacan, "Analysis and Truth," *The Four Fundamental Concepts of Psycho-Analysis*, ed. Jacques-Alain Miller, trans. Alan Sheridan (New York: Norton, 1981), 137.

[38]Lacan, "The Function and Field of Speech and Language in Psychoanalysis," *Ecrits*, 91.

[39]Leo Bersani, *The Freudian Body: Psychoanalysis and Art* (New York: Columbia University Press, 1986), 4.

other matter is to join the characters onstage in offering to master events with yet another flawed and arbitrary interpretation. Finally, the play doesn't stand anywhere, which is what makes it so fascinating to under-stand. To attempt closure in discussing a play so ambivalent toward closure is as futile a gesture as it is inappropriate. *The Comedy of Errors* proliferates meanings as a means of escaping containment and at the same time generates narratives that seek to effect closure. It preys upon itself and yet is divided against itself, and we repeat this pattern in our efforts to describe or contain it. Its intricate structure and symbolism, like its elaborate patterns of plot and imagery, betray its compulsive efforts to master meaning and so to repress its own discovery of repression. We can stage this disjunction here only by interrupting and upstaging our own readings; we can only proliferate splits in the play's codes as we attempt to encompass them.

Not surprisingly, Freud denies the importance of automata to the uncanny—or rather, Freud considers, only to dismiss, the importance of objects and events that "excite in the spectator the impression of automatic, mechanical processes at work behind the ordinary appearance of mental activity."[40] And yet "The 'Uncanny'" marks Freud's first connection of repetition compulsions to the superego, and of both to the uncanny, repression, and doubling. Suitably, "The 'Uncanny'" is a fragmented essay that never ties together its insights. As critics have observed, it is as significant for its repressions as for its treatments of the repressed.[41] From such fragmented texts we best glean a sense of the uncanny at work—an awareness of unconscious processes interrupted, observed, and caricatured.

The literature of the uncanny blends the familiar and the strange, makes us feel that we are awake while dreaming, that we see and do not see into our deepest fears and wishes. But such literature also sees that it does not see and where it does not see. It engages representations that do not sufficiently protect us, that do not sufficiently

[40]Freud, "The 'Uncanny,'" 226.

[41]See Hélène Cixous, "Fiction and Its Phantoms: A Reading of Freud's 'Das Unheimliche,'" *New Literary History* 7 (1976), 525–48; Samuel Weber, "The Sideshow, or Remarks on a Canny Moment," *Modern Language Notes* 88 (1973), 1102–33; and Neil Hertz, "Freud and the Sandman," in *Textual Strategies: Perspectives in Post-Structuralist Criticism*, ed. Josué V. Harari (Ithaca: Cornell University Press, 1979), 296–321.

disguise the repressed in the service of the ego, but that mock and subvert the ego's representations. The uncanny recapitulates the processes it exposes: it infiltrates unconscious representation, interrupts it, and stages it. This consciousness of unconsciousness, this representation of interrupted representation, is what makes farce in particular, and the uncanny in general, "significant." Perhaps now we can appreciate Freud's example of the uncanny from Johann Nestroy's farce *Der Zerrissene*, [*The Torn Man*], in which "the fleeing man, convinced that he is a murderer, lifts up one trap-door after another and each time sees what he takes to be the ghost of his victim rising up out of it. He calls out in despair, 'But I've only killed *one* man. Why this ghastly multiplication?'"[42]

[42]Freud, "The 'Uncanny,'" 252.

4

Taming Difference and
The Taming of the Shrew:
Feminism, Psychoanalysis, Theater

This problem of dealing with difference without constituting an opposition may just be what feminism is all about (might even be what psychoanalysis is all about). Difference produces great anxiety. Polarization, which is a theatrical representation of difference, tames and binds that anxiety. The classic example is sexual difference which is represented as a polar opposition (active-passive, energy-matter—all polar oppositions share the trait of taming the anxiety that specific differences provoke).

—Jane Gallop, The Daughter's Seduction:
Feminism and Psychoanalysis

I

Jane Gallop correctly assesses the shared goals of feminism and psychoanalysis in the postmodernist enterprise: both are predicated upon subverting the structuration of difference as opposition.[1] Structuralism and semiotics, the twin harbingers and now culprits of postmodern theory, process experiences into polarities that offer an illusion of alternatives: nature/culture, passive/active, male/female, conscious/unconscious. Postmodern theorists explore how these binarisms are ideologically coercive systems that privilege and procure one term at the expense of the other and so function to repress a

---

[1]Jane Gallop, *The Daughter's Seduction: Feminism and Psychoanalysis* (Ithaca: Cornell University Press, 1982), 93.

114

larger range of differences. Gilles Deleuze and Claire Parnet explain what is at stake: "It is false [to say that] the binary machine only exists for reasons of convenience. It is said that 'base two' is the easiest. But in reality the binary machine is an important piece of the apparatuses of power."[2]

Yet in seeking to escape binarisms, are we not also trapped within binarisms? How to intervene in the cultural reproduction of difference without being entangled in it? Any group previously defined by exclusion from and oppression by a social order faces the question of how to redefine itself without destroying itself. Should it celebrate the scorned values with which it has been identified, adopt the values of the prevailing order, or challenge an oppressive social structure with a more inclusive sense of difference? Luce Irigaray and Hélène Cixous would have feminists reverse the negative value assigned to woman and would locate her specificity in a multileveled libidinal energy shaped by female bodily drives that find their way into the style of feminist writings.[3] But as Ann Rosalind Jones points out, celebrations of the feminine are problematic to the extent that they assume an essential feminine to be celebrated; as a result, "theories of *féminité* remain fixated within the metaphysical and psychoanalytic frameworks they attempt to dislodge."[4] Monique Wittig also blames the universalizing tendencies of *néoféminité* for fetishizing difference and so keeping us locked in an oppositional gender structure. But Wittig demands that we "dissociate 'women' (the class within which we fight) and 'woman,' the myth. For 'woman' . . . is only an imaginary formation, while 'women' is the product of a social relationship," and so a group capable of effecting change.[5]

[2]Gilles Deleuze and Claire Parnet, *Dialogues* (Paris: Flammarion, 1977), 29.

[3]See, for example, Hélène Cixous, "The Laugh of the Medusa," trans. Keith Cohen and Paula Cohen, in *New French Feminisms*, ed. Elaine Marks and Isabelle de Courtivron (Amherst: University of Massachusetts Press, 1980), 245–64; and Luce Irigaray, *Speculum of the Other Woman* (Ithaca: Cornell University Press, 1985), and *This Sex Which Is Not One* (Ithaca: Cornell University Press, 1985).

[4]Ann Rosalind Jones, "Inscribing Femininity: French Theories of the Feminine," in *Making a Difference: Feminist Literary Criticism*, ed. Gayle Greene and Coppélia Kahn (London: Methuen, 1985), 106. See also Jones, "Writing the Body: Toward an Understanding of *l'Ecriture Féminine*," *Feminist Studies* 7 (1981), 247–63; and Jones, "Julia Kristeva on Femininity: The Limits of a Semiotic Politics," *Feminist Review* 18 (1984), 56–73.

[5]Monique Wittig, "One Is Not Born a Woman," *Feminist Issues* 1 (1981), 50–51.

Staging the Gaze

Other critics employ deconstructive strategies to define feminism in terms of an opposition to oppositions. Julia Kristeva argues
that "the very dichotomy man/woman as an opposition between
two rival entities may be understood as belonging to metaphysics."[6]
In its place, she offers a model of pulsion between the semiotic
(preoedipal, prelinguistic energy and desire) and the symbolic (made
possible by the repression of the semiotic). To work from the semiotic is to adopt "a *negative* function: reject everything finite, definite,
structured, loaded with meaning, in the existing state of society." It is
to work "on the side of the explosion of social codes: with revolutionary moments."[7] Like Kristeva, Shoshana Felman defines femininity as a "real otherness . . . [which] is uncanny in that it is not the
opposite of masculinity but that which subverts the very opposition
of masculinity and femininity."[8] The answer provided by avant-
garde feminism, then, is that woman does not take (a) place but,
rather, re-visions positionality itself.[9] In what sense does a feminism
so defined differ from deconstruction, which both acknowledges the
symbolic and disrupts it from within, subverting positionality on a
continuous basis? What is a position that denies its position?

Feminists who employ Lacanian methodology in turn find themselves framed by a discourse of castration and phallic signifiers which
they may well not seek to reproduce. Whereas Lacan employs the
term *phallus* to refer to sexual identity as fraudulent, he champions an
equally implacable place for a theory of displacement couched in the
terms of a phallocentric discourse. Gallop rightly acknowledges that
"the penis is what men have and women do not; the phallus is the
attribute of power which neither men nor women have. But as long
as the attribute of power is a phallus which refers to and can be
confused . . . with a penis, this confusion will support a structure in

6Julia Kristeva, "Women's Time," trans. Alice Jardine and Harry Blake, *Signs* 7
(1981), 33.
7Julia Kristeva, "Oscillation between Power and Denial," in *New French Feminisms*, 166.
8Shoshana Felman, "Rereading Femininity," *Yale French Studies* 62 (1981), 42.
9See Kristeva's "Modern Theater Does not Take (a) Place," trans. Alice Jardine
and Thomas Gora, *Sub-stance* 18/19 (1977), 131–34, and "Oscillation between Power
and Denial," where she identifies "the moment of rupture and negativity which
conditions and underlies the novelty of any praxis 'feminine,'" and adds: "No 'I' is
there to assume this 'femininity,' but it is no less operative, rejecting all that is finite
and assuring in *(sexual) pleasure* the life of the concept" (167).

which it seems reasonable that men have power and women do not. And as long as psychoanalysts maintain the separability of 'phallus' from 'penis,' they can hold on to their 'phallus' in the belief that their discourse has no relation to sexual inequality, no relation to politics."[10] Teresa de Lauretis identifies the frame here, complaining that "while psychoanalysis recognizes the inherent bisexuality of the subject, for whom femininity and masculinity are not qualities or attributes but positions in the symbolic processes of (self)-representation, psychoanalysis is itself caught up in 'the ideological assignation of discourse,' the structures of representation, narrative, vision, and meaning it seeks to analyze, reveal, or bring to light."[11]

Given the extent of feminist rethinkings of narrative and cinema, an exploration of how theater figures difference would seem long overdue.[12] Laura Mulvey and Teresa de Lauretis have persuasively argued that the pleasure of traditional Western cinematic narratives is predicated upon coercive identifications with a position of male antagonism toward women.[13] Since the male is traditionally envisioned as the bearer of the gaze and the woman as the fetishized object of the gaze, the staging of any spectacle is always already a matter of sexual difference. Since classical theater incorporates not only spectacle but narrative—so that the male is represented as an agent of change, the female as the passive object to be actively transformed by him—its action would also appear to reveal the work of gender ideology. Not only pleasure but plot is derived from male fantasies

[10]Gallop, *Daughter's Seduction*, 97.

[11]Teresa de Lauretis, *Alice Doesn't: Feminism, Semiotics, and Cinema* (Bloomington: Indiana University Press, 1984), 164; her quotation is from Ben Brewster, Stephen Heath, and Colin MacCabe, "Comment," *Screen* 16 (1975), 83–90.

[12]See, for example, Laura Mulvey, "Visual Pleasure and Narrative Cinema," *Screen* 16 (1975), 6–18; Kaja Silverman, *The Subject of Semiotics* (Oxford: Oxford University Press, 1983); E. Ann Kaplan, *Women and Film: Both Sides of the Camera* (London: Methuen, 1983); *Re-Vision: Essays in Feminist Film Criticism*, ed. Mary Ann Doane, Patricia Mellencamp, and Linda Williams (Los Angeles: American Film Institute, 1984); de Lauretis, *Alice Doesn't*; de Lauretis, *Technologies of Gender: Essays on Theory, Film, and Fiction* (Bloomington: Indiana University Press, 1987); and Jacqueline Rose, *Sexuality in the Field of Vision* (London: Verso, 1986). Sue-Ellen Case's groundbreaking *Feminism and Theater* (New York: Methuen, 1988) is the first full-length study to treat this topic.

[13]See Mulvey, "Visual Pleasure and Narrative Cinema"; and de Lauretis, *Alice Doesn't*; de Lauretis is far more critical of the dichotomies Mulvey sets up in this classic essay, as is Mulvey in her later work.

that depend on the scopic and narrative exploitation of woman. She is the linchpin in the system: her losses propel the relay of looks and her sins move the plot forward. If traditional Western theater as well as cinema relies on the fetishized spectacle of woman and the narrative of her domination and punishment, at stake is the potential of feminism, psychoanalytic theory, and theater to reflect and effect change—to insert a difference in our construction of the subject and so to make a difference.

The question that arises when we return to Gallop's statement is why she refers to polarization as "a *theatrical* representation of difference." Whereas the relationship of ideology and genre is hardly Gallop's subject, the identification of theater with a defensive, ideologically complicit ordering of difference constitutes a serious challenge to those for whom theater offers a model of epistemological inquiry. Is theater the guarantor of polarities—part and parcel of the great semiological myth of the versus—or, as Roland Barthes contends, designed to subvert this myth?[14] Is deconstruction the enemy of theater or its double? Are deconstructive techniques that function to unsteady such rigid oppositions theatrical? Are feminism and psychoanalysis theatrical when they stage these oppositions or when they subvert them?

II

Given its overtly misogynistic subject matter, its narrative of the domination and punishment of woman, its specular fascination with the image of woman, *The Taming of the Shrew* would seem to confirm rather than to challenge the feminist critique of theater. Yet what fascinates me about the work is its marked resistance to enclosure; whereas the play exhibits all the major strategies of gender ideology I have described, it also problematizes feminist readings. In its concern with avoiding entrapment, in its use of theatricality to subvert a spectator consciousness, *The Taming of the Shrew* displaces any stable relation of the spectator to the play.

The Taming of the Shrew appears to tame the critic more than the

[14]Roland Barthes, *Roland Barthes by Roland Barthes*, trans. Richard Howard (New York: Hill and Wang, 1977), 68–71, 177.

shrew. Its ability to contain us is vividly evidenced both in its onstage containment of an audience and in its success in engaging critics in debate. Whether Kate is a shrew or merely a misunderstood young woman, whether Petruchio is a bully or a philosopher, whether the play upholds or undermines degree, is farce or philosophical comedy, should be staged with or without its Induction—all are matters of heated debate in Shakespearean scholarship. For those critics who take Kate's final speech and Petruchio's bullying at face value, the characters are rather stereotypical, the moral is clearly in favor of male supremacy, and the genre is closer to farce.[15] Others read the characters as more realistic, the genre as closer to comedy, and the argument as an ironic, if veiled, attack on a doctrine of male superiority.[16] Whether they write about plot, characters, argument, genre, or structure, critics routinely adopt one of two diametrically opposed positions on this play.

Perhaps the most famous critical controversy regards the argument or moral of the play. For most critics, *The Taming of the Shrew* upholds faith in an intrinsic hierarchical order, or great chain of being, and simply must be read historically to be read correctly. For others, the play attacks this belief in degree by exposing social roles as theatrical rather than natural. Whereas there are many sly approaches to this controversy, there is no certain way out of it. If *The Taming of the Shrew* upholds an inherent hierarchical order, then why does Shakespeare end the play with Tranio still a servant? In Shakespeare's source play—Ariosto's *Supposes*—the same character (Du-

[15]See, for example, George Bernard Shaw, *Shaw on Shakespeare*, ed. Edwin Wilson (London: Arno, 1961); E. K. Chambers, *Shakespeare: A Survey* (1925; rpt. New York: Hill and Wang, 1958); H. B. Charlton, *Shakespearian Comedy* (London: Methuen, 1938); Mark Van Doren, *Shakespeare* (1939; rpt. New York: Doubleday-Anchor, 1953); Donald Stauffer, *Shakespeare's World of Images* (1949; rpt. Bloomington: Indiana University Press, 1966); Robert B. Heilman, Introduction to *The Taming of the Shrew*, in the Signet Classic Shakespeare (New York: New American Library, 1966); and Larry S. Champion, *The Evolution of Shakespeare's Comedy* (Cambridge: Harvard University Press, 1970).

[16]See, for example, Nevill Coghill, "The Basis of Shakespearian Comedy," *Essays and Studies* 3 (1950), 1–28; Harold Goddard, *The Meaning of Shakespeare* (Chicago: University of Chicago Press, 1951); and Coppélia Kahn, *Man's Estate: Masculine Identity in Shakespeare* (Berkeley: University of California Press, 1981). These critics differ on the extent to which Kate and Petruchio take part in this attack; some view Petruchio's bullying behavior as a crude exaggeration of patriarchal values, and others do not.

lypo) discovers his aristocratic birth, which "explains" why he could mimic his master so successfully. Why would Shakespeare delete this twist unless his purpose was to question "right supremacy"? And yet if this was indeed his intent, then why did he conclude the play with a speech in favor of an intrinsic hierarchical order?

Similar contradictions abound when we try to decipher Petruchio's character. Does he really prize riches above all—"I come to wive it wealthily in Padua; / If wealthily, then happily in Padua" (1.2.75–76)—or the philosophic mind—"For 'tis the mind that makes the body rich" (4.3.172)? Is he a chauvinist—"Marry, peace it bodes, and love, and quiet life, / An aweful rule, and right supremacy" (5.2.108–9)—or is he mocking Paduan marriage rituals— "She is my goods, my chattels, she is my house, / . . . My horse, my ox, my ass, my any thing" (3.2.230–32)? Is he simply a fool—"Why, give him gold enough, and marry him to a puppet or an aglet-baby. . . . Why, nothing comes amiss, so money comes withal" (1.2.78–82)—or is he a trickster figure—"I say it is the moon" (4.5.4)? If he is a strong master, why can't he once get his servant Grumio to obey him? If he is only role playing and so mimicking Kate's tantrums, then why does he throw a tantrum in the streets with Grumio before he has even met Kate? Is he from the country or the city? Rich or poor? A gentleman or a self-made man?

Not only is the basic action of the play under suspicion (has a shrew been tamed?), but the characters are as well (is there a shrew; is there a tamer?), and these suspicions result in controversies over genre that have led critics to devalue the play. E. M. W. Tillyard summarizes the problem: "A Mark Van Doren finds the play quite satisfactory as a hearty farce, a Hardin Craig as a comedy where the farcical elements are remotely vestigial and need not trouble us. For myself, I can neither ignore nor reconcile the two elements and am forced to conclude that the play fails in so far as it misses such a reconciliation."[17] M. R. Ridley suggests that if the play were farce, "our subtler feelings would lie contentedly quiescent. . . . But Shakespeare, being Shakespeare, cannot restrain his hand from making Petruchio more of a man, and Kate more of a woman, than from the

[17]E. M. W. Tillyard, *Shakespeare's Early Comedies*, ed. Stephen Tillyard (London: Chatto and Windus, 1965), 214.

artistic point of view was wise."[18] John Bean repeats this complaint, concluding that "this uneasy mixture of romance and farce suggests that Shakespeare's own sense of purpose is unclear, that he is discovering possibilities of one kind of comic structure while working within the demands of another."[19] In the new Oxford edition of the play, H. J. Oliver concurs; the result is "a young dramatist's attempt, not repeated, to mingle two genres that cannot be combined." He concludes: "Shakespeare was already too good a dramatist for the material he was dramatizing: characterization and farce are, finally, incompatible."[20]

The structure of the play is another source of controversy.[21] Most performances excise the Induction to *The Taming of the Shrew* because the frame plot, featuring Sly as audience to a play, is never picked up at the conclusion. Scholars have offered a variety of explanations for this oddity: some argue that Shakespeare simply forgot about the frame plot, others that this part of the play was lost; some suggest that the actors in the frame plot reappear in the main plot; and still others hypothesize that Shakespeare revived these characters in a dance (jig) that concludes the play. Yet the problem remains unsolved, raising still more. When does *The Taming of the Shrew* begin? When does it end? And what does this labyrinthine structure tell us about beginnings and endings?

Faced with these problems, the honest critic may admit dissatisfaction, frustration, and confusion. Some may simply agree with Tillyard that "the last scene of the play with Kate's great speech on

[18]M. R. Ridley, *William Shakespeare: A Commentary*, Introductory Volume to the New Temple Shakespeare (London: Dent, 1936), 24.

[19]John C. Bean, "Comic Structure and the Humanizing of Kate in *The Taming of the Shrew*," in *The Woman's Part: Feminist Criticism of Shakespeare*, ed. Carolyn Ruth Swift Lenz, Gayle Greene, and Carol Thomas Neely (Urbana: University of Illinois Press, 1980), 74.

[20]H. J. Oliver, Introduction to the Oxford edition of *The Taming of the Shrew* (Oxford: Clarendon Press, 1982), 56, 52.

[21]See Thelma N. Greenfield, "The Transformation of Christopher Sly," *Philological Quarterly* 33 (1954), 34–42; Richard Hosley, "Was There a 'Dramatic Epilogue' to *The Taming of the Shrew*?" *Studies in English Literature* 1 (Spring 1961), 17–34; Peter Alexander, "The Original Ending of *The Taming of the Shrew*," *Shakespeare Quarterly* 20 (Spring 1969), 111–16; and Arthur Colby Sprague and J. C. Trewin, *Shakespeare's Plays Today* (Columbia: University of South Carolina Press, 1970), 54.

the subordination of wives readily accommodates itself to whatever notions we have acquired in the course of reading the play."[22] But that is no reason to presume, along with Bean, that "Shakespeare's own sense of purpose is unclear"—as if we knew Shakespeare's thoughts, or lack thereof. Rather than remain trapped within these arguments over characters, moral, and genre, we might accept that we can no more resolve them conclusively than we can decide whether Bellman or Silver was faster at the hunt. Of more concern is what we make of being put in situations where we cannot choose. What does the construction of this play tell us about our construction as subjects?

The Taming of the Shrew is a trap. Even those who proclaim the unlimited semiotic pleasure of the text must agree that this is not a pleasurable text. Like Grumio's menu, *The Taming of the Shrew* is a tempting but ultimately depriving text that forces us to choose between impossible alternatives. It is a world of choices and no choice, of ambivalence and deprivation, bisexuality and castration. Grumio's mock offering of mustard and beef is in this regard no different from Petruchio's games with the sun and the moon. The play tantalizes us with a variety of choices and then forces us to choose a limited subject position in a way that cannot help but frustrate. And no discovery of hidden thematic harmonies can change this experience.

Again and again we are confronted with an illusion of alternatives and forced to make a choice. When the Lord plots to reconstruct Sly's class identity, for example, he asks his servant whether Sly will accept the part. "Believe me, lord, I think he cannot choose" (Ind. 1.42), replies the servant, who is in a woefully similar situation. When asked by Kate which suitor she fancies, Bianca replies—with hands literally tied—"Believe me, sister, of all the men alive / I never yet beheld that special face / Which I could fancy more than any other" (2.1.10–12). Can we choose the mustard? What critic would argue for the sun? Is Gremio preferable to Hortensio? Bianca to Kate? Tranio to Lucentio? Is there a "thirdborough" who can decide whether Sly or the Hostess, Petruchio or Grumio, Bianca or Kate was at fault? Not only can we not choose the correct reading of characters, plot, theme, argument, genre, and structure, but we cannot choose who is who, because everyone is "really" someone

---

[22]Tillyard, *Shakespeare's Early Comedies*, 84.

else. Yet as soon as we take on the task of acting in, viewing, or writing about this play, we are forced to make choices all the same.

For the reader or critic who is unprepared to have his or her critical tenets equated with folly, *The Taming of the Shrew* offers a maddeningly intransigent and contradictory experience. Rather than docilely submit to such traditional interpretive strategies as character analysis or clarification of moral stance, *The Taming of the Shrew* comments on their folly. It questions the hierarchy of meanings that we would impose upon it and initiates us into a world where the logic of paradox reigns. It foregrounds the impulse to dichotomize and so impose a logic of oppositional structures upon experience. And yet it does so through a paradoxical structure that both tantalizes us with a way of getting outside of these binarisms and yet denies its possibility.

The history of critical controversy over the true nature of the characters reveals the play's success in demonstrating the coalescence of theatrical role and social reality. The more we attempt to distinguish the "real" Kate and Petruchio from the roles they assume, the more we are trapped. Petruchio's stance of paradoxical self-reference calls to mind the paradox of Epimenides the Cretan, who announced: "All Cretans are liars." If the statement is true, then it is also false. Since the character Petruchio tells us he is always playing roles, there is no single character who we can say plays these roles. The history of controversy over the play's refusal to retrieve the frame plot at its conclusion further evinces an interest in double-binding paradoxes. Since the frame plot with Sly and the Lord as audience to a play is not picked up, since both "plays" end at once, the characters of the frame plot are no longer outside of the play that they witness; the frame is subsumed by the vision. The numerous plays within plays redefine each enclosed play as a frame as well and emphasize the problem of separating frame from vision, play from reality, and character from role. Biondello brings the "old news" that Petruchio comes but comes not, since "A horse and a man / Is more than one, / And yet not many" (3.2.84–86). Grumio informs Petruchio that "the oats have eaten the horses" (3.2.205–6), and Tranio plots that "A child shall get a sire" (2.1.411). These jests further underline the play's interest in the paradox of the enclosed enclosing its frame.

The most inclusive reading of *The Taming of the Shrew* describes the play as a metadrama designed to confuse and later clarify the relation between social roles and theatricality.[23] The only problem with this interpretation is that it denies the contradictions we actually experience in reading and watching the play. If the moral of the play is that we cannot escape theater, any reading that would stand outside of the play denies that the play refuses any stance outside of it. If we correlate play and paradox, we are still not clear of the problem, since a reading of the play as paradox must acknowledge the play of paradox at the level of its own discourse. As soon as we seek to resolve the contradictions in character by arguing that Petruchio is a wise fool who displays the paradox of character, we betray the felt experience of the play in which he is both a cruel authoritarian and a witty philosopher who infuriates and confuses. If we resolve the controversy over genre by suggesting that the play veers toward comedy to show a freedom over the mechanical or arbitrary roles of farce, we are faced with the task of staging a production that can reflect this paradox. If we are right about *The Taming of the Shrew* then we are wrong, and there is no easy way out of this dilemma.

We can find a visual analogy of this frame-up in any number of works by M. C. Escher, of which *The Print Gallery* may serve as an example (see figure 10). To read the picture we may trace a path from the bottom right-hand corner or entrance into the print gallery, past the man near the entrance, and finally on to the young man on the far left who is examining a framed print of a harbor scene. Just as the windowpane of the gallery through which we see the young man frames him, so the print the young man beholds is constructed so as to escape the boundaries of its frame. In the upper right-hand corner

---

[23]Richard Henze, "Role Playing in *The Taming of the Shrew*," *Southern Humanities Review* 4 (1970), 231–40, is the first extensive treatment of this argument. According to Henze, Petruchio "trains Kate to play roles so expertly that one cannot separate Kate's part in the pageant from Kate's function in life" (231); "Petruchio plays contradictory roles with equal effectiveness" (235) that we cannot determine his true nature; and "the final pageant of incredibly obedient shrew reflects most nearly the comedy of life where irony and multiple role-playing obscure reality exactly because irony and multiple role-playing are reality" (239). See also J. Dennis Huston, *Shakespeare's Comedies of Play* (New York: Columbia University Press, 1981), for an even fuller study of play here; as well as Marianne Novy, "Patriarchy and Play in *The Taming of the Shrew*," *English Literary Renaissance* 9 (1979), 264–80, and the extension of that essay in her later *Love's Argument: Gender Relations in Shakespeare* (Chapel Hill: University of North Carolina Press, 1984).

Figure 10. M. C. Escher, *The Print Gallery* (1956). © 1989 M. C. Escher Heirs/Cordon Art, Baarn, Holland. Collection Haags Gemeentemuseum, The Hague.

of the picture, the print becomes the building in which the young man stands, and so the viewer is truly "lost" in the picture he beholds. The left side of the picture emphasizes the frame; the right side emphasizes how the framed material encloses its frame. *The*

Print Gallery contains a viewer, already framed, and a framed print; it ultimately denies the boundary between the two, contains its viewer, and so reminds us that we are part of the picture we see. *The Taming of the Shrew* contains an audience, already dramatized onstage, and a framed play. By denying the boundary between the two, the play reminds us that we are part of the play we see and that we cannot escape it.

In its games with both characters and spectators *The Taming of the Shrew* enacts the problem of getting outside of the system in which one operates. It confuses ground and figure, frame and vision; it refuses to complete its stories, to decide its debates, to resolve its contradictions, to finish what it begins. The critic who would tame and trap the play finds her attempts frustrated and her role mocked. To interpret becomes equivalent with an attempt to dominate, to transform, to tame, to fix a shifting ludic surface with a single master perspective. This play, structured like a paradox, reminds us of the way in which paradox works so as to deny a frame of reference outside of its infinite regressions. The question remains: what does *The Taming of the Shrew* tell us about our construction as subjects?

III

One answer is provided by the essay "Ideology and Ideological State Apparatuses," in which Louis Althusser explains how the construction of the subject and its interpellation into an ideologically constrictive symbolic order are one and the same:

Ideology "acts" or "functions" in such a way that it "recruits" subjects among the individuals (it recruits them all), or "transforms" the individuals into subjects (it transforms them all) by that very precise operation which I have called *interpellation* or hailing, and which can be imagined along the lines of the most common everyday police (or other) hailing: "Hey, you there!" Assuming that the theoretical scene I have imagined takes place in the street, the hailed individual will turn round. By this mere one-hundred-and-eighty-degree physical conversion, he becomes a *subject*. Why? Because he has recognized that the hail was "really" addressed to him, and that "it was *really him* who was hailed." . . . Naturally, for the convenience and clarity of my little theoretical theatre I have had to present things in the form of a temporal succession. . . . But in reality these things happen without any succession. The existence of ideology and the hailing or interpellation of individuals as subjects are one and the same thing.[24]

One of the best examples of Althusser's argument is the opening of *The Taming of the Shrew*, where Sly is "hailed" and made a new man. But perhaps the best example is the way in which this play repeats in its games with its audiences the games it plays with Kate; both re-enact the taming of the shrew, the uncomfortable introduction to the arbitrary and divisive subject positions of the symbolic which is considered socialization.

Critics who resist teaching *The Taming of the Shrew* explain that literary works are ideologically complicit discourses that actively construct their audiences: "Since each invocation of a code is also its reinforcement or reinscription, literature does more than transmit ideology: it actually creates it. . . . To invoke the conventional narrative resolutions . . . [is] to sanction them . . . to perpetuate them as the working myths of the culture."[25] Since *The Taming of the Shrew* offers a virtual manual of techniques devised to persuade women of the natural basis of culturally determined differences, an exploration of the work of gender ideology provides a useful *class* exercise. Rather than refuse to recognize sexist texts, we can subvert the relation of frame, gaze, and pleasure in the theater of a sexist culture by identifying these sites of misrecognition.

The history of criticism reminds us that the play has served as a vehicle for engendering gender. As a text that encourages controversy and divisiveness, *The Taming of the Shrew* forces us to take sides, and so to take our places on either side of the gender line. Most readers are familiar with the story Lacan tells of the engendering of the subject through language: a little boy and little girl are seated in a train facing both each other and the opposing sides of the station which they are fast approaching. " 'Look,' says the brother, 'we're at

---

[24]Louis Althusser, "Ideology and Ideological State Apparatuses," *Lenin and Philosophy and Other Essays*, trans. Ben Brewster (London: Monthly Review Press, 1971), 174–75.

[25]Gayle Greene and Coppélia Kahn, "Feminist Scholarship and the Social Construction of Woman," in *Making a Difference*, 4–5.

Ladies!' 'Idiot!' replies his sister, 'Can't you see we're at Gentlemen.'
For these children," Lacan concludes, "Ladies and Gentlemen will be
henceforth two countries towards which each of their souls will
strive on divergent wings, and between which a truce will be the
more impossible since they are actually the same country and neither
can compromise on its own superiority without detracting from the
glory of the other."[26] Lacan maintains that language and sexual
difference are intertwined in arbitrary gender identifications that
(mis)direct our libidinal energies. To illustrate his argument Lacan
draws two identical doors, writes the words "Ladies" and "Gentlemen" under them, and explains that the signifier does not "stand for"
the thing but only makes sense in relationship to another signifier.
Similarly, male and female, regardless of biological differences, are
products of a linguistic signifying system, so that male is necessarily
"not female" and female "not male." Jacqueline Rose explains: "In
Lacan's account, sexual identity operates as a law—it is something
enjoined on the subject. For him, the fact that individuals must line
up according to an opposition (having or not having the phallus) makes
that clear."[27]

Lacan's work on the splitting and so procuring of the subject in
language led him to correlate the instability of sexual identity with
the instability of ego identity and to see both as a function of the
ordering fictions by means of which the ego as supplement is set into
place. For Lacan, the assumption of a sexual identity is accompanied
by the sacrifice of free libidinal energy necessitated by signification,
which demands that we be one thing and not another. As identity
demands the fiction of closure, so sexual identity requires a fiction
which, however fostered by biology or in its service, is essentially
linguistic, ideological, and fetishistic. A more telling illustration of
Lacan's thesis can be discovered in the painting by Larry Rivers titled
Parts of the Face (figure 11). For Rivers, as for Lacan, the problem is
the *representation* of sexuality—the way in which libidinal energy is
parceled up and channeled through socially appropriate bodily zones,
the way in which we are inscribed and so caught in a linguistic order.
Rose observes that we have "failed to see that the concept of the

[26]Jacques Lacan, "Agency of the Letter in the Unconscious," *Ecrits: A Selection*,
trans. Alan Sheridan (New York: Norton, 1977), 152.
[27]Jacqueline Rose, Introduction—2, to *Feminine Sexuality: Jacques Lacan and the
Ecole Freudienne*, ed. Juliet Mitchell and Jacqueline Rose, trans. Rose (New York:
Norton, 1985), 29.

Figure 11. Larry Rivers, *Parts of the Face* (1961), oil on canvas. Courtesy of the Tate Gallery, London / Art Resource, New York.

phallus in Freud's account of human sexuality was part of his awareness of the problematic, if not impossible, nature of sexual identity itself," and as a result, we have "lost sight of Freud's sense that sexual difference is constructed at a price and that it involves subjection to a

129

law which exceeds any natural or biological division. The concept of the phallus stands for that subjection, and for the way in which women are very precisely implicated in its process."[28] And yet most suspect here is the way in which any text about the problem of oppositional structures, including Lacan's, is inevitably caught up within them.

The Taming of the Shrew records a powerful myth in our society—one so prevalent in our culture that we hardly recognize it. The myth of the transformation of nature into culture through the incest taboo was celebrated by Claude Lévi-Strauss and in turn adopted by Lacan as the truth of the symbolic order. This myth privileges men over women, sanctions the exchange between men of their daughters and wives, and equates misogyny with civilization itself. "The prime role of culture is to ensure the group's existence as a group," writes Lévi-Strauss, "and consequently, in this domain as in all others, to replace chance by organization. The prohibition of incest is a certain form, and even highly varied forms, of intervention. But it is intervention over and above anything else; even more exactly, it is *the* intervention."[29] As an exogamy rule, the incest taboo functions to establish a system of social relationships by replacing the intrafamilial marriage with interfamilial marriage. Yet given such an account, we might as well make up our own myth of difference.

Consider. Once, long ago, there was a shrew, a she-demon, a woman-who-frightened-men. She refused to submit to our laws of marriage; refused to be traded as her father ordered; and threatened to undo the very system of exchange by enjoying her sexuality freely. No marriages could take place until she was controlled, for by her actions the identity-conferring status of marriage in our tribe—the very basis of our systems of exchange and assignment of subject positions—was threatened. None of the men in the village could control her; she was called demon and witch, devil and whore. The natural order suffered as a consequence; the places at table and church

[28]Ibid., 28.

[29]Claude Lévi-Strauss, *The Elementary Structures of Kinship*, trans. James Harle Bell, John Richard von Sturmer, Rodney Needham (Boston: Beacon Press, 1969), 32. On the role of women as objects of exchange in the work of Lévi-Strauss, see Gayle Rubin, "The Traffic in Women: Notes on the 'Political Economy' of Sex," in *Toward an Anthropology of Women*, ed. Rayna R. Reiter (New York: Monthly Review Press, 1975), 157–210.

stood empty; the harvest was spoiled. In time, her father went to a trickster figure and struck a bargain with him. As the trickster understood the law of no-difference and of difference, he agreed to undertake the taming of this she-man and so to restore difference to the society. The trickster ushered in a period of festive nondifference, and pandemonium ensued with the advent of his misrule. Sons refused to obey their fathers, servants refused to obey their masters—everyone enjoyed a change of place. The shrew felt the entire community to be mocking her, however, and, shamefaced, soon repented. From then on the couple symbolized the triumph of difference and of the sacred role of marriage in creating systems of exchange which assure identity and order.

Is this story so different from *The Taming of the Shrew*? Like this play, it offers a compendium of devices of gender ideology. It universalizes its sexism as natural and inevitable and parades the instance of female submission as the basis of civilization. It not only repeats the classic separation between woman as angel and as devil, fetishized object and castrating bitch, but also repeats the classic distinctions between woman as nature/man as culture, woman as object of the gaze/man as bearer of the gaze, woman as obstacle/man as hero who by mastering the dangerous otherness of nature brings about civilization. Finally, like *The Taming of the Shrew*, our story employs a trickster figure who appears to subvert a particular social order, and yet does so only to strengthen it. For example, Petruchio's mad actions reveal the folly of Paduan society; his reversal of the traditional categories of mad and sane, foolish and wise suggest his affinities with the trickster, jester, or wise fool. The Paduans call him "lunatic," "madcap ruffian," "madbrain rudesby," "a frantic fool," "a devil," "a very fiend." Kate suggests that he wear a coxcomb, Petruchio dresses himself in a clown's costume, and the play's folk sources confirm Petruchio's roots in the rustic clown.[30] The influence

---

[30]Petruchio is treated as a type of clown or fool by Marianne Novy as well as by Charles Baskervill and W. B. Thorne; his character seems to be based on both the rustic clown and the witty fool. For the folk tradition in *Shrew*, see Charles Baskervill, *The Elizabethan Jig and Related Song Drama* (1929; rpt. New York: Dover, 1965); Jan Brunvand, "The Folktale Origin of *The Taming of the Shrew*," *Shakespeare Quarterly* 17 (1966), 345–59; W. B. Thorne, "Folk Elements in *The Taming of the Shrew*," *Queen's Quarterly* 75 (1968), 482–96; Michael West, "The Folk Background of Petruchio's Wooing Dance: Male Supremacy in *The Taming of the Shrew*," *Shakespeare*

of a festive carnival tradition on *The Taming of the Shrew* is evident in the play's inversion of the roles of master and servant through disguise, its reported mockery of religious authority at the wedding, its mockery of paternal authority at the conclusion, as well as its focus on paradox.[31]

Since the carnival tradition subverts only to restore difference in a given social order, it is simultaneously subversive and conservative. Similarly, *The Taming of the Shrew* both recognizes the work of gender ideology and seeks to justify it. Such contradictions are in fact typical of the genre of Renaissance humanist defenses in favor of extending women's rights, texts that have since become more paradoxical than originally intended. In the sixteenth century, the term *paradox* referred not only to apparently self-contradictory yet valid statements but to statements contrary to received opinion, as in *Hamlet*'s "This was sometime a paradox, but now the time gives it proof" (3.1.113–14). Renaissance humanist defenses of woman were therefore doubly paradoxical, since they were both unconventional and, to some readers, inherently self-contradictory. Further, as Rosalie Colie points out, "most of them were truly paradoxical in that they both defended and did not defend their subject, incorporating elements from the long tradition of misogyny into their general

---

Studies 7 (1973), 65–74. See also Barbara Swain, *Fools and Folly during the Middle Ages and the Renaissance* (New York: Columbia University Press, 1932); Enid Welsford, *The Fool: His Social and Literary History* (London: Faber and Faber, 1935); and William Willeford, *The Fool and His Scepter: A Study in Clowns and Jesters and Their Audience* (Chicago: Northwestern University Press, 1969). In "Shakespearean Comedy and the Uses of Reason," *South Atlantic Quarterly* 63 (1964), 1–9, Ronald Berman all too briefly reads Petruchio as "a wise fool in a world of the foolish wise, and in this he brings to life the great comic document of his day, Erasmus' *Praise of Folly*" (7). One might also consider the possibility that Shakespeare was playing *Praise of Folly* against Eramsus's humanist treatise on women.

[31]For studies that relate Shakespearean comedy to folk traditions of carnival, inversion, and dramatized paradox, see C. L. Barber, *Shakespeare's Festive Comedy: A Study of Dramatic Form and Its Relation to Social Custom* (Princeton: Princeton University Press, 1959); Mikhail Bakhtin, *Rabelais and His World*, trans. Helene Iswolsky (Cambridge: MIT Press, 1968); Ian Donaldson, *The World Upside-Down: Comedy from Jonson to Fielding* (Oxford: Clarendon Press, 1970); Robert Weimann, *Shakespeare and the Popular Tradition in the Theater: Studies in the Social Dimension of Dramatic Form and Function*, ed. Robert Schwartz (Baltimore: Johns Hopkins University Press, 1978); Michael Bristol, *Carnival and Theater: Plebeian Culture and the Structure of Authority in Renaissance England* (New York: Methuen, 1985); and Peter Stallybrass and Allon White, *The Politics and Poetics of Transgression* (Ithaca: Cornell University Press, 1986).

arguments for the relative emancipation of women."[32] A prominent example is Erasmus's famous defense of women, *A Merry Dialogue Declaring the Properties of Shrewd Shrews and Honest Wives*, which advises us to employ the humanist strategy of firm persuasion rather than force in dealing with shrews.

Colie reminds us that paradoxes fail when the values they question are no longer widely held: "To deliver a paradoxical encomium, the rhetorician assumed certain values on the part of his audience, values which he would then proceed to question, to undermine, or to overthrow by means of his *epideixis*. Whether or not he believed in his argument is not in question: but his audience, representing 'received opinion,' had to believe in its dialectical opposite."[33] One of many paradoxes in *The Taming of the Shrew* is the advice that one may humanize a shrewish wife by treating her as if she were an object or animal. Of course, misogynistic farce had always suggested this strategy, following the assumption that a husband would be happy with an object or pet. In *The Taming of the Shrew*, however, this tactic is paradoxical since it is employed so that the wife may reject the role of object or pet and recognize the value of social roles instead. In her conscious agreement to play an arbitrary role, she will be fully "humanized." Critics unfamiliar with misogynistic farce miss Shakespeare's parody of it to reach very different aims. *The Taming of the Shrew* disturbs not simply because it is sexist, then, but because its supposed correction of misogynistic practices renders its remaining misogyny all the more disturbing. The play's efforts to put socialization on display as comic drama and to break some mirrors of misrecognition merely highlight its blatant failure to break other mirrors.

To explore sexism in *The Taming of the Shrew* is to recognize that the relationship between ideology and cultural reality as transmitted through literature is never easy to analyze. Yet the mere existence of propagandistic literature, as Carolyn Lougee points out, implies "the reality of prohibited behavior which alone made the prescriptions necessary."[34] Like the misogynistic farces upon which it is modeled,

[32]Rosalie L. Colie, *Paradoxia Epidemica: The Renaissance Tradition of Paradox* (Princeton: Princeton University Press, 1966), 58.

[33]Ibid., 8–9.

[34]Carolyn Lougee, "Review Essay: Modern European History," *Signs* 2 (Spring 1977), 635.

The Taming of the Shrew blames and punishes woman. It merely offers new tactics of punishment and domination, replacing physical violence with double-binding mind games, deprivation of food and sleep, and emotional hypnosis. The replacement of violence by propaganda may indicate no more than increased artfulness in the manipulation of the oppressed. The replacement of shrew-taming farces by shrew-taming comedies is simply a more covert form of oppression. Precisely because *The Taming of the Shrew* appears less overtly sexist than misogynistic farces, it is all the more dangerous. As disturbing as Kate's taming is the way in which she is portrayed as happily tamed and actively spreading the practice of her indoctrination. The play renders woman into an apologist for the phallocentric system that oppresses her. It offers as a corrective to a blatantly diseased aristocratic society the scapegoating of woman as solution; the rebellious woman becomes the cause rather than the symptom of class struggle. Since comedies about the illness of society still masquerade as comedies about the illness of women, it appears that we have not yet escaped the scene of shrew taming.[35]

Shakespearean comedy typically deflects class problems onto the instance of the rebellious female whose punishment and correction constitute the narrative action. *The Comedy of Errors* concludes with the correction of Adriana, *A Midsummer Night's Dream* solves its problems by punishing Titania, and *The Taming of the Shrew* pretends to treat a failing aristocratic order by reconciling a rebellious female critic to its ways. That Kate has become the apologist for a misogynistic society that she vows to hold to certain standards of truth and decency cannot help but strike us as ridiculous. Petruchio has taught Kate sublimation: she exchanges one halter for another. She hates not men but less "masculine" men than Petruchio; hates not women but less "feminine" women than herself; hates not rules but those that contradict Petruchio's. She is still the naive opponent of hypocrisy, the unwitting pawn in a much larger game, the scapegoat for a failing social order. Petruchio will never "watch the night in storms, the day in cold" (5.2.150); Kate will never lift a finger except to wag it at her disobedient house servants—the future audiences to even lengthier speeches on duty. Petruchio will continue to show men how un-

[35]See Mary Ann Doane, "The 'Woman's Film': Possession and Address," in *Re-Vision*, ed. Doane et al., 67–82.

manly they are, Kate will reveal the women as unfeminine; both will continue to perform in games of one-upmanship. The two have become principles of differentiation—yet only in a theater. And as we watch their triumphant exit off to bed, we remember what a sterile gesture this is. We look back at the male actor playing Sly's wife. We remember that Kate is a character played by a man. We remember that we are in a theater, multiple theaters. And we begin to hope for another kind of theater, one that accepts difference without making it the obstacle to be defeated, tamed, or raped.

IV

That we have to pay a price in entering any social order is not in question; that we must go back and repay the price that Kate pays, however, is. Like Shakespeare, Lacan recognizes gender roles as arbitrary but necessary and parades the specific price that women have paid under a patriarchal order as a symbol of that cost. What disturbs is not cost itself but the mistaken identification of a culturally specific cost with its universality and inevitability. Like Petruchio, Lacan is a trickster figure who undermines and yet proclaims his mastery. Like Petruchio, Lacan articulates the dilemma of breaking the mirror of ideology and yet exemplifies in his "corrected" misogyny his inability to stand outside of the system he would change. Both argue that woman does not exist except as a fantasy or theatrical construct and yet both seek to reify a cultural myth of the exchange of women as the basis of civilization.

Lacan's theory of the symbolic order is limited by the structural anthropology upon which it depends and by the early forms of object-relations theory that it was designed to subvert. Lacan equates a particular configuration of social power with the symbolic order, universalizes the oedipal law, and identifies the paternal metaphor as the privileged level of representation that must intervene between mother and child to bring "nature" to a state of "culture." Lacanians respond to such complaints by explaining that the specific configurations of the symbolic are indeed open to change: "We must remember that the Symbolic here does not mean anything representative of a second hidden thing or essence," Ellie Ragland-Sullivan cautions. "Rather, it refers to that order whose principal function is to mediate between the Imaginary order and the Real. The Symbolic order interprets, symbolizes, articulates, and universalizes both the experiential and the concrete which, paradoxically, it has already shaped contextually."[36] Yet Lacan's theory of the symbolic order was developed in the context of a specific historical period of intellectual thought, one heavily influenced by a highly sexist form of structural anthropology. After studying Lacan's reliance on Lévi-Strauss, Rose concludes that "Lacan's use of the symbolic" "is open to the same objections as Lévi-Strauss's account" since "these remarks . . . most critical of the order described . . . are in another sense complicit with that order and any argument constructed on their basis is likely to be circular."[37]

Lacanian theorists answer that Lacan's phallocentric discourse intentionally reflects the problems he sought to portray. But the tricky question of intentionality is further complicated by Lacan's fondness for paradox. "In the psyche, there is nothing by which the subject may situate himself as a male or female being" asserts Lacan valiantly.[38] The sentence is a marvelous example of the problems here: whereas it suggests the ways in which language directs biology and subverts the sexual drive into an identificatory one, it also repeats this strategy by interpellating the female reader as "he," "him," and "men." At what level Lacan's awareness of such problems operates is impossible to discover. Juliet Flower MacCannell rightly warns us against the "tendency . . . to over-identify Lacan's analysis of the culture of the signifier . . . with his own stance *on* that culture." She maintains that "just as the physician may be said to be apart from the disease s/he discovers, even if s/he has been constrained by it, Lacan's analysis of the systems formed by the signifier, metaphor, the phallus, stand apart from his own 'system.'"[39] But can it? Since the popular return to Freud owes as much to deconstruction as to Lacan, the acknowledgment that Lacan is implicated in that which he attacks need not detract from his insights. We now acknowledge, for example, that Freud repressed the idea of repression, and wished away

[36]Ellie Ragland-Sullivan, *Jacques Lacan and the Philosophy of Psychoanalysis* (Urbana: University of Illinois Press, 1986), 268.

[37]Rose, Introduction—2, 45.

[38]Lacan, "Alienation," *The Four Fundamental Concepts of Psycho-Analysis*, ed. Jacques-Alain Miller, trans. Alan Sheridan (New York: Norton, 1981), 204.

[39]Juliet Flower MacCannell, *Figuring Lacan: Criticism and the Cultural Unconscious* (Lincoln: University of Nebraska Press, 1986), 19.

threats to his theory of wish fulfillment. We admit that Freud refused to abandon the search for primal scenes which he elsewhere acknowledged exist only at the level of fantasied reconstruction. And we accept that Freud denied the bisexuality and gender instability he elsewhere theorizes with conviction. Why deny that Lacan is framed by what he describes?

"Taking the experience of psychoanalysis in its development over sixty years," Lacan observes expansively, "it comes as no surprise to note that, whereas the first outcome of its origins was a conception of the castration complex based on paternal repression, it has progressively directed its interests towards the frustrations coming from the mother, not that such a distortion has shed any light on the complex."[40] Lacan charged early object-relations theory with denying the fundamental role of the unconscious, sexuality, and representation in psychoanalysis in favor of a new emphasis on the study of the quality of actual maternal care.[41] To stress the importance of his intervention, Lacan introduced the name of the father as the third term that interrupts the asocial mother–infant dyad and brings to bear upon it the law of language and symbolic positions. And that intervention is indeed designed to reframe mother–infant relations as always already outside of language and representation. In Lacan's dramatization of psychoanalytic history, the son figure (Lacan) intervenes and rescues the dead father's authority (Freud) from the mother's tyranny (object-relations theory). Since gender ideology is obviously at work in Lacan's portrayal of the mothering function as asocial, we may conclude with Rose that "there is, therefore, no question of denying here that Lacan was implicated in the phallocentrism he described, just as his own utterance constantly rejoins the mastery which he sought to undermine."[42]

Teresa de Lauretis rightly critiques Lacanian theory for the way

[40]Lacan, "Guiding Remarks for a Congress on Feminine Sexuality," in *Feminine Sexuality*, ed. Mitchell and Rose, 87.

[41]Ironically, early object-relations theory is also charged with failing to explore *actual* child care rigorously enough. D. W. Winnicott points out that "Melanie Klein represents the most vigorous attempt to study the earliest processes of the developing human infant *apart from the study of child-care*. She has always admitted that child-care is important but has not made a special study of it," in "Classification: Is There a Psycho-Analytic Contribution to Psychiatric Classification?" (1959), in his collected papers, *The Maturational Process and the Facilitating Environment* (New York: International Universities Press, 1965), 126.

[42]Rose, Introduction—2, 56.

in which its descriptive features all too easily become prescriptive. She complains that "in opposing the truth of the unconscious to the illusion of an always-already false consciousness, the general critical discourse based on Lacanian psychoanalysis subscribes too easily . . . to the territorial distinction between subjective and social modes of signification and the cold war that is its issue." More concerned with misrecognition as sites for change, de Lauretis suggests we redirect attention to the dialectical relationship between the means by which signs are produced and the codes themselves, and so explore meaning as a cultural production "not only susceptible of ideological transformation, but materially based in historical change."[43] Insofar as Lacan's writings ignore the material and historical nature of social organization and social change, they betray a disturbing complacency toward structuralist and phallocentric versions of a transcendent law—whether in the form of the phallic signifier, the law of the father, or the law of the symbolic order.

V

In question here are the role theater has played in the development of psychoanalytic narratives and the role it can play in rethinking them. As a psychoanalyst and teacher of Freudian theory, Lacan reads human psychic development in terms of narratives that he discovered in Freud. Not surprisingly, the locus for Freud's theories of childhood sexuality and male castration anxieties is the Greek tragedy *Oedipus*, which places incestuous desire in the context of a communal law that condemns it. According to Freud's myth of difference, the male child's sexual fantasies in relation to his mother are accompanied by fears of punishment in the form of castration. The result is the internalization of social taboos and the acceptance of the law of place, achieved simultaneously through superego development and the ordering and repression of sexuality.

Traditional Western narratives of tragedy and comedy alike champion a view of civilization as castration—a phallocentric concept that equates the organization of human sexuality and gender with the birth of language and repression, and so with a psychic

[43]De Lauretis, *Alice Doesn't*, 180–81, 172.

displacing-as-ordering that alienates the subject even as it guarantees it a place in the symbolic order. Theater enacts the costs of assuming the displacing image returned back by society—the mask that alienates as it procures entry into society. Traditional narratives of comedy and tragedy therefore typically promote a culturally determined form of the socialization process, juxtaposing the deconstruction of the gaze against the inevitability of a theater of representation, the imaginary as alterity against the symbolic of oedipally inscribed inevitability.

But the key word here is *narrative*, not *theater*. We may agree with Gallop that theater stages and so reinforces polar oppositions—but only if we equate the word *theater* with the term *Western narrative drama*. The term *theater*, as Keir Elam reminds us, customarily refers to the performance aspects of a work, whereas the term *drama* is traditionally reserved for its narrative forms.[44] Since theater is always performative but not necessarily narrative, we cannot equate a theatrical ordering of difference with strict polarities. We can, however, acknowledge that traditional Western narrative theater has been obsessed with repeating Freud's version of the Oedipus myth—the scene of a founding crime of sexuality and a payment that decisively orders sexuality and gender. And we cannot help but observe that *The Taming of the Shrew* rehearses and preserves that myth today, insofar as it identifies the achievement of civilization itself with the domination of women through patriarchal exogamy rites, physical violence, and double-binding mind games. If we compare the complementary narratives of *Oedipus* and *The Taming of the Shrew*, we have the tragedy of the man who discovers his sexuality and the comedy of a woman who learns to disavow her own in submission to a repressive patriarchal law. One scenario identifies civilization with male payment for his own sexuality, the other identifies civilization with male control over disordered female sexuality. Both not only record but promulgate the values of a repressive patriarchal culture.

Traditional Western theater thus offers us two stages, comic and tragic, upon which are always playing some version of *Oedipus* or its sister play, *The Taming of the Shrew*. A setup is therefore always being staged as well—one that places its spectators in the positions of Kate, Oedipus, and Christopher Sly, all of whom "cannot choose" but

[44]Keir Elam, *The Semiotics of Theatre and Drama* (London: Methuen, 1980), 2.

accept the interpellation, or hailing, that indoctrinates the subject into a confusing and limiting identity. Whereas cinema can challenge or deconstruct the symbolic by dissolving or dispersing the image, traditional theater would appear to be more tied to the symbolic, to the ego, and to the mask of the unitary individual. Whereas theater questions the validity of masks by virtue of their ability to be exchanged, it cannot dissolve or otherwise destroy them. Master and servant, husband and wife may exchange roles in a comedy, but they never escape the tyranny of social roles; in short, they can never escape being seen, caught in a scene, and so interpellated by a social order. Given traditional theater's superimposition of narrative inevitability, given its scopic regime of voyeurism and exhibitionism, and given its narrative regime of domination and mastery—a feminist theater would indeed appear to require an Oedipus wrecked. Accordingly, feminist theater requires a performance that exposes and stages this taming of the gaze by the symbolic order.

Josette Féral points the way. While arguing that theater is on the side of inscription in the symbolic, Féral maintains that performance is on the side of deconstruction in the semiotic. She suggests that feminist theater is possible—but only when theater is not theater per se. Féral's use of the term *theater* would seem to correspond to Keir Elam's definition of drama, and her use of the term *performance* corresponds to Elam's description of theater. "In contrast to performance, theatre cannot keep from setting up, stating, constructing, and giving points of view," Féral explains, for it requires a unified subject that performance deconstructs into drives and energies and since it assumes representational models that performance rejects in favor of discontinuity and spillage. If performance highlights the *"realities of the imaginary,"* "originates within the subject and allows his flows of desire to speak," she concludes, theater "inscribes the subject in the law and in theatrical codes, which is to say, in the symbolic."[45]

Féral finds theater and performance "mutually exclusive" "when it comes to the position of the subject." Yet finally she is describing a dialectic essential to both subjectivity and to theater, which she acknowledges by arguing that "theatricality arises from the play

[45]Josette Féral, "Performance and Theatricality," trans. Terese Lyons, *Modern Drama* 25 (1982), 178.

between these two realities" and by describing performance as that within theater which deconstructs it. Féral notes: "In its very stripped-down workings, its exploration of the body, and its joining of time and space, performance gives us a kind of theatricality in slow motion: the kind we find at work in today's theatre. Performance explores the under-side of that theatre." Criticized for assuming that performance reaches a presence outside of representation, Féral merely observes that "performance seems to be attempting to reveal and to stage something that took place before the representation of the subject (even if it does so by using an already constituted subject)."[46]

Like much theater theory and practice, Féral's thesis is symptomatic of the battle within theater to differentiate presence from representation. Insofar as theater stages presence, it enacts the contest between being and representation and so renews itself by continually re-posing that relationship. If theater presents a funhouse of mirrors we never escape, it also rehearses the quest for presence by shifting its point of view. If theater suggests Jean Baudrillard's "generation by models of a real without origin or reality: a hyperreal,"[47] it also grounds this paradox in the physical realities of time, space, and society and keeps posing the question of the performance present. As a displacing of the object by its display, theater stages the way it can never get to itself, the way in which the scene always displaces what is shown. Similarly, the actor presents herself to us as always already displaced by a look and seeks, in the process of exhibitionism, the nature of exhibitionism. Theatrical showing is a framing that, by putting frames on stage, necessarily displaces itself. If theater reveals that objects exist only insofar as they are displaced by a look, it also offers various reactive and interactive means of displacing and renewing the act of seeing.

The relation between performance art and traditional theater is therefore not a polar opposition but a dialectic. We seek in theater that moment when our looking is no longer a looking (as in film) but a being seen, a return of the look by the mirror image. Theater

---

[46]Ibid., 177, 178, 176.

[47]Jean Baudrillard, "The Precession of Simulacra," in *Art after Modernism: Rethinking Representation*, ed. Brian Wallis (New York: New Museum of Contemporary Art, 1984), 253.

provides a way of interrupting the frame from a point of view both within and outside it, much as the unconscious is the blind spot in our vision which in turn is constructed through and reflected by the look of the other. Feminist performance art thus poses a challenge to traditional dramatic theater by foregrounding a subversive force always already within it. In *Swan Lake, Minnesota* a stripper performs to a fascinated crowd of men by throwing down cardboard cutouts of her body in various states of undress; the last cutout is a mirror that reflects their gaze. In the performance piece *Waiting*, the author holds up sheets upon which are projected images of waitresses, and then inserts her body and voice in filmed images and narratives of restaurant life, simultaneously positioning herself as author, actor, screen, and the source of their mutual confusion and deconstruction. Thus the paradox of avant-garde theater: in seeking to stage a moment outside of representation it cannot avoid the play of looks that constitutes representation, and yet in speaking of the costs of representation it evokes a sense of rebellion against symbolic form.

Since theater is always placing the living body's energies in tension with a constraining form, it is always recording the cost of entry into the symbolic. But by staging that form we displace it; we view from another angle the looks that inscribe us, and so look back. Neither ideologically conservative nor anarchic, theater is always about the relationship of what is seen and the fact that it is seen, and always renewing the relation of what is seen to the social gaze in which it is inscribed. Rather than deny the look by means of which we are seen and socialized, theater creates energy from the resistance and tension generated by the reversal of that look in the moment of exhibitionism. Since theater is always replaying the battle of presence and representation which occasions it, even classical drama can return us to the theatrical body and to the disruptive gaze by which it is constituted.

For example, *The Taming of the Shrew* not only stages theatricality but can be said to be "about" the very problem of theater's degenerating into mere show, insofar as it explicitly calls out for a performative mode capable of interrupting and revisioning social roles. Paduan society threatens to degenerate into the merely theatrical, which we may define as a stale crystallization of dramatic roles and narratives. Yet the term *theater* also refers to a subversive tension that threatens to displace traditional roles and narratives. Similarly, whereas the term *drama* refers to the conventional narrative aspect of theater, the term *dramatic* implies a breaking of containers by their contents.

Paduan society is given over to mere show without substance, and on that basis may be condemned as bad theater. Controlled by reified roles and stale narratives, this society resists the energy and tension generated by an awareness of the relation of appearance and reality, container and contained. Padua operates according to an aristocratic code; order is maintained by an elaborate fiction that requires allegiance to the sanctity and prerogative of theatrical roles. Human identity need never be discovered in such a world; will, reason, and justice are exchanged for a smoothly oiled social system in which perspective is arbitrarily determined with mechanical efficiency. With its superficial equation of appearance and reality, social codes and justice, Padua might as well be operated by costumed dummies or robots. The various reactions to Petruchio's costume suggest how the means we use to express what is within have come instead to define it. If clothes don't "make the man," speech may similarly be "goodly talk" of which we should be suspicious. Insofar as appearance, lineage, and role work as a veneer to disguise our needs, the frame of show has falsely come to define its contents. As the home of the arts, Padua boasts of its culture but ceremoniously contains the materialism, sexuality, and aggression upon which it is based; Petruchio therefore endorses each openly. Its order depends upon servitude; Petruchio bullies his servant. Its continuance depends upon the sexuality that Petruchio openly celebrates in his antiromantic courting. Its maintenance depends upon wealth; Petruchio praises riches as the highest good. The peace, perspective, and culture are dependent upon taming; the civilizing is dependent upon trapping; the order has been achieved through a form of brutality.

Petruchio's paradoxical actions function both to teach Paduan society the value of the living and the animal, the mercenary and the violent, and to teach Kate the opposing value of the arbitrary social roles she disdains. In this sense his actions serve to emphasize the necessity of keeping the relationship between human being and social role, contained and container, in lively tension. Petruchio's actions function to reverse and so reframe the *relationship* of performance and theatricality, human beings and their social roles, through subversive action that reverses the categories of civilized and crude, rational and animal. When he champions that which is considered low or denigrates whatever is considered high, he is not simply playing games but exposing the arbitrary game of making such distinctions. Petruchio's behavior reminds us that the low can also be reframed as the elemental and so essential; his mockery of Paduan conventions suggests what happens when social conventions are divorced from use. When Petruchio pronounces materialism to be the chief good, we are shocked—until we find ourselves questioning the dependency of Paduan society's peace, idealism, and culture upon the very materialism he champions. Bianca's love, representative of Padua's highest value, goes to the "lowest" value—riches. When Petruchio demands money or sexual attractiveness in a wife, he reasserts priorities hypocritically denied in Lucentio's idealized wooing. Only a society that recognizes and preserves its connection with the material and the animal will survive, he suggests, and Paduan society deceives itself of this truth at its peril.

Even in the most misogynistic of dramatic narratives, then, we may discover a subversive strain characterized by a disruptive gaze that never rests secure. At the level of narrative, *The Taming of the Shrew* is not appreciably different from a medieval farce of shrew taming. Yet at the level of performance, *The Taming of the Shrew* conveys the sense of being maddened by such oppositions and turns it against the audience in a way that alone suggests why this play continues to fascinate. *The Taming of the Shrew* repeats with the audience or critic what it does to Kate: it maddens us with contradictory experiences until we agree to find resolution in either reductive readings or ideologically suspect resolutions. This activity doesn't make it a less sexist text, but it does make it a more productive one, as well as a more complicated one for feminist inquiry.

To be sure, *The Taming of the Shrew* not only resists but succumbs to a feminist analysis. The farcical confusions suggest that relations between master and servant or husband and wife need not be dictated by external show but must be determined by mutual dependencies and their acknowledgment. And yet the discrepancy between the play's lesson of mutual dependency and service and its enforcement of a sexist and aristocratic order cannot fail to disturb. The message that a plumed hat cannot make a master, nor a ceremony a marriage, like the argument that these roles are defined by active service, may continue to make sense today. But when Petruchio seeks to impose upon Kate the values of the formal, the ritual, and the conventional by recourse to physical force and patriarchal custom, we are less inclined to rediscover the "natural" basis of social roles in mutual dependency than a form of sex and class struggle that must be reframed.

Reframing can be an important strategy of change, depending upon how and why it is employed. Reframing emphasizes the arbitrariness of class assignments, acknowledges and enforces alternative class memberships, and so changes one's perspective on a problematic situation.[48] Whenever Kate disagrees with patriarchal law, she is forcefully reminded that her protest against theatrical roles is in itself a role. When Kate refuses to accept Petruchio's will and contradicts him, he recasts her disagreements as a form of playful agreement. His double-binding games of reframing the opposition as agreement make it impossible for Kate to negate or to differ, and so have the effect of returning her again to the same position. By reversing traditional categories of value, by calling angry words or behavior mild, Petruchio calls attention to the ways in which the equation of appearance and reality in Padua has led to confusing and false appraisals of character and value.

All this behavior takes place within the context of another game of reframing called punning, a game which unexpectedly reveals that words have membership in two different semantic classes. When Kate refuses to sit on Petruchio's lap by noting, "Asses are made to bear, and so are you" (2.1.199), Petruchio counters with the observation that "women are made to bear, and so are you" (2.1.200). This subtle reframing of insults leads to more explicit reframing when Petruchio announces to Kate's family that Kate has agreed to marry him. Confronted with her angry denial—"I'll see thee hang'd on Sunday first" (2.1.299)—Petruchio reframes the scene: " 'Tis bargain'd 'twixt us twain, being alone, / That she shall still be curst in company" (2.1.304–5). By reframing Kate's behavior as a temporary role, Petruchio implies that her behavior is a game over which she has

---

[48]See Paul Watzlawick, John Weakland, and Richard Fisch, *Change: Principles of Problem Formation and Problem Resolution* (New York: Norton, 1974); and Paul Watzlawick, Janet Beavin Bavelas, and Don D. Jackson, *Pragmatics of Human Communication* (New York: Norton, 1967).

control. By playing the game "Let's be shrews," by putting shrew-ishness into the category of acceptable behavior instead of in the category of a problem that must be solved, Petruchio forces Kate into a position from which her rebellion has no meaning, and so no power.

As a strategy for rethinking the relation between container and contained, between the energies of the living body and the constraints of social roles, reframing can be employed just as easily to disenfranchise as to empower another. For example, reframing strategies are often employed to tame and so control feminist and cultural-materialist approaches today. Psychoanalytic and deconstructive approaches that demonstrate that we cannot escape the text, the symbolic, or ideology remind us of the means by which Kate is encouraged to believe that she can never escape the theater of difference in which she exists. The means by which critical theory contains difference are therefore not that different from the techniques employed by Petruchio to tame Kate, insofar as both seek to prove that we are trapped by the terms that we use and so can never escape or revise them.

VI

The use of reframing to control and prevent women from differing is an all too familiar strategy, still in practice in film and theater criticism today. Consider the interaction between Constance Penley and Peter Gidal on feminism and film theory as perceived by Stephen Heath. First Penley: "If filmic practice, like the fetishistic ritual, is an inscription of the look on the body of the mother, we must now begin to consider the possibilities and consequences of the mother returning the look." Gidal replies: "The last words of your piece say it all. You search for the simple inversion, the *mother looking back*. I consider the possibilities of the not-mother, not-father (looking or not)." Heath joins Gidal: "To invert, the mother returning the look, is not radically to transform, is to return as well the same economy . . . (and cinema in the fiction film has always and exactly been concerned to consider the possibilities and consequences within the fetishistic ritual, including the *constitutive* threat of its endangerment, the play of eye and look, vision and lack); the difference inverted is also the difference maintained."[49]

Like Kate, Penley differs and is told that she has made no difference; she is told that her reframing of traditional narrative cinema is merely a reversal that cannot effect change. The difference inverted, however, is not always the difference maintained. Gidal's impulse is cinematic; he wants to dissolve images of women. Penley's impulse is theatrical; her response is a looking back that looks forward. Why should it be more effective to delete women from films than to present their responses to their reflections? Responding to this tactic in contemporary film practice, Rose protests that any such dissolution of the image, any equation of women with a beyond or before language is actually more regressive than progressive:

> The impetus is clear: the attempt to place woman somewhere *else*, outside the forms of representation through which she is endlessly constituted as image. The problem is that this sets up notions of drive, rhythmic pulsing, eroticisation of energy pre-representation, a space of "open viewing," which then makes film process itself socially—and sexually—innocent. Film process is then conceived as something archaic, a lost or repressed content ("continent"), terms to which the feminine can so easily be assimilated, as it has been in classical forms of discourse on the feminine as outside language, rationality, and so on; arguments which are now being revived as part of the discussion of psychoanalysis and feminism, the search for a feminine discourse, specific, outside. The dangers are obvious. That such arguments overlook the archaic connotations of these notions of energy and rhythm for women, at the same time that they render innocent the objects and processes of representation which they introject onto the screen, seems again to be not by chance.

In a critique of Lyotard's exploration of a nontheatrical representational space, Rose pointedly remarks: "We have to ask what, if the object itself is removed (the body or victim), is or could be such a space of open viewing (fetishisation of the look itself or of its panic

---

[49]Constance Penley, "The Avant-Garde and Its Imaginary," *Camera Obscura* (1978), 26, and Peter Gidal, as quoted by Stephen Heath with his comments in "Difference," *Screen* 19 (1978), 97–98.

and confusion)? And what does this do for feminism? Other than strictly nothing, dropping all images of women; or else an archaising of the feminine *as* panic and confusion, which is equally problematic, simply a re-introjection as feminine—the pre-mirror girl—of the visual disturbance against which the image of woman classically acts as guarantee."[50]

Penley wants to reverse the look by rethinking the limits of the cinematic apparatus. She cites the films of Yvonne Rainer, Chantal Ackerman, and Marguerite Duras, all of which do indeed "run counter to the Oedipal structuring of Western narrative form and the imaginary and fetishistic imperatives of the cinematic apparatus," effect changes in "narrative organization, point of view and identi-fication," and designate "both the spectator and the narrator as 'out-side' the scene . . . not caught up in or radically circumscribed by a masculine gaze or logic of desire."[51] Yet none of these films deletes or dissolves the image of woman; none of them suggests a feminist style that has so succumbed to its manipulation by an avant-garde as to be virtually indistinguishable from it.

The subtext in this game of two against one is a doubling of its content—the problem of woman. Since the cinematic look is read by these male theorists as constituted by the threat of woman's lack (that is, her castration), she had better not look back, nor, by implication, should Penley. Especially disturbing here is the argument that the cinematic look is constituted by the threat of its endangerment—which in turn is associated with woman's castration ("the play of eye and look, vision and lack"). However successful the application of a phallocentric theory for a reading of phallocentric films, this model stymies the development of film theory and practice in new direc-tions. It encourages us to simplify the complex series of identifica-tions actually at work when gendered subjects view a film, and it results in such peculiar avant-garde stances as Gidal's refusal to por-tray women in his films *since* woman is always already the castrated fetishized object.

According to Freudian theory, in a deferred reading of his "first" sight of his mother's genitalia the subject-as-little-boy interprets the

[50]Rose, *Sexuality in the Field of Vision*, 209, 210.
[51]Constance Penley, "'A Certain Refusal of Difference': Feminist Film Theory," in *Art after Modernism*, ed. Wallis, 386, 387.

mother's "lack" in terms of the threat of the father's punitive, castrating "no" made good. In other words, he associates his mother's "actual" castration with his potential castration. That Lacan rereads this scenario symbolically does not, finally, save it for feminist theory. The castration theory is made no more palatable by the argument that, insofar as we are all lacking, woman is even more aware of her incomplete status. Instead, this rereading keeps a sexist account of the construction of the subject alive and maintains an association of the look with a negative view of female sexuality.

A more theatrical paradigm empowers women to look back and forward, to see how their looking back is interpreted and disrupted by another gaze in a continuing theater of interactive reflections. Accordingly, it may be useful to reformulate the implications of the Lacanian gaze for feminist theory and practice. To reframe this schema we might rethink the development of gender as identificatory and rooted in the problem of the gaze. Feminist applications of object-relations theory, such as the work of Robert Stoller and Nancy Chodorow on gender roles, for example, explore how certain so-called male behavior in our society results from a denial of identification with the maternal figure.[52] The male infant's primary identification with the female as mothering person is disrupted in a way that the female infant's is not. Whereas the female subject resolves maternal prohibitions by moving from being the mother's desire to imitating the mother's desire, the male subject is not free to resolve the problem in this way. Deprived of the shift toward mimetic desire open to the female subject, the route offered to the male is typically one of rapid disidentification, which in turn results in ambivalence toward the nurturing object.

As object-relations theory further reminds us, a main task of mothering is to enable the child to accept separation and disillusionment.[53] The disruptive maternal look reflects back to the child some-

[52]Robert Stoller, "The Sense of Femaleness," and "The 'Bedrock' of Masculinity and Femininity: Bisexuality," in *Psychoanalysis and Women*, ed. Jean Baker Miller (Baltimore: Penguin, 1973), 231–43, 245–68; Stoller, "Fact and Fancies: An Examination of Freud's Concept of Bisexuality," in *Women and Analysis*, ed. Jean Strouse (New York: Grossman, 1974); Nancy Chodorow, *The Reproduction of Mothering: Psychoanalysis and the Sociology of Gender* (Berkeley: University of California Press, 1978).

[53]See Jay R. Greenberg and Stephen A. Mitchell, *Object Relations in Psychoanalytic Theory* (Cambridge: Harvard University Press, 1983); Margaret Mahler, *On Human Symbiosis and the Vicissitudes of Individuation* (London: Hogarth Press, 1969);

thing other than what it wants to see, but which alone makes identity possible. Ironically, the greater repression is not the mother's castration (what the child doesn't want to see) but the subject's loss-of-face (what the mother doesn't want to see or can't see in the child). Consider Hamlet's "Do you see nothing there?" and his mother's shocked reply: "Nothing at all, yet all that is I see" (*Hamlet*: 3.4.131–32). What assures entry into the symbolic is not the father's intervention but the disillusionment offered by the real mother. Lacanians might argue that this disillusionment is the intervention itself, and so repeats the move from the real mother to the symbolic mother, but Lacan's early writings on object-relations theory repudiate any such interpretation. If we cannot ascribe the maternal gaze to a period prior to or outside of representation, we can inscribe it as recording the tension of representation, insofar as the maternal gaze both introduces the infant into the social order and questions that identification. Since the maternal gaze offers the infant not a stable, cohesive image but one that by definition changes, the disruptive maternal look reacts to the infant's look and reflects it differently. The paradox of the contained breaking out of its contents, of a deferred disruption always already contained within the mother-infant dyad, yields a maternal disruptive gaze characteristic of theater. We can therefore theorize the mother's look as that which functions to displace in advance the father as the privileged level of representation—without identifying the woman with panic, confusion, or a space before language and representation.

The difference inverted is not always the difference maintained. Since neither Heath nor Gidal proves capable of considering the "possibilities and consequences" of the mother's returning the look—except as a reversal of the terms of the male look, which in itself is castrating—they project that threat onto Penley. Asks Heath: "What then of the look for the woman, of woman subjects in seeing? The reply given by psychoanalysis is from the phallus. If the woman looks, the spectacle provokes, castration is in the air, the Medusa's head is not far off; thus, she must not look, is absorbed herself on the side of the seen, seeing herself seeing herself, Lacan's femininity."[54] Castration

---

and D. W. Winnicott, *Playing and Reality* (London: Tavistock, 1971).
[54]Heath, "Difference," 92.

is indeed in the air—insofar as male fears of a reversal of their fantasies are projected onto a rethinking of representation which begins on the other side of the screen.

The difference inverted is not always the difference maintained. The reply given by psychoanalysis is not always from the phallus. Penley realizes that no reversal of the look in the same terms is possible—except when Woman as a homogenized construct of the male imaginary is doing the looking, in which case she does not look from the point of view of *women*. Following Laura Mulvey's critique of traditional cinematic practice as voyeuristic and fetishistic, Penley is calling for the development of new ways of looking—for a rethinking of what it means to be a spectator. To return the look in this context is to break up performance space, deconstruct the gaze, subvert the classic organization of showing and seeing, and rethink the very notion of spectatorship.

Heath summarizes one of the arguments that stalls this movement when he asks if it is "possible for a woman to take place in a film without representing a male desire," since "any image of a woman in a film, by the fact of its engagement in a process of representation . . . inevitably re-encloses women in a structure of cultural oppression that functions precisely by the currency of 'images of women.' "[55] He quotes Hélène Cixous, who complains that "one is always in representation, and when a woman is asked to take place in this representation, she is, of course, asked to represent man's desire."[56] But Heath ignores the key word "asked." When women are not asked to take place in a representation created by and for men but occupy and share the sites of production and consumption, a different economy obtains. Women take place, and refigure that taking place, in ways that challenge traditional forms of representation.

The associations I have drawn here suggest that theatricality offers a constructive path for both psychoanalytic theory and feminist theory to accept the implications of their own displacing looks. Theatrical reading is ambivalent reading, dedicated *not* to varying the look (which simply amounts to critical pluralism) but to disrupting it, (up)staging theories through one another. It requires that psycho-

[55]Ibid., 96–97.
[56]Ibid., 96; this comment first appeared in "Entretien avec Françoise van Rossum-Guyon," *Revue des sciences humaines* (1977), 487.

analysis read cinema and theater read psychoanalysis and—following the motto each proclaims—that none of these disciplines ever rests secure in itself. Why is it that theater alone has always staged identity as unstable, exposing gender and class as a masquerade? Insofar as theater cannot rest in the *abyme* but stages the displacing gaze, the bursting of the container by its contents, theater offers a way of dislodging the current critical standstill whereby we must use language to describe an experience of being outside of it.

The performative aspect of theater emerges here as a process of staging the disturbance and reversal of the gaze. Theater's techniques for reframing offer a model for feminist theory insofar as they move beyond both the quest for the mysterious essence of the feminine, beyond the acknowledgment of woman as an object of a male gaze, and on to an exploration of the potential of women to break that gaze by reframing it. Feminism poses the problem of reframing in the Kristevan paradox of the semiotic and the symbolic; psychoanalysis confronts this problem in the relationship of the imaginary and the symbolic; but theater alone is capable of staging the paradox of the frame in a way that subverts it. Unlike feminism and psychoanalysis, theater has no allegiance but to ambivalence, to a compulsion to subvert its own look, to split itself through a reflected image. Theater comfortably allies with feminism against psychoanalysis, with psychoanalysis against cinema, and with cinema against itself, without ever finding a resting point except as provisional and always already undermined. Whereas feminism and psychoanalysis seek to reflect the subject from a place where it can never see itself, be it gender, ideology, or the unconscious, theater provides the tools—the stages, the mirrors, or reflecting gazes—through which perspectives are fragmented, shattered, and set into play against one another. A methodology necessarily tied to no master, theater poses a methodological challenge to feminism and psychoanalysis to escape its terms, its goals, its identity.

Against the *mise en abyme* paradoxes of cinema and deconstructive philosophy we may posit the disruptive potential of the theatrical gaze, which is always ambivalent, always displacing one view and threatened in turn by another. Hélène Cixous complains that "men and women are caught up in a network of millennial cultural determinations of a complexity that is practically unanalyzable: we can no more talk about 'woman' than about 'man' without getting caught up in an ideological theater where the multiplication of representations, images, reflections, myths, identifications constantly transforms, deforms, alters each person's imaginary order and in advance, renders all conceptualization null and void."[57] Yet given these terms, is theater a mere showing or a radical staging of the gaze? Is Peggy Kamuf's "a woman writing as a woman writing as a [woman]"[58] a means of breaking out of the label "woman" or of showing how we can never hope to do so? The question is not whether a feminist or a deconstructive theater is possible but whether feminism and deconstruction can recognize and utilize theatrical strategies. Can either feminism or deconstruction stand outside of theater as techniques to be used upon it, or are they always already within it? To theatricalize one must deconstruct, insert a difference in a term which splits it, mimics it, then displaces or usurps it. A woman writing like a woman writing like a woman is never the same woman. If feminism, psychoanalysis, and deconstruction can never frame theater, but only mine or mime it, this may be because their techniques have long been trapped inside it. The cost of exit may be denial or repression—or perhaps another frame-up.

[57]Cixous, "Sorties," in *New French Feminisms*, ed. Marks and Courtivron, 96.
[58]Peggy Kamuf, "Writing like a Woman," in *Women and Language in Literature and Society*, ed. S. McConnell-Ginet et al. (New York: Praeger, 1980), 298.

5

Dis/Figuring Power:
Censorship and Representation
in *A Midsummer Night's Dream*

> It is precisely at the legislative frontier between what can be repre-
> sented and what cannot that the postmodernist operation is being
> staged—not in order to transcend representation, but in order to
> expose that system of power that authorizes certain representations
> while blocking, prohibiting, or invalidating others.
>
> —Craig Owens, "The Discourse of Others:
> Feminists and Postmodernism"

I

In a recent study of Renaissance censorship, Annabel Patterson
maintains that the incidents of physical torture and dismember-
ment we uncover are less startling than their statistical infrequency.
Considering the power that a prince could wield against a playwright, what is surprising is not Queen Elizabeth's recognition of the
topical implications of the 1601 revival of *Richard II* or James I's less
speedy response to Thomas Middleton's *Game at Chess* but the conclusion of both productions with their players intact. Since dismem-
berment and trial signal the dissolution of codes governing censorship, Patterson reasons, their marked infrequency in the history of
this period of drama attests to the healthy functioning of an "implicit
social contract between authors and authorities . . . intelligible to all
parties at the time."[1]

---

[1]Annabel M. Patterson, *Censorship and Interpretation: The Conditions of Writing
and Reading in Early Modern England* (Madison: University of Wisconsin Press, 1984),

A Midsummer Night's Dream articulates this social pact by openly celebrating the shaping vision of an aristocratic ideology. The harmless question "What hempen home-spuns have we swagg'ring here, / So near the cradle of the Fairy Queen?" (3.1.77–78) is also a question of the precise and limited conditions under which the different classes of poets and patrons can meet. And *A Midsummer Night's Dream* promptly answers that question through its fawning collaboration with state ideology. The terms governing the prince-poet relationship in *A Midsummer Night's Dream*, like those governing the husband-wife relationship in *The Taming of the Shrew*, are nostalgically tailored along the lines of an idealized pact between feudal lord and gratefully submissive servant. The play fashions itself as a mediator between court and poet as if charged with legislating their proper interaction; it genially mocks offensive playwrights while humbly requesting that they be pardoned. At the same time, the play panders to an aristocratic ideology by wreaking comic punishment on all those who defy the prince's legislation of desire. Finally, the play sets out a self-serving and conciliatory relationship between poet and prince with its gestures of flattery, apology, and self-abasement.[2] By flattering the prince as the only poet with the natural wisdom, imagination, and magnanimity to determine licensed comparisons, the play works to justify the role of the poet in the state.

A Midsummer Night's Dream's open collaboration with the aristocracy is of particular interest to the study of ideology—the means by which cultural configurations of inequitable social relationships are presented as natural and so serve the interests of a given ruling class. Critics have discovered in *A Midsummer Night's Dream* a variety

---

17. In *Power on Display: The Politics of Shakespeare's Genres* (London: Methuen, 1986), Leonard Tennenhouse observes that "no other Tudor monarch maintained such tight control over the plays and players as Elizabeth" (106); he cites information from Glynne Wickham's *Early English Stages, 1300–1600* (London: Routledge and Kegan Paul, 1963), 2:75–90. In *The Politics and Poetics of Transgression* (Ithaca: Cornell University Press, 1986), Peter Stallybrass and Allon White note that Ben Jonson was arrested in 1597 for cowriting *The Isle of Dogs*, accused of treason for *Sejanus* in 1603, and imprisoned in 1605 for cowriting *Eastward Ho*; it was reported that he would have his nose and ears cut off for the latter work (74).

[2]For a fascinating account of this relationship, see Frank Whigham, *Ambition and Privilege: The Social Tropes of Elizabethan Courtesy Theory* (Berkeley: University of California Press, 1984). Whigham outlines a variety of strategies employed by Elizabethan writers to further their status, including tropes of personal promotion, tropes of rivalry, and tropes of social hierarchy.

of rationalizations for gender and class oppression. James Kavanagh examines how, by drawing "ideological raw materials from both insurgent bourgeois-individualist and entrenched feudal-absolutist discourses," *A Midsummer Night's Dream* subverts authoritarian rule only to pander to it, "finally trivializing any threat with a comic resolution that magically reconciles rebellious 'feminine' and individualist desire to a rigid social hierarchy of aristocratic and patriarchal privilege."[3] Louis Montrose studies how this play not only reflects but shapes culturally specific fantasies which convey ideological configurations of gender and class relationship, particularly in the context of the influence of the cult of Elizabeth on the collective political unconscious.[4] And Leonard Tennenhouse explores how the play figures the relation between queen and poet in terms of the mating of the aristocratic body and the grotesque public body.[5]

Despite the sophistication of these critiques, scholars have yet to read *A Midsummer Night's Dream* in a way that brings psychoanalytic, deconstructive, and cultural-materialist discourses together. That the play is about the mind knowing itself is hardly a new idea, although James Calderwood states the proposition most promisingly: "A major kind of knowledge made available to its audience by *A Midsummer Night's Dream* is that of the inner forms and impulses of the human mind itself—the tricks and shaping fantasies of strong imagination and the forces directing it but also the range and limits of cool reason. The mind that comes to focus on the play and especially on the drama of the forest comes to focus on itself."[6] Since *A Midsummer Night's Dream* remains one of our culture's most important theoretical texts on dreaming, it should have something to tell us about the Renaissance mind and how it organizes experience.

[3]James Kavanagh, "Shakespeare in Ideology," in *Alternative Shakespeares*, ed. John Drakakis (London: Methuen, 1985), 155–56.

[4]Louis Montrose, " 'Shaping Fantasies': Figurations of Gender and Power in Elizabethan Culture," *Representations* 1 (Spring 1983), 61–94, rpt. in a shorter, revised version as "*A Midsummer Night's Dream* and the Shaping Fantasies of Elizabethan Culture: Gender, Power, Form," in *Rewriting the Renaissance: The Discourses of Sexual Difference in Early Modern Europe*, ed. Margaret W. Ferguson, Maureen Quilligan, and Nancy J. Vickers (Chicago: University of Chicago Press, 1986), 65–87.

[5]Tennenhouse, *Power on Display*, 43–44.

[6]James Calderwood, *Shakespearean Metadrama* (Minneapolis: University of Minnesota Press, 1971), 137.

A reductive simplification of cultural-materialist, deconstructive, and psychoanalytic discourses is one factor that has stalled productive dialogue in this direction. Reductive versions of psychoanalysis have been partly to blame, as has the failure of literary critics to consider the more radical implications of psychoanalytic theory for literary theory. For many critics, psychoanalytic criticism is simply a helpmeet to New Criticism, and ego psychology offers a means of neatly closing up the text, like the well-analyzed personality, through "terminable" analysis. By filling in the text's blank spaces, however, these critics neglect Freud's emphasis on discovering the *laws governing the construction of blank spaces.*

Reductive versions of cultural-materialist theory are also partly to blame for the delayed production of this dramatic scene. And we can trace this tendency to the failure of much political criticism to come to terms with the deconstructive critique of representation, as evidenced in the variety of exclusionary tactics employed to invalidate deconstructive techniques. The reduction of deconstructive theory to a naive celebration of the impossibility of knowing, like the charge that deconstruction could offer any of us a safe retreat into the indeterminacy of meaning, simply doesn't hold up. Derrida's conclusion to "Structure, Sign, and Play," for example, contrasts two "interpretations of interpretation"—one denying, the other celebrating radical uncertainty—only to argue that no choice between the two is possible: "Although these two interpretations must acknowledge and accentuate their difference and define their irreducibility, I do not believe that today there is any question of *choosing* . . . because we must first try to conceive of the common ground, and the *différance* of this irreducible difference."[7]

The tendency of critics from these two camps to avoid rather than engage with one another is evidenced in the way they side with only one of Derrida's two interpretations of interpretation—or with only one of two stances on the imagination offered by *A Midsummer Night's Dream.* Critical responses to the play routinely take the form of a defense of one of its two concluding statements regarding the status of a knowledge that escapes logical proof. Theseus argues for a knowledge situated within the representable; Hippolyta's silenced

[7]Jacques Derrida, "Structure, Sign, and Play," *Writing and Difference,* trans. Alan Bass (Chicago: University of Chicago Press, 1978), 293.

voice reminds us of the conditions of repression that render such knowledge possible. Psychoanalytic critics tend to read *A Midsummer Night's Dream* through Lacanian narratives of social conditioning which privilege the wresting of the infant from the maternal as the only valid means of entry into the symbolic. They argue that to privilege Hippolyta's position or to take sides in this debate is to miss the point, precisely because psychoanalysis stresses the *interdependence* of knowledge and repression. To champion Hippolyta's cause, they claim, is tantamount to a denial of the boundaries through which knowledge is constituted. To side with Hippolyta, from this standpoint, is to deny the loss and distortion that inevitably accompany our construction in the social order.

From a cultural-materialist stance, however, the celebration of Hippolyta's vision over Theseus's law is not the result of a naive idealism that presupposes one can attain a knowledge without repression or distortion. Rather, this critical stance acknowledges the *specificity* of repression instead of universalizing its form or proclaiming its inevitability. Admittedly, we can no more deny the force of law, *in the abstract*, than we can deny the truth of that which escapes it. Yet we have a responsibility both to acknowledge the shape that repression takes against specific people and to rethink how to teach a play that celebrates this particular shaping vision. Simply because the structuralist and patriarchal assumptions of Lacanian narratives dovetail with the patriarchal ideology of *A Midsummer Night's Dream*, for example, is no reason to collaborate with those assumptions. By encouraging us to recognize how our explanatory narratives are ideologically constructed to privilege and so reinforce certain social formations, cultural-materialist approaches are finally more practical and revisionary than idealistic.

Rather than refuse to teach *A Midsummer Night's Dream* because of its colonialist fantasies or *The Taming of the Shrew* because of its overt sexism, we can learn from both. Rather than censor either work, a more productive approach would be to explore how censorship operates within them. Granted, *A Midsummer Night's Dream* stages a disturbing relationship among social formation, text, and psyche: it presents knowledge as an effect of right censorship and figures metaphor as a dangerous instrument requiring close state control. And yet precisely because *A Midsummer Night's Dream* poses the question of interpretation within this specific ideological framework, its exploration of strategies that legitimize vision can alert us to the ways in which we censor meaning today.

Since *A Midsummer Night's Dream* foregrounds a complex relationship among censorship, knowledge, and interpretation, the act of censorship serves as a conceptual lever through which ideological, deconstructive, and psychoanalytic discourses may be brought into productive dialogue. Throughout *A Midsummer Night's Dream* the audience is asked to determine the status of various imaginative experiences. Yet insofar as social conditions determine the means by which the categories of true and false, real and fantastic are figured and so licensed, these categories are always subject to change. Censorship refers to social activity that constructs the boundaries between real and imaginary; neither exterior nor interior, censorship works at the boundaries of representation in both culture and psyche.

Commenting on Freud's "Note upon a 'Mystic-Writing Pad,'" Derrida explains how censorship as a writing function mediates among text, state, and psyche:

> It is no accident that the metaphor of censorship should come from the area of politics concerned with the deletions, blanks, and disguises of writing. . . . The apparent exteriority of political censorship refers to an essential censorship which binds the writer to his own writing. . . . The "subject" of writing does not exist if we mean by that some sovereign solitude of the author. The subject of writing is a *system* of relations between strata: the Mystic Pad, the psyche, society, the world. . . . The *sociality* of writing as *drama* requires an entirely different discipline.

Derrida complains that "a psychoanalysis of literature respectful of the *originality of the literary signifier* has not yet begun, and this is surely not an accident. Until now, only the analysis of literary *signifieds*, that is, *nonliterary* signified meanings, has been undertaken."[8] New historicists such as Francis Barker and Peter Hulme point the way in their study of how discourse is "instrumental in the organization and legitimation of power-relations—which of course involves, as one of its components, control over the constitution of meaning."[9] Whether or not we seek to develop "a *history of writing*" or "a new

[8] Jacques Derrida, "Freud and the Scene of Writing," ibid., 226–27, 230.
[9] Francis Barker and Peter Hulme, "Nymphs and Reapers Heavily Vanish: The Discursive Con-Texts of *The Tempest*," in *Alternative Shakespeares*, ed. Drakakis, 197.

psychoanalytic graphology,"[10] in question here is how to bring psycho-analytic, deconstructive, and cultural-materialist readings of dreams and of *A Midsummer Night's Dream* together. Can psychoanalytic and deconstructive approaches be aligned with a study of their complicity in social and cultural censorship? Can psychoanalytic theory prove useful to the study of the history of the signifier? And can cultural-materialist theory become more attuned to the play of meaning and repression at the level of its own discourse? If we cannot take sides in the debate between a knowledge that moves in the direction of a myth of a real and a knowledge that exposes the omissions by means of which discourses of truth and mastery operate, we can explore the politics governing the relation of these two interpretations of interpretation today.

II

Peter Quince's bungled prescription for his play aptly describes the laws governing representation in *A Midsummer Night's Dream*: "One must come in with a bush of thorns and a lantern, and say he comes to disfigure, or to present, the person of Moonshine" (3.1.59–61). By mistakenly associating presentation and disfigurement, Quince reminds us that Elizabethan playwrights whose comparisons were perceived as a threat to the status quo could be physically disfigured by the state. By punishing those who make unlawful comparisons between themselves and others, *A Midsummer Night's Dream* seeks to preserve a rigidly hierarchical social order against the threats of encroaching bourgeois individualism.

Throughout this comedy, the agreement to play one's assigned role and to accept one's social status constitutes licensed comparison, whereas the desire to change one's role or status is portrayed as a criminal act that warrants disfigurement. Hermia is condemned for seeking to play both her own and her father's parts; she expects not only to marry the bridegroom but to choose him. Helena is guilty of coveting Hermia's role as a means of winning back the love of Demetrius. She confides to Hermia: "Were the world mine, Demetrius being bated, / The rest I'll give to be to you translated"

[10]Derrida, "Freud and the Scene of Writing," 230–31.

(1.1.190–91); yet she rightly attributes her plight to her jealousy: "What wicked and dissembling glass of mine / Made me compare with Hermia's sphery eyne!" (2.2.98–99). Titania's desire to play both lord and lady in questioning Oberon's control over the Indian boy is portrayed as an offense to nature itself. Bottom's desire to play every part in the production of *Pyramus and Thisby* is a comic version of the same crime. Bottom not only threatens the success of *Pyramus and Thisby* but, by extension, the success of the collaborative production we term Elizabethan social reality.

According to the terms of this play, the metaphoric language through which we map our world has clear-cut positive and negative implications. To compare love to a rose is useful only if that comparison contributes to our sense of what love is like. Order in comparison depends on a firm sense of priorities—state before individual, lord before lady, and both before the hempen homespun. When used to strengthen or extend the boundaries of the state and its power, comparison is positive. Theseus and Hippolyta, for example, speak a triumphant metaphoric discourse; secure in their vision of an ordered hierarchy, their sentences are indeed "in government." When comparisons are unlicensed, however, they threaten the social order: the four lovers lose all sense of identity in their rivalry, and in the darkness of the woods, the power to disfigure turns against these unlicensed poets with a vengeance. Comic punishment is carried out by that licensed principle of unlicensed comparisons, Puck. Puck adopts the strategy of "rope tricks" that Petruchio employed in *The Taming of the Shrew*: "He will throw a figure in her face, and so disfigure her with it" (*The Taming of the Shrew*: 1.2.113–14). Since Puck functions as a type of court fool or licensed clown, his punitive dramas are sanctioned because staged in the service of his master: "Sometime a horse I'll be, sometime a hound, / A hog, a headless bear, sometime a fire" (3.1.108–9).

Theseus lavishly employs metaphors in reprimanding Hermia and thereby parades his license to make such comparisons. What for us is an obvious case of gender ideology is for Theseus a simple matter of rational classification: as an object of meaning and value, Hermia cannot seek to determine how meaning and value function. Like words, women are merely objects to be compared and exchanged and so incapable of determining whether, how, or by whom they will be exchanged. The hempen homespuns confront the problem of unlicensed comparisons when they seek to put on a play. Their disfigured speech is described as "a sound, but not in government," "a tangled chain; nothing impair'd, but all disorder'd" (5.1.123–26). Their sole virtue is an impaired imagination that renders them incapable of effecting economic or social advancement. When they carefully inform the court that they are not to be confused with their dramatic roles, they preserve the production of Elizabethan ideology at the expense of the play at hand.

Not surprisingly, in his bid to play court propagandist Shakespeare mocks others' pretensions to advance their status as a means of advancing his own. Yet if we must castigate Shakespeare for his role in this game of comparisons, we should also acknowledge how we are implicated in the game. Given the importance of visual imagery to critics' appreciation of this play, the source of that appeal deserves examination. One of Shakespeare's most richly visual plays, *A Midsummer Night's Dream* makes us *feel* rich with its images of gold and silver, traders and merchandise, luxury and power. It continually tempts us to collaborate in fantasies of unbridled consumption. Theseus opens the play with a description of the moon as a wealthy woman who withholds her riches: "She lingers my desires, / Like to a step-dame, or a dowager, / Long withering out a young man's revenue" (1.1.4–6). Hippolyta responds with a more lucrative comparison, observing that in a speedy four days, "the moon, like to a silver bow / [New] bent in heaven, shall behold the night / Of our solemnities" (1.1.9–11). In a rush to depart, Lysander leisurely extends his discourse to describe the evening more poetically: "Tomorrow night, when Phoebe doth behold / Her silver visage in the wat'ry glass, / Decking with liquid pearl the bladed grass" (1.1.209–11). Furious with Oberon, Titania conveys her decision to keep the changeling boy by describing in lush detail how she and the boy's mother used to sit and pass the time "on Neptune's yellow sands, / Marking th' embarked traders on the flood; / When we have laugh'd to see the sails conceive / And grow big-bellied with the wanton wind; / Which she, with pretty and with swimming gait, / Following (her womb then rich with my young squire) / Would imitate, and sail upon the land / To fetch me trifles, and return again, / As from a voyage, rich with merchandise" (2.1.126–34).

A Midsummer Night's Dream seduces not merely by virtue of its metaphoric language but by the precise nature of its comparisons. Is it not the silver bow and the pearls that are so beautiful, the fantasy of having trifles fetched for one that is indulgent, the spices and luxuries that are delightful? The poetry is exquisite insofar as it encourages us to enjoy colonialist fantasies with neither guilt nor obligation. Oberon knows of lush worlds we haven't seen and offers to share with us their secret powers: "I know a bank where the wild thyme blows, / Where oxlips and the nodding violet grows, / Quite over-canopied with luscious woodbine, / With sweet musk-roses and with eglantine" (2.1.249–52). With Puck's help, we can enjoy these riches without delay: "I'll put a girdle round about the earth / In forty minutes" (2.1.175–76). We can look on at others, invisible ourselves, and play pranks or indulge in fantasies of omnipotence with no concern for others' welfare. More disturbing than "how easy is a bush suppos'd a bear" (5.1.22) is how easily we first steal an Indian boy and then argue between ourselves over who deserves him. Appropriative, narcissistic fantasies of self-indulgence and power are the order of the day. Whereas *The Comedy of Errors* fascinates us with its uncanny sensibility, *A Midsummer Night's Dream* indulges us by making the strange familiar. Metaphor both appropriates and invalidates otherness by proving that everything strange can, in a moment of high narcissism, be made to reflect a part of oneself. When we imagine that everyone is like us, or can be compared to us, we are exploiting otherness as a commodity.

Metaphor not only makes a world but makes it according to certain relationships of power, since it offers precise strategies of taming and appropriating the unfamiliar. Writing on metaphor, Julian Jaynes observes that cognitive psychologists use the term *assimilation* to refer to an automatic process "where a slightly ambiguous perceived object is made to conform to some previously learned schema."[11] When the act of assimilation is conscious and intended, it is termed *conciliation* or *compatibilization*. But the act of fitting things together or making them compatible is also a strategy by means of which difference is forced into paradigms that sanction the status quo.

For Theseus, the difference between comprehension and apprehension is crucial: "Such tricks hath strong imagination, / That if

[11]Julian Jaynes, *The Origin of Consciousness in the Breakdown of the Bicameral Mind* (Boston: Houghton Mifflin, 1976), 64, 65.

it would but apprehend some joy, / It comprehends some bringer of that joy" (5.1.18–20). When we read *A Midsummer Night's Dream*, we comprehend or grasp things together; understanding is not a means of standing under something but of grabbing hold by force and assimilation. And we comprehend in the same way when we employ New Critical strategies to map out a play or piece together its parts in a hierarchical order. Walter Ong identifies as "the most fundamental stylistic difference between ancient writing and modern writing— the immeasurably greater exploitation today of visualist metaphors and of imagery which in one way or another admits of diagrammatic analysis."[12] Could it be that *A Midsummer Night's Dream* so neatly illustrates New Critical techniques because both play and critical style reflect appropriative strategies developed at triumphant points in the history of Western European hegemony?

Many of us were taught to read and to teach *A Midsummer Night's Dream* in New Critical terms that equated the discovery of meaning with the scope of our assimilative powers; the aim of literary criticism was to find the most encompassing theme, or to "find the concord of this discord" (5.1.60). In the 1960s and 1970s we followed such critics as D. A. Traversi, Philip Edwards, and David Young through various takes of the "structure and theme" variety, so that among British and American Shakespeareans the commentary on the play had indeed grown to "something of great constancy" (5.1.26).[13] And we liked to think of that line as *our* line, as the natural and well-earned product of our superior organizational skills. The prominence of Young's chapter in the anthology *Modern Shakespearean Criticism* suggested as much; here was New Criticism at its best, at everyone's disposal.

In classrooms around the English-speaking world (was there any other?) the play was diagramed on blackboards as if its coordinates were no less than the four corners of the known world. Our *Dream*

[12]Walter J. Ong, S.J., "System, Space, and Intellect in Renaissance Symbolism," *The Barbarian Within and Other Fugitive Essays* (New York: Macmillan, 1962), 76.

[13]See David Young, *Something of Great Constancy* (New Haven: Yale University Press, 1966), a section of which is reprinted in the anthology *Modern Shakespearean Criticism*, ed. Alvin Kernan (New York: Harcourt, Brace, and World, 1970), 174–89, under the title "*A Midsummer Night's Dream*: Structure." See also Philip Edwards, *Shakespeare and the Confines of Art* (London: Methuen, 1968); and D. A. Traversi, *An Approach to Shakespeare,* 3d ed. rev. (New York: Doubleday-Anchor, 1969).

not only had a bottom but a top and sides; we could neatly chart its beginning, middle, and end. We followed the characters from a harsh legalistic world, through a green world of desire, and on toward a compromise conclusion in which law is tempered by mercy and society accommodates individual desire. We located sources for this pattern in Renaissance pastorals, romances, and morality plays alike. We mapped the characters' progression from a flawed society, through a wilderness, to a new, improved society; from separation, through bewilderment, and on to reunion and harmony. We even discovered in this framework a morality pattern in which despair gave way to punishment and penance, yet ultimately led to redemption. That our critical efforts mirrored the play's treatment of how the mind organizes experience was not of concern, or of as much concern, as demonstrating the prowess of New Critical techniques. How meaning is produced or resisted, channeled or erased—for whom, when, or why—was none of our concern. This was a case of perfect dovetailing, and we didn't want to know the price of our success. We didn't want to know that the result of all our minds "transfigur'd so together" (5.1.24) was less a matter of truth than of that "something of great constancy" termed *ideology*.

Postmodernism is often described in terms of a loss of faith in Western narratives of mastery.[14] In literary theory it has taken the form of an exploration of the plurality of meanings and traditions previously repressed by traditional notions of the author, reader, work, and canon. In "From Work to Text," Roland Barthes describes this paradigm shift in terms of a move away from the single meaning of the closed, unified work in favor of an awareness of the multiple meanings, both privileged and censored, of the open text.[15] Ironically, Barthes would have us forgo the term *work* for *text* at the same time that he encourages us to focus on the real work that is involved in the performance of meaning. If the grand production that is *A Midsummer Night's Dream* has anything to do with the production of

[14]See Craig Owens, "The Discourse of Others: Feminists and Postmodernism," in *The Anti-Aesthetic: Essays on Postmodern Culture*, ed. Hal Foster (Port Townsend, Wash.: Bay Press, 1983), 57–82, for descriptions of postmodernism. Also see the other essays in this volume, as well as Jean-François Lyotard, *The Postmodern Condition* (Minneapolis: University of Minnesota Press, 1984).

[15]Roland Barthes, "From Work to Text," *Image/Music/Text* (New York: Hill and Wang, 1977), 155–64.

our dreams, then the collaborative work of the various parts of the mind as they legislate meaning may further clarify the relation between power and discourse on the stage of contemporary critical theory.

III

One of the paradoxes that critical theory continually confronts is the problem of figuring the mind without disfiguring it. "Perhaps the happiest moment the human mind ever knows," Stephen Booth suggests, "is the moment when it senses the presence of order and coherence—and before it realizes the particular nature (and so the particular limits) of the perception. At the moment of unparticularized perception the mind is unlimited. It seems capable of grasping and about to grasp a coherence beyond its capacity."[16] Lysander's description of the difficulty of comprehending love applies just as well to the difficulties we experience in self-apprehension: both situations yield an insight that is "momentany as a sound, / Swift as a shadow, short as any dream, / Brief as the lightning in the collied night, / That, in a spleen, unfolds both heaven and earth; / And ere a man hath power to say 'Behold!' / The jaws of darkness do devour it up: / So quick bright things come to confusion" (1.1.143–49). No sooner do we figure the mind than we disfigure it with terms of comparison.

Julian Jaynes describes how consciousness both "narratizes and conciliates . . . in a metaphorical space where such meanings can be manipulated like things in space."[17] To the extent that meanings are indeed manipulated like things in space, our descriptions of the mind are necessarily distorted by spatial metaphors. *A Midsummer Night's Dream* offers numerous descriptions of the mind meditating upon itself, but all compare the mind to some external apparatus, such as a mirror, a writing tablet, or a picture. Lysander describes the shining moon as a moment of literal self-reflection: "To-morrow night, when Phoebe doth behold / Her silver visage in the wat'ry glass" (1.1.209–

[16]Stephen Booth, *An Essay on Shakespeare's Sonnets* (New Haven: Yale University Press, 1969), 14.
[17]Jaynes, *Origin of Consciousness*, 65–66.

10). If to know the mind is to know that it works by comparison, this is also to know that we can never properly locate the mind.

And yet the terms by which we know the mind are themselves instructive. Perhaps most striking about *A Midsummer Night's Dream* is the highly self-conscious use of metaphors to serve an aristocratic ideology. So many Elizabethan texts state as their goal the presentation of the mind as a microcosm of a divinely ordered hierarchical universe that it would be surprising indeed if cultural and psychic formations were presented as anything other than harmonious. Elizabethan authors were continually working to bring the new technology into line with prevailing ideology. Clearly the accommodation of the ideologically coercive discourses of the so-called "great chain of being" to meet and control the fantasies of a rising bourgeoisie in Shakespearean comedy is a prominent example of this trend. It is therefore reasonable to ask ourselves whether we are really uncovering political metaphors and social configurations in Renaissance descriptions of the mind or merely recovering them, since Renaissance authors were obviously serving a vested interest in depicting how text, psyche, and society could be harmoniously interrelated. In *A Midsummer Night's Dream*, for example, the real is an elaborate collaborative production, dependent upon the work of imagination which makes comparisons and the work of reason which licenses those comparisons. The mind's parts are figured as interacting according to a model of good government; the faculties of hearing and sight create the fantasies that in turn are corrected by reason.

The open acknowledgment of the limits of metaphor in modernist accounts of the mind contrasts sharply with the self-serving deployment of comparisons in Renaissance texts. For example, Freud repeatedly states his plan to "replace a topographical way of representing things by a dynamic one"[18]—and repeatedly fails in that attempt. He is continually generating models of the psychic apparatus only to realize that the aim of locating consciousness entraps him in metaphors of mirroring, picturing, and mapping which distort the thing he would describe. Caught between the desire for and the failure of metaphor, Freud describes spatial and temporal metaphors of the mind as both inevitable and impossible. The writing machine, the camera, the political process—all are metaphors that are at-

[18]Freud, *The Interpretation of Dreams* (1900), *SE*, 5:610.

tempted and discarded. "Strictly speaking," writes Freud, "there is no need for the hypothesis that the psychical systems are actually arranged in a *spatial* order. It would be sufficient if a fixed order were established by the fact that in a given psychical process the excitation passes through the systems in a particular *temporal* sequence."[19]

In a study of Freud's ambivalence toward his own topological models, Derrida observes that even this temporal model is based on a metaphysics of presence and so is flawed: "The text is not conceivable in an originary or modified form of presence. The unconscious text is already a weave of pure traces, differences in which meaning and force are united—a text nowhere present, consisting of archives which are *always already* transcriptions. . . . Always already: repositories of a meaning which was never present, whose signified presence is always reconstituted by deferral, *nachträglich*, belatedly, *supplementarily*: for the *nachträglich* also means *supplementary*." Even when Freud openly rejects a topological model, Derrida points out, he still cannot avoid the metaphor of psychic machinery:

> Metaphor—in this case the analogy between two apparatuses and the possibility of this representational relation—raises a question which, despite his premises, and for reasons which are no doubt essential, Freud failed to make explicit. . . . Metaphor as a rhetorical or didactic device is possible here only through the solid metaphor, the "unnatural," historical production of a *supplementary* machine, *added to* the psychical organization in order to supplement its finitude. . . . It opens up the question of technics: of the apparatus in general and of the analogy between the psychical apparatus and the nonpsychical apparatus.

Derrida concludes that whereas Freud seeks to avoid "freezing energy within a naive metaphorics of place" and acknowledges "the necessity not of abandoning but of rethinking the space or topology of this writing," he "still insists on *representing* the psychical apparatus in an artificial model, has not yet discovered a mechanical model adequate to the graphematic conceptual scheme he is already using to describe the psychical text."[20]

As Freud becomes more convinced of the limits of topological models, he develops the hypothesis that "thoughts and psychical

[19]Ibid., 537.
[20]Derrida, "Freud and the Scene of Writing," 211, 228, 212–13.

structures in general must never be regarded as localized in organic elements of the nervous system but rather, as one might say, *between* them, where resistances and facilitations provide the corresponding correlates." And so he finally describes psychic functioning in terms of a virtual image, using the model of a camera:

> Everything that can be an object of our internal perception is *virtual*, like the image produced in a telescope by the passage of light-rays. But we are justified in assuming the existence of the [perceptual] systems (which are not in any way psychical entities themselves and can never be accessible to our psychical perception) like the lenses of the telescope, which cast the image. And, if we pursue this analogy, we may compare the censorship between two systems to the refraction which takes place when a ray of light passes into a new medium.[21]

As Freud strives to picture the psyche both as object and as process, he conveys the confusion of categories in which these descriptions are necessarily trapped. The mind is both an object to be compared and the act of comparison itself, both like a map and a mapping function of which the self is a mirage, both like a camera and itself a projection or image.

Of all Freud's models of the mind, the one most relevant to Derrida's concerns is his "Note upon the 'Mystic Writing-Pad'": "If we imagine one hand writing upon the surface of the Mystic Writing-Pad while another periodically raises its covering-sheet from the wax slab, we shall have a concrete representation of the way in which I tried to picture the functioning of the perceptual apparatus of our mind." Here Freud visibly inscribes the process of repression: "On the Mystic Pad the writing vanishes every time the close contact is broken between the paper which receives the stimulus and the wax slab which preserves the impression. This agrees with a notion which I have long had about the method by which the perceptual apparatus of our mind functions, but which I have hitherto kept to myself."[22] Elizabethan table books were also constructed of heavily waxed, erasable cardboard leaves.[23] These are the tables to which Hamlet

---

[21]Freud, *Interpretation of Dreams*, 611.

[22]Freud, "A Note upon the 'Mystic Writing-Pad'" (1925), *SE*, 19:232, 231.

[23]See, for example, the 1581 Elizabethan table book, now in Harvard College Library, in the Riverside Shakespeare, ed. G. Blakemore Evans (Boston: Houghton Mifflin, 1974), 146.

refers, and of which Theseus speaks when figuring to Hermia her construction under a patriarchal order: "To you your father should be as a god; / One that compos'd your beauties; yea, and one / To whom you are but as a form in wax, / By him imprinted, and within his power, / To leave the figure, or disfigure it" (1.1.47–51). Is Shakespeare imagining the mind as a sort of table book? It seems oddly fitting that Freud admits to having concealed or withheld this model, that he admits to having refrained from *ex-pressing* his theory. Since Freud's theory is riddled with the censorship that it describes, his writing pad returns us not only to Elizabethan models of repression but to Derrida's idea that "writing is unthinkable without repression."[24] Can we think of the unconscious as a trace, or an inscription that erases? Did Shakespeare?

The influence of the printing press in determining how we know exemplifies how a change in visual conventions affects basic cognitive and epistemological assumptions. Walter Ong explains:

> In many ways, the greatest shift in the way of conceiving knowledge between the ancient and the modern world takes place in the movement from a pole where knowledge is conceived of in terms of discourse and hearing and persons to one where it is conceived of in terms of observation and sight and objects. This shift dominates all others in Western intellectual history. . . . Stress on induction follows the stress on deduction as manifesting a still further visualization in the approach to knowledge, with tactics based on "observation," an approach preferably through sight.[25]

One result of this shift was widespread ambivalence toward a growing print culture, which explains why a play like *A Midsummer Night's Dream* is so suspicious of sight and so concerned with legislating vision. We delight in Peter Quince's efforts to teach his uneducated actors to follow a play script. We laugh when he responds to Flute's "Must I speak now?" and "Ninny's tomb" with a curt " 'Ninus' tomb,' man. Why, you must not speak that yet. That you answer to Pyramus. You speak all your part at once, cues and all" (3.1.89, 97, 98–100). Yet we delight even more when Peter Quince gets lost in

---

[24]Derrida, "Freud and the Scene of Writing," 226.
[25]Ong, "System, Space, and Intellect," 69–70.

deciphering punctuation in the Prologue to *Pyramus and Thisby*. Just as the phrase "to know" shifted from a sense of "being in the know" to a sense of being able to *envision* what one knows, so we now expect that we can *follow* another's speech according to a strict linear pattern.

Another effect of this burgeoning print culture was a tendency to think inductively, to conceive of the mind as territory that could be mapped though never seen directly. The Renaissance mind is often described as a physical container with concealed spaces: as a house with hidden rooms, a map that contains vast uncharted territories, or a perspective picture that contains hidden images. When Lysander tells Helena of his secret plans, he states: "Helen, to you our minds we will unfold" (1.1.208). Hermia speaks of her secrets with Helena as things contained within her mind and heart; she reminds Helena of the years that they have spent "emptying our bosoms of their counsel [sweet]" (1.1.216). "The mind now 'contains' knowledge," Ong explains, "especially in the compartments of the various arts and sciences, which in turn may 'contain' one another, and which all 'contain' words."[26]

Not only does the mind contain knowledge, but its manner of mediating between its various containers is distinctly political. Not surprisingly, a rigidly hierarchical society with disparate social levels envisions the mind in terms of hierarchical modes of organization according to which various parts can be interrelated yet kept strictly separate. *A Midsummer Night's Dream* figures psychological processes through acts of partitioning discrete entities between which there is no communication. The fairyland, court, and wood are clearly delineated from one another. All these realities exist simultaneously, as if nothing but imaginary walls separated them. Puck can taunt an angry Demetrius without being caught, and Oberon can bless a house unseen. No one level of reality encompasses all the others; although the fairies can see what the mortals cannot, spirits of another sort worry Puck, and even Titania can never fully comprehend Bottom's ways.

A Midsummer Night's Dream explores the function of such partitions by showing us what happens when they break down. It encourages us to hold various "levels" of imaginative experience in our minds at once, only to confuse our sense of their priority, exclusivity,

[26]Ibid., 75.

and autonomy. The play encourages us to grant equal imaginative reality to groups operating at conflicting levels of cognitive experience. As members of different groups infiltrate the others' domains, the possibility of discovering an objective standpoint from which to delineate truth from fantasy becomes increasingly less plausible. When these characters return to their usual "worlds," they have no shared language or interpretive conventions to make sense of their experience. By invalidating their own and others' perceptions, these characters lead us to question how we construct such categories as knowledge and fantasy.

IV

A Midsummer Night's Dream interrogates the status of a knowledge constructed through erasures and partitions. It stages privileged and unauthorized acts that encode and enclose knowledge, that wall it up and wall it off. *The Comedy of Errors* both figures and resists repression as its narrative moves in the opposing directions of recognition and denial, recovery and splitting. Yet by openly staging repression, *A Midsummer Night's Dream* offers a productive means of mapping both knowledge and that which escapes it. To represent censored material, *A Midsummer Night's Dream* employs a strategy similar to Freud's mystic writing pad; it visibly inscribes something only to make it appear as having disappeared. This strategy anticipates Heidegger's strategy of publishing crossed out words and so putting concepts "under erasure." To point to the inadequacy of language Heidegger writes the word "Being," crosses it out, and leaves the crossed out word in the text. The strategy of putting things "under erasure" enables us to make a mark and, without negating it, to indicate with another mark the problems such a term poses. A famous example is Derrida's phrase "The sign ✗ that ill-named ~~thing~~, the only one, that escapes the instituting question of philosophy: 'what is . . . ?' "[27]

A Midsummer Night's Dream stages visions only to discredit them

[27]Derrida, "The End of the Book and the Beginning of Writing," *Of Grammatology*, trans. Gayatri Chakravorty Spivak (Baltimore: Johns Hopkins University Press, 1976), 19.

later, as if charming them into oblivion. Not only have we shared with Bottom and the four lovers "a most rare vision" (4.1.204–5), not only have we joined the court in witnessing a play that is not for us, but as an audience we have seen a play that questions its own status. Oberon orders Puck to stage a play only to make it later "seem a dream and fruitless vision" (3.2.371); again, at the end of *A Midsummer Night's Dream*, Puck encourages us to regard Shakespeare's play as "no more yielding but a dream" (5.1.428). Theseus seeks entertainment to "beguile / The lazy time" (5.1.40–41), and so commands Philostrate: "Say, what abridgment have you for this evening?" (5.1.39). The three hours fly by as we watch the play *A Midsummer Night's Dream*. The fairy scenes not only stage the invisible but seek to make invisible that which is already present. The fairies sing lullabies to banish all that might disturb a sound sleep: "Thorny hedgehogs, be not seen, / Newts and blind-worms, do no wrong, / . . . Weaving spiders, come not here; / Hence, you long-legg'd spinners, hence!" (2.2.10–11, 20–21). Moreover, Puck himself is an invisible creature made present only to be erased or made absent. He is "that merry wanderer of the night" (2.1.43) responsible for errors, the one "that frights the maidens of the villagery, / Skim milk, and sometimes labor in the quern, / And bootless make the breathless huswife churn, / And sometime make the drink to bear no barm, / Mislead night-wanderers, laughing at their harm" (2.1.35–39). As a visible invisible spirit, Puck makes himself invisible when he fights with Demetrius and Lysander. He removes himself as the source of the voice that commands the two rivals to "Follow my voice" (3.2.412). As a result, Demetrius and Lysander seek to conquer an absent presence that moves and so is both present and invisible. Lysander complains: "He goes before me, and still dares me on. / When I come where he calls, then he is gone" (3.2.413–14).

A Midsummer Night's Dream is filled with references to nothing— and yet these references are of two kinds. The play firmly distinguishes between the act of creating something out of nothing and the act of staging the process of repression itself. When Philostrate describes the play that he would censor as "nothing, nothing in the world" (5.1.78), Theseus responds, "The kinder we, to give them thanks for nothing" (5.1.89). Like poets, lunatics and lovers fabricate something out of nothing, Theseus explains, since "as imagination bodies forth / The forms of things unknown, the poet's pen / Turns them to shapes, and gives to aery nothing / A local habitation and a name" (5.1.14–17). Proving himself a poet, Theseus suggests that he can make something out of the nothing that is the play by reminding us of his ability to read duty in silence: "Out of this silence yet I pick'd a welcome; / And in the modesty of fearful duty / I read as much as from the rattling tongue / Of saucy and audacious eloquence" (5.1.100–3). And yet the real poetry of *A Midsummer Night's Dream* derives from in its ability to embody dream, to represent the nothing or "it" of the unconscious which can only be defined as that which escapes representation.

To refuse the conventional literary critic's game of making the unseen visible is to choose the more perverse game of exploring how *A Midsummer Night's Dream* makes the visible unseen, the spoken silenced. More difficult than creating something out of nothing is the act of staging nothing itself. Herein, Foucault suggests, lies the value of psychoanalysis:

> In setting itself the task of making the discourse of the unconscious speak through consciousness, psychoanalysis is advancing in the direction of that fundamental region in which the relations of representation and finitude come into play. Whereas all the human sciences advance towards the unconscious only with their back to it . . . psychoanalysis . . . points directly towards it . . . towards what is there and yet is hidden, towards what exists with the mute solidity of a thing, of a text closed in upon itself, or of a blank space in a visible text, and uses that quality to defend itself.[28]

Is the unconscious that which is not there, that which has no locality? Lacan avows: "We don't even know if the unconscious has a being in itself, and . . . it is because one could not say *that's it* that it was named the *'it'* [*id*]. In fact, one could only say of the unconscious, *that's not it*, or rather, *that's it*, but *not for real*."[29] As the product and process of erasure that takes on a specific form, however, the unconscious is *not* "that's it, but not for real," but part of the very process of constructing "the real." *A Midsummer Night's Dream* thus moves toward what

[28]Michel Foucault, *The Order of Things: An Archaeology of the Human Sciences* (New York: Random-Vintage, 1973), 374.

[29]Lacan, "La méprise du sujet supposé savoir," *Scilicet* 1 (1968), 35, as translated by Shoshana Felman, in *Writing and Madness* (*Literature/Philosophy/Psychoanalysis*), trans. Martha Noel Evans and the author (Ithaca: Cornell University Press, 1985), 124.

Foucault terms "a *positive unconscious* of knowledge: a level that eludes the consciousness of the scientist and yet is part of scientific discourse." Foucault adds: "We know that psychologists and philosophers have dismissed all this as Freudian mythology. It was indeed inevitable that this approach of Freud's should have appeared to them in this way; to a knowledge situated within the representable, all that frames and defines, on the outside, the very possibility of representation can be nothing other than mythology."[30] As if in response, Theseus answers: "I never may believe / These antic fables, nor these fairy toys" (5.1.2–3).

V

Derrida's stated aim in his essay "Freud and the Scene of Writing" is to prove that "the Freudian concept of trace must be radicalized and extracted from the metaphysics of presence which still retains it." The question, as he sees it, is "not if the psyche is indeed a kind of text, but: what is a text, and what must the psyche be if it can be represented by a text?" Derrida's attempts to replace a model of the unconscious as a space or place with a model of the unconscious as a trace suggest that he too is caught in the spatial and technological metaphors that he discovers in Freud. One response to his question might be to consider what the psyche must be if it can *never* be represented by a text—if it can never be represented at all. And one answer to that question is provided by Derrida's title, since his interest in figuring the psyche as text is undermined by his fascination with theatricality. Derrida's work is riddled with theatrical references—to Artaud, to the *scene* of writing, to the *staging* or *performance* of theory—and these references have serious implications for theater theory. He concludes the essay with an appropriately theatrical flair: "Thus Freud performs for us the scene of writing. Like all those who write. And like all who know how to write, he let the scene duplicate, repeat, and betray itself within the scene." Since the "scene" of writing "must be thought in the horizon of the scene/stage of the world, as the history of that scene/stage,"[31] since all Freud can do is perform for us the scene of writing, as Derrida claims, then the

---

[30]Foucault, *Order of Things*, xi, 374–75.
[31]Derrida, "Freud and the Scene of Writing," 229, 199.

relationship between theatricality and writing requires closer scrutiny. If we cannot figure without disfiguring, can we not put these disfiguring processes on stage by acknowledging their role in representation?

In *The Interpretation of Dreams*, Freud advances the provocative thesis that censorship "imposes upon the dream-work *considerations of representability*" which restrict the dream "to giving things a new form." Since censorship determines representation, he reasons, dream interpretation must follow the distorting form of the dream work. Freud reproaches analysts for reductive models of interpretation that seek to retrieve an undistorted original: "They seek to find the essence of dreams in their latent content and in so doing they overlook the distinction between the latent dream-thoughts and the dream-work. At bottom, dreams are nothing other than a particular *form* of thinking. . . . It is the *dream-work* which creates that form, and it alone is the essence of dreaming—the explanation of its peculiar nature."[32] The mistake such analysts make, according to Freud, is the same error for which Derrida took literary critics to task: they adopt a simplistic model of representation which depends upon the dream of an origin, an originating wish, motive, or meaning that can be faithfully reproduced or retrieved.

Freud repeatedly acknowledges that undistorted knowledge of dreams is impossible: "Our memory of dreams is not only fragmentary but positively inaccurate and falsified." Like our memories of dreams, dream interpretation is riddled with distortions: "It is true that we distort dreams in attempting to reproduce them. . . . But this distortion is itself no more than a part of the revision to which the dream-thoughts are regularly subjected as a result of the dream-censorship." Freud concludes that "one can reconstruct from a single remaining fragment not, it is true, the dream—which is in any case a matter of no importance—but all the dream-thoughts."[33] Once Freud dismisses the importance of reconstructing the dream per se, and focuses instead on the dream work, the ontological status of both dreams and dream interpretation is, as Samuel Weber points out, radically redefined: "It [the dream] can no longer be regarded as a self-contained, fully determinable *object*, susceptible of being ren-

[32]Freud, *Interpretation of Dreams*, 506–7.
[33]Ibid., 512, 514, 517.

dered or represented faithfully—'*dargestellt*'—by an interpretation. Rather, the dream comes to be only through a process of revision and distortion that even the best of interpretations can only hope to continue. What results . . . is a situation of interpretation that is quite different from that presumed by a hermeneutics that defines its task in terms of *explication* or of *disclosure*."[34]

Observing that Freud always considered dreams a form of distortion, of *Entstellung*—which implies both disfigurement and dislocation—Weber explains what is at stake:

> The interpretation of a dream thus does indeed constitute a process of deformation; yet far from invalidating itself, this alone constitutes, paradoxically, its sole claim to legitimacy. For the dream "itself" is already an *Entstellung*: not merely by virtue of what Freud describes as "secondary elaboration" . . . but also because the specific mechanisms of articulation that constitute the distinctive language of the dream are all forms of *Entstellung*: a word that must be read as an alternative to *Darstellung*, "presentation" or "exposition." . . . The "form" of thinking peculiar to dreams . . . is that of a de-formation that dissimulates its deformative character by creating a representational facade. "*Darstellung*" thus becomes one of the means by which the dream achieves its goal of "*Entstellung*."[35]

The key phrase here is "a de-formation that dissimulates its deformative character by creating a representational facade." Is representation always already a distortion? If "the essence of dreams" is not to be found in some original wish but in the process of a distorting yet constitutive inscription, if representation is a form of dislocation or distortion, then the entire interpretive process, whether of dreams, literature, or history, indeed must be rethought. Interpretation is itself subsumed under the disfiguring effects of performance. Not only is reading a reproduction that necessarily distorts the original, but the "original" is itself a product of distortion because it too is "always already" in representation. At the core of the dream there is

[34]Samuel Weber, "The Blindness of the Seeing Eye: Psychoanalysis, Hermeneutics, *Entstellung*," in his *Institution and Interpretation* (Minneapolis: University of Minnesota Press, 1987), 79. I am indebted to Weber's discussion (pp. 73–84) throughout these pages.
[35]Ibid., 78–79.

no desire that is not also a result of censorship; in essence there is no essence, no core of the dream at all. At bottom we have reached the dream that has no bottom. Is this critique of referentiality the limit of deconstructive analysis?

If there is no undistorted inscription or intent "underneath" or "behind" the work of play or dream, how do we define the work of critical theory today? Once Freud establishes that we can never reconstruct the dream itself, he turns his attention to the acts of distortion and censorship that he terms the dream work. Similarly, rather than forgo theory, we return it to theater by rethinking meaning as performative. In a remarkable passage, Freud directly relates theatricality to psychoanalysis: "Condensation, together with the transformation of thoughts into situations ('dramatization'), is the most important and peculiar characteristic of the dream-work."[36] If the dream work is all that we can study and if its defining characteristic is dramatization, then the revival of theatrical terms and concepts would appear crucial to the redirection of critical theory.

Rather than conceive of the meaning of a dream or a play as a thing to be retrieved, we might rethink meaning as a social production or enactment. And theater provides an intriguing model for that production. Terry Eagleton explains: "The literary text is not the 'expression' of ideology, nor is ideology the 'expression' of social class. The text, rather, is a certain *production* of ideology, for which the analogy of a dramatic production is in some ways appropriate. A dramatic production does not 'express,' 'reflect,' or 'reproduce' the dramatic text on which it is based; it 'produces' the text, transforming it into a unique and irreducible entity."[37] The analogy of production is more than appropriate; it is necessary—which explains why Derrida must stage a scene in order to critique representation. If the literary work is displaced by the active work through which meaning is produced, we cannot avoid rethinking reading as enactment and enactment as a constitutive distortion.

The acts of staging a play that will escape censorship and producing a dream that can never be adequately translated are remarkably similar. Play production, like dream production, is a matter of a translation that effaces as it reaches toward an original. A play is, after

[36]Freud, *On Dreams* (1901), *SE*, 5:653.
[37]Terry Eagleton, *Criticism and Ideology* (London: New Left Books, 1976), 64.

all, a projected performance of an original that can never be retrieved or realized as such. Like a dream, the original play is "nothing, nothing in the world" (5.1.78); it can only be located as "not that," or as a simulacrum of a simulacrum, a distortion of an origin that is itself constituted by distortions. Peter Quince knows that to represent is to disfigure. Should Bottom follow up on his plans to have Peter Quince write a ballad of his dream, that ballad would also be a disfiguring translation. Censorship doesn't end with the construction of a work but continues in its reconstruction on stage and page. Dreams, like plays, are always censored translations, since presentation is a constitutive distortion of an original that is nowhere to be found.

Both dream and play production are based on "considerations of representability"—on the materiality of the signifier, on the conditions of staging, on the conventions of audience reception. Elizabethan play production, for example, was a highly collaborative activity over which no one individual maintained complete or autonomous control. Stephen Orgel observes: "The company commissioned the play, usually stipulated the subject, often provided the plot, often parcelled it out, scene by scene, to several playwrights. The text thus produced was a working model, which the company then revised as seemed appropriate. The author had little or no say in these revisions: the text belonged to the company, and the authority represented by the text—I am talking now about the *performing* text—is that of the company, the owners, not that of the playwright, the author."[38] Shakespeare's content with the collaborative aspects of theatrical production, unlike the discontent of his contemporary Ben Jonson, suggests an acceptance of the distortion that plagues all representation.[39] Not surprisingly, Freud stressed the collaborative and distorting nature of dream production as well: "Each element in the content of a dream is 'overdetermined' by material in the dream-thoughts; it is not derived from a *single* element in the dream-thoughts, but may be traced back to a whole number."[40] Yet Freud's

---

[38]Stephen Orgel, "What Is a Text?" *Research Opportunities in Renaissance Drama* 2 (1981), 3.
[39]See, for example, Stallybrass and White on Ben Jonson and problems of authorship in *Politics and Poetics of Transgression*, 66–79.
[40]Freud, *On Dreams*, 652.

focus on "considerations of representability" suggests these distorting representations. Insofar as cultural formations determine conditions of representability, the play of distortion is itself limited to a local form.

VI

To what extent, then, does *A Midsummer Night's Dream* figure interpretation as distortion or acknowledge its politics? At first glance, *A Midsummer Night's Dream* follows the traditional categories of Renaissance faculty psychology, in which reality is a collaborative production of the hearing and the seeing senses in cooperation with imagination and reason. Since reason must control imagination in the production of reality, vision is "corrected" as in trick perspective paintings. But in fact, *A Midsummer Night's Dream* differs from this account in one important respect: patriarchal law rather than reason actually controls perspective in this play, and its vision is depicted as necessarily distorted and distorting. Since all power is necessarily a distortion, the problem the play poses is not how to correct distorted perspective but how to legitimize the distorted vision of the patriarchy. The problem it faces is how to bring Elizabethan faculty psychology into the service of a patriarchal aristocracy that openly employs distortion to construct truth.

Renaissance faculty psychology was a kind of cognitive psychology which explored how memory and judgment work with sight and hearing. Bottom aptly describes his experience in the wood by confusing sight and hearing in his bungled rendering of a passage from 1 Corinthians: "The eye of man hath not heard, the ear of man hath not seen, man's hand is not able to taste, his tongue to conceive, nor his heart to report, what my dream was" (4.1.211–14). Despite its rich visual imagery, *A Midsummer Night's Dream* keeps reminding us that the eye, the chief organ by which we know, is the most deceptive. Rather than cite the many references to erring vision in the play, consider the exceptions to the rule. The few references to erring hearing are connected to lovers' singing: Egeus charges Lysander with having bewitched his daughter not only with sight but with sound: "Thou hast by moonlight at her window sung / With faining voice verses of faining love" (1.1.30–31). When Titania is awakened by Bottom's singing, she responds: "I pray thee, gentle mortal, sing again. / Mine ear is much enamored of thy note; / So is mine eye enthralled to thy shape" (3.1.137–39). For the rest of the play, erring knowledge is figured as visual and the hearing sense is privileged.

The lengthy and seemingly irrelevant speech Hermia delivers as she discovers the erring lovers is in fact an argument concerning the limits of the seeing sense:

> Dark night, that from the eye his function takes,
> The ear more quick of apprehension makes;
> Wherein it doth impair the seeing sense,
> It pays the hearing double recompense.
> Thou art not by mine eye, Lysander, found;
> Mine ear, I thank it, brought me to thy sound.
> But why unkindly didst thou leave me so?
>
> (3.2.177–83)

Perhaps just as valid as Hermia's concluding question is why she spends such an important moment philosophizing upon the relative merits of the hearing and seeing senses.

Even the play's celebration of order is an auditory epiphany of "the musical confusion / Of hounds and echo in conjunction" (4.1.110–11). Hippolyta boasts of what she has heard, not seen, when she was with Hercules and Cadmus. What she remembers best is the sound of the Spartan hounds: "Never did I hear / Such gallant chiding; for besides the groves, / The skies, the fountains, every region near / Seem all one mutual cry. I never heard / So musical a discord, such sweet thunder" (4.1.114–18). Theseus responds boastfully that his Spartan-bred hounds bark according to a musical scale; they are "match'd in mouth like bells, / Each under each. A cry more tuneable / Was never hollow'd to, nor cheer'd with horn, / In Crete, in Sparta, nor in Thessaly. / Judge when you hear" (4.1.123–27). The question is not why Theseus employs a musical scale to champion a rigidly hierarchical social order, or even why one can judge best when one hears but not when one sees, but how right sight can be legitimized.

Shakespeare's early comedies repeatedly contrast categories of true and false perspective to stage the legislation of right perspective. *The Taming of the Shrew* carefully deletes the information upon which decisions are based in order to focus our attention on the decision-making process. It presents us with undecidable situations and then offers us a variety of alternatives through which they can be resolved. The question is never who is factually correct but which system should determine "right perspective." As in the famous scene of Kate and Petruchio's return to Padua, or as in the dispute between the Lord and First Huntsman concerning the better dog at the hunt, the emphasis is less on who is correct than on how perspective is both constructed and enforced.

A Midsummer Night's Dream is another early comedy in which the control of meaning takes precedence over any particular meaning, and in which that control is accomplished through the manipulation of sight. Theseus's reputation as a wise judge identifies him with the act of legislating right vision. He is flanked on either side by representatives of mastered fantasy; both Hippolyta and Philostrate embody imaginative forces held in check by his rule. Philostrate, as master of revels, is both the source of imaginative material and the means by which it is censored or transformed in accordance with Theseus's "right vision." Hippolyta evokes and reflects Theseus's sexual desire, which the law demands he restrain until his wedding day. When *A Midsummer Night's Dream* opens, then, the three characters on stage emblematically set out the relationship between the right vision of law and the erring vision of imagination.

The right relationship between imagination and patriarchal law is threatened when Egeus and Hermia enter and present their quarrel. By refusing to marry Demetrius, Hermia openly challenges the perspective of the Athenian patriarchy: "I would my father look'd but with my eyes" (1.1.56). Theseus upholds the "ancient privilege of Athens" (1.1.41) and responds sharply: "Rather your eyes must with his judgment look" (1.1.57). Lysander may be worthy, Theseus admits, but "wanting your father's voice, / The other must be held the worthier" (1.1.54–55). Hermia's refusal "to choose love by another's eyes" (1.1.140) has disastrous consequences: since she challenges the interpretive conventions by means of which her society measures truth, her privileges as a reader are withdrawn and her interpretation of events is discredited. Power in *A Midsummer Night's Dream* is both optical and patriarchal; patriarchal law determines perspective and operates through the control of that perspective.

Yet how valid is patriarchal perspective in this play? Consider the competing visions held by Oberon and Titania regarding the changeling boy. According to Oberon, as Puck informs us, Titania is caring for "A lovely boy stolen from an Indian king" (2.1.22). Titania, however, offers a different account: "His mother was a vot'ress of my order, / . . . And for her sake do I rear up her boy" (2.1.123, 136). Since only patriarchal law legislates right vision in this play, Titania's competing perspective must be discredited. In order to place Titania in the position of an erring spectator, Oberon squeezes the juice of the flower love-in-idleness on her eyelids while chanting: "What thou seest when thou dost wake, / Do it for thy true-love take; / . . . In thy eye that shall appear / When thou wak'st, it is thy dear: / Wake when some vile thing is near" (2.2.27–28, 32–34). No sooner is Titania's viewpoint rendered distorted than Oberon's perspective is triumphantly equated with right sight. By successfully distorting Titania's perspective, Oberon presents his own interpretation of events as unerring.

An analogy for this complicated plot of competing visions is a 1638 description by Jean-François Niceron of a trick perspective in which various images, drawn from multiple points of view, are superimposed on a painting with straightforward images, so that they "represent two or three wholly different things, such that being seen from the front, they represent a human face; from the right side a death's head, and from the left something different."[41] From one perspective, Lysander and Demetrius look exactly the same—two rather uninteresting young Englishmen. Lysander points to the similarity: "I am, my lord, as well deriv'd as he, / As well possess'd; my love is more than his; / My fortunes every way as fairly rank'd / (If not with vantage) as Demetrius'" (1.1.99–102). From Egeus's standpoint, however, Demetrius appears the ideal suitor and Lysander an unrecognizable blur, whereas from Hermia's perspective the reverse is true. Again, from one standpoint, Hermia and Helena appear to be interchangeable. Helena reminds us that she and Hermia are widely considered to be of comparable beauty: "Through Athens I am thought as fair as she" (1.1.227). Yet from Lysander's perspective, Hermia appears fair and Helena disordered, whereas in the past it appears that for Demetrius the reverse was true. The problem *A Midsummer Night's Dream* presents is how to achieve not truth in

---

[41]Jean-François Niceron, *Perspective curieuse* (1652), as quoted and translated by Ernest B. Gilman, *The Curious Perspective: Literary and Pictorial Wit in the Seventeenth Century* (New Haven: Yale University Press, 1978), 41.

vision but optical power; when Demetrius shifts his affections, he fights to stand where Lysander does. Since neither of the two will share the viewing space, each must fight to present the other's vision as distorted.

This fact alone explains why Demetrius's vision is left magically distorted at the end. Even a correction of sight is yet another distortion of sight. In *A Midsummer Night's Dream*, right vision is a social construct achieved through its own form of distortion. The play openly admits that all figuration is distortion; the problem it confronts, however, is how to legitimize the distorted vision of a patriarchal order. Oberon's manipulation of vision, however tricky, ultimately affirms a patriarchal ideology that equates men with right perspective and women with an irrational nature that defies orderly sight. Even if Titania isn't wrong, her vision is so drastically impaired by Oberon that she learns to distrust her sight. Even if Hippolyta is correct, she is silenced as speaking inappropriately and so proven incorrect in advance. Shakespeare's depiction of the relationship of the gaze to narratives of women's punishment and correction holds steady from *The Comedy of Errors* to *The Winter's Tale*. Woman is the guilty object—whether Titania or Hippolyta, Helena or Hermia, Kate or Adriana—whose erring vision, traditionally figured in her guilty sexuality, must be punished.

Similar examples of the use of distorted sight to control women are plentiful in Hollywood films of the 1940s and 1950s. At the level of narrative, these films commonly portray women as irrational, unable to see clearly and unable to trust what they see. At the level of representation, such films provide a variety of techniques for distorting, dehumanizing, and idealizing the image of woman as fetish. In Busby Berkeley's film *Dames*, the image of woman is continually distorted and then corrected in ways that deny women either individuality or humanity (see figure 12). In one shot, a group of women lift their skirts to create an idealized image of the face of woman—in the form of the face of the film star Ruby Keeler (see figure 13).[42] The women are seen correctly only when they have utterly effaced their individuality and merged together to form an idealized representation of Woman. Such doubling apparently reassures the male gaze: it

---

[42]Lucy Fischer makes this point in her fascinating essay "The Image of Woman as Image: The Optical Politics of *Dames*," *Film Quarterly* 30 (Fall 1976), 1–10.

Figures 12 and 13. Film stills from Busby Berkeley, *Dames* (Warner Brothers, 1934). Courtesy of the Museum of Modern Art Film Stills Archive.

185

suggests that Woman is not only the means by which we are re-produced, but an object that we can reproduce, in turn; women are nothing more than Woman—an image that can be multiplied end-lessly without ever being confronted. Since women may be seen but not heard in *A Midsummer Night's Dream*, some of the most powerful productions of the play flood the stage with visions of identical women. In a Canadian Stratford production of the play with Maggie Smith, the stage was peopled with multiples of the major figures. The effect was to stage dream mechanisms, so that image distortion fed into the play's exploration of the role of censorship in the dream work. Just as uncanny repetition counteracts repression in *The Comedy of Errors*, so in this production of *A Midsummer Night's Dream* the figure of woman could not be repressed; the idea that woman should be seen but not heard was enacted with a vengeance.

Both contemporary and Elizabethan strategies of power are di-rectly related to the control of the spectator's gaze. Jean Baudrillard claims: "Power did not always consider itself as power, and the secret of the great politicians was to know that power *does not exist*. To know that it is only a perspectival space of simulation, as was the pictorial space of the Renaissance, and that if power seduces, it is precisely—what the naive realists of politics will never understand—because it is a simulacrum and because it undergoes a metamorphosis into signs and is invented on the basis of signs."[43] Baudrillard's claim is overstated, but it aptly describes the strategies of optical power employed throughout Shakespearean comedy. The long-standing quarrel over whether Hal's "reformation" in *1 Henry IV* is real or staged exemplifies the claim that at issue is how the real is staged. That Hal's power is optical is suggested by his description of his strategy as a manipulation of others' perceptions of his image: "My reformation, glitt'ring o'er my fault, / Shall show more goodly and attract more eyes / Than that which hath no foil to set it off" (1.2.213–15). Oberon gains power, as Hal does, by presenting cer-tain images as unquestionably distorted so that less obviously dis-torted images will be perceived as accurate. The curious anamorphic portrait of Edward VI (see figure 2, chapter 1) makes good political sense when read in the context of this strategy. Just as Hal manipu-lates his political image by disguising himself as distorted, so Ed-

[43]Jean Baudrillard, "Forgetting Foucault," *Humanities in Society* 3 (Winter 1980), 108–9.

ward's portrait physically and cognitively constrains the viewer to reject a distorted image of Edward in favor of an idealized image.

Stephen Heath reminds us that trick perspectives were less subversive than we might at first imagine, since "the 'wit' of anamorphosis is constantly a reference to a rational and stable system that it assumes in the very moment it parodies or questions and is thus always available as a final image of order."[44] And yet the rational and stable system assumed is itself presented as constructed only through distortion. The Renaissance use of distortion to construct right vision suggests that interpretation was always already a question of censorship and legitimization. *A Midsummer Night's Dream*'s exploration of the means by which knowledge and fantasy are generated is therefore less dependent upon some hidden or unconscious content per se than on the work involved in authorizing and censoring perspectives.

VII

In his early writings on dreams, Freud employs political metaphors to figure the process of representation. He maintains: "A dream-element is, in the strictest sense of the word, the 'representative' of all this disparate material in the content of the dream."[45] Further, he acknowledges the shaping role of specific social formations in the production of imaginative experience:

> A dream is not constructed by each individual dream-thought, or group of dream-thoughts, finding (in abbreviated form) separate representation in the content of the dream—in the kind of way in which an electorate chooses parliamentary representatives; a dream is constructed, rather, by the whole mass of dream-thoughts being submitted to a sort of manipulative process in which those elements which have the most numerous and strongest supports acquire the right of entry into the dream-content—in a manner analogous to election by *scrutin de liste*.[46]

[44]Stephen Heath, *Questions of Cinema* (Bloomington: Indiana University Press, 1981), 70 n. 12.

[45]Freud, *On Dreams*, 652.

[46]Freud, *Interpretation of Dreams*, SE, 4:284.

The more Freud's metaphors veer away from the spatial, the local, the topological, however, the less political they become as well. Whereas Freud was reluctant to develop a politics of the unconscious, Gilles Deleuze and Félix Guattari are not. In their groundbreaking *Anti-Oedipus*, they maintain that desire is necessarily constituted by repression, and so can never be understood outside of a social context: "The law tells us: You will not marry your mother, and you will not kill your father. And we docile subjects say to ourselves: so *that's* what I wanted!"[47] By reading psychoanalysis as an ideological instrument of capitalism, Deleuze and Guattari redefine the unconscious as a social production. Rather than complain that desire can never be singled out from its representation and production, they urge us to explore how desire functions. Rather than avoid a local habitation and a name for our shaping fantasies, they encourage us to acknowledge, use, and change the metaphors we have. They urge us to stage the political and psychological problems inherent in the act of representation, to reinstate within critical discourse the materiality of the signifier by exploring the production, distribution, and circulation of meaning.

Louis Althusser's study of the relationship of ideology and psychoanalysis has been attacked on the grounds that it construes, and so constructs, ideology as a transcendental signified, as a specific form of the unknowable. But Althusser relates psychoanalysis and ideology in far more constructive ways: "It is not enough to know that the Western family is patriarchal and exogamic . . . we must also work out the ideological formations that govern paternity, maternity, conjugality, and childhood: what are 'husband-and-wife-being,' 'father-being,' 'mother-being' and 'child-being' in the modern world? A mass of research remains to be done on these ideological formations. This is a task for *historical materialism*."[48] If the conditions of representability play a major role in the construction of desire, such an analysis extends to the construction of the critic's desire, as well. *A Midsummer Night's Dream* urges its audience, as well as Hermia, to "question your desires" (1.1.67).

[47]Gilles Deleuze and Félix Guattari, *Anti-Oedipus: Capitalism and Schizophrenia*, trans. Robert Hurley, Mark Seem, and Helen R. Lane (Minneapolis: University of Minnesota Press, 1983), 114.

[48]Louis Althusser, *Lenin and Philosophy*, trans. Ben Brewster (London: Monthly Review Press, 1971), 211.

Further, *A Midsummer Night's Dream* offers a model for this sort of analysis. Critics have long prized Hermia's dream as a model of text and dream interpretation.[49] It suits New Critical approaches in that it can be read according to the conventional interpretive devices of imagery, theme, and structure. Yet Bottom's account of his "dream" resists this critical approach by openly acknowledging its status as an incomplete and censored translation: "I have had a dream, past the wit of man to say what dream it was," Bottom sighs, acknowledging: "Man is but an ass, if he go about [t'] expound this dream" (4.1.205–7). When Bottom finally meets up with his friends, he keeps beginning and then refusing to recount that dream in a curious act of self-censorship: "Masters, I am to discourse wonders; but ask me not what; for if I tell you, I am [no] true Athenian. I will tell you every thing, right as it fell out. . . . Not a word of me. All that I will tell you is, that the Duke hath din'd. . . . No more words" (4.2.29–32, 34–35, 45).

Bottom's account mediates between certain knowledge and its impossibility, or between Derrida's two interpretations of interpretation, in that it conveys *certain knowledge of uncertainty*. As in discourse theory, which examines the legitimation of meaning, the focus of Bottom's account is less a particular meaning than the *performance and control of meaning itself*. Since his account of his dream is largely a record of what he cannot say, it shifts our attention away from content and onto the *legitimating process as content*. In this sense, *A Midsummer Night's Dream* suggests a model of interpretation as a socially determined activity of privileged and censored perspectives. Whereas *A Midsummer Night's Dream* does not urge us to explore the construction of an individual or personal unconscious, it does inquire into the modes of production, translation, and representation of collective imaginative experiences. It seems less appropriate, therefore, to seek to reconstruct Hermia's personal fantasies than to study the social construction of fantasy.

Even at the level of dramatic narrative, *A Midsummer Night's Dream* keeps stalling the activity of putting on a play to show us what

---

[49]See, for example, Norman Holland, "Hermia's Dream," in *Representing Shakespeare: New Psychoanalytic Essays*, ed. Murray M. Schwartz and Coppélia Kahn (Baltimore: Johns Hopkins University Press, 1980), 1–20, rpt. from *Annual of Psychoanalysis* 7 (1979).

is involved in the process. It puts representation on stage, displacing content with the disfiguring process of censorship itself. Dreams stage not only content but process as content, and what they tell us about the dream work may be more revealing than the content itself; similarly, Shakespearean comedy is to be valued for the means by which it stages its own representational strategies. The comedies resist arguments regarding the absolute certainty or uncertainty of knowledge because they study that which resists meaning as a form of knowledge. Their treatment of learned ignorance suggests an effort to understand that which escapes comprehension rather than an easy means of denying what we know. The comedies fascinate because they refuse to retreat into ignorance. They demonstrate that we can know and do know, even when we do not know. The mind may only know itself through a mirroring that displaces as it procures self-consciousness, but we can know how it unfolds through that distorting process.

A Midsummer Night's Dream may present itself to us as but another dream to be interpreted; yet we succumb to a naive form of dream interpretation indeed if we simply seek to force into place privileged signifieds, including the politics of the signifier. If *A Midsummer Night's Dream* cannot figure itself, if the mind can only know itself as not itself or through a distorting enactment, the scene of its performance nonetheless offers a kind of knowledge. Finally, *A Midsummer Night's Dream* offers a knowledge that subverts the possibility of knowledge, a knowledge that collapses neat distinctions between psyche and text, writing and censorship, or truth and distortion. We *miss* when we try to read the play from the perspective of the privileged viewer, just as we *miss out* when we assert that meaning is inaccessible. But if we follow erasures, blind spots, and distortions, we discover a different kind of truth. In "Les non-dupes errent" Lacan develops this hypothesis, and Shoshana Felman presents it concisely:

> Lacan makes it clear that we are in no way dealing with the myth of "non-knowledge" [*non-savoir*] that a superficial avant-garde used to its advantage: for not only is it not *sufficient* not to know; the very ability not to know is not granted to us, and cannot thus be taken for granted. What we are dealing with is a knowledge that is, rather, indestructible; *a knowledge which does not allow for knowing that one knows;* a knowledge,

therefore, that is not supported by *meaning* which, by definition, *knows itself.* The subject can get a hold on this unconscious knowledge only by the intermediary of his *mistakes*—the effects of non-sense his speech registers: in dreams, slips of the tongue, or jokes.[50]

If it is *not* sufficient *not* to know, then the distinction between suppression and repression deserves rethinking. Is it possible that the theory of repression is really a fantasy of repression—a dream of unknowingness? From this standpoint, what dreams, trick perspectives, jokes, and comedies share is a reminder of the impossibility of not knowing, of the fantasy that *is* not knowing. Since our desire to uncover the original meaning of a given work is an impossible dream, we must attend to the disfiguring processes by means of which we continually reconstruct ourselves and our knowledge. As we continue to write at the margins of representation and to posit our unknowingness, however, we do so not to reify our blind spots but to keep them on the move.

Here psychoanalytic theory and Shakespearean comedy intersect at their most puzzling and promising, as doubled discourses of non-knowledge. Riddled with meaning, both comedy and psychoanalysis set themselves the task of knowing that which they define in advance as impervious to meaning; both bear witness to what Foucault terms a "positive unconscious" of knowledge. Both stand at the limits of meaning, move by indirections to find directions out, and work through and against themselves. Between as well as within both systems is a wall. Yet it is perhaps "the wittiest partition that ever I heard discourse" (5.1.167–68), since it makes referentiality possible and representation paradoxical.

[50]Felman, *Writing and Madness*, 121.

6

Naming Loss:
Mourning and Representation
in *Twelfth Night*

What, then, is this function of traumatic repetition if nothing—
quite the reverse—seems to justify it from the point of view of the
pleasure principle? To master the painful event, someone may
say—but who masters, where is the master here, to be mastered?
Why speak so hastily when we do not know precisely where to
situate the agency that would undertake this operation of mastery?
—Lacan, *The Four Fundamental Concepts of Psycho-Analysis*

I

To read Shakespeare's *Twelfth Night* is to take part in an intriguing game of lost and found, since the play returns us to
the earlier comedies, to the problem of (re)presentation as repetition
and return, and to the question of our desire in relation to the letter.
Why do we return to *Twelfth Night*, and what is the compulsion
behind the repetition of the signifying chain that is *Twelfth Night*?
How does the twelfth night come to mark and so keep alive the
previous eleven, and how does the play *Twelfth Night* serve as the site
where the earlier comedies are found? In short, how do we understand the relationship between loss and repetition, desire and representation?

Given its obsessive play with the transcription, transmission, and
retrieval of various letters, with pen and ink, and with the *inviolable*
sealing of a letter, *Twelfth Night* suggests a preoccupation with a lack
inscribed in subjectivity, and so a theory of the letter as the signifier of

a primal loss. Yet if *Twelfth Night* encourages an analysis of the loss inscribed in the letter, by the same token it encourages an analysis of the losses inscribed in a theory of loss-in-the-letter—particularly any theory that repeats this insight as truth and cannot move beyond it. The play therefore encourages a return to those theories of loss and representation that Lacan sought to replace as well as to those theories that have displaced Lacan's. But must *Twelfth Night* get hollowed out as another "Purloined Letter," as the space where a battle over the text is performed by Derrida and Lacan, the "two brothers . . . [who] both have attained reputation in letters"?[1] In question is whether we can move beyond a deconstructive stance that seeks to prove that Lacan and Derrida are not, finally, free of each other; in question is the success of the transference model itself, the possibility of something *other* entering into the *en abyme* structure, however mediated by its frame. The allegory of the frame being framed by its contents is itself capable of becoming allegorized in any writing on writing. Rather than deny this paradox, we can develop it in the context of repetition and representation in *Twelfth Night*.

Given its fascination with repeating loss, *Twelfth Night* offers a useful site for figuring out figuration. Yet given a critical scene where warring theories of representation and loss challenge one another in an oedipally inscribed game of rivalry, where each theory makes the other "gone" in order to find itself, the problems of re-presenting loss through theory and representing the losses facing theory are intricately interwined. For example, do we read loss in terms of object-relations theory, Lacanian theory, or Derridean theory? Do we read *Twelfth Night* in terms of the characters' represented losses or in terms of the characters' losses in representation, in terms of an allegory of loss and desire which reads both literature and psychoanalysis or in terms of the scene of their writing, this writing? To choose one theory, do we need to make the others gone? To choose any, do we need to complete and so make *Twelfth Night* gone? How to pass on this chain letter and yet escape the allegorizing that closes up or closes off? Whereas object-relations theory always finds, as Lacan reminds us, the loss of the other in relationship, and Lacanian

[1]Edgar Allan Poe, "The Purloined Letter," in *Collected Works of Edgar Allan Poe*, vol. 3: *Tales and Sketches, 1843–1849*, ed. Thomas Olive Mabbott (Cambridge: Harvard University Press, 1978), 986.

theory always finds, as Derrida reminds us, the subversion of the subject by the signifier, and Derridean theory always finds, as Barbara Johnson reminds us, the subversion of theory by the scene of its writing—how are we (to reverse the Shakespearean motto) not to find ourselves as lost?[2]

At the most basic level we might read the characters in *Twelfth Night* according to their strategies for coping with loss and disillusionment. Some deny loss through parasitism; others keep loss alive by playing "gone" with themselves.[3] Some characters reenact loss by setting others up to be disillusioned; still others use poetry and song to help others deal with loss. Whereas Malvolio fails to see the letter or his division by it, characters like Olivia and Orsino frantically seek to find, incorporate, or possess the letter; only Viola and Feste accept their division by the letter, as well as the fact that it is always already purloined. Rather than chart these responses in terms of developmental stages, we might better convey this sense of loss-in-repetition with a repetition that knows it misses as it returns.

In *Beyond the Pleasure Principle*, for example, Freud offers a useful model for examining theories of loss and representation in his readings of the *fort-da* game played by his grandson, Ernst, with a toy reel.[4] The game at first involves nothing more than making the object lost; later, the game becomes two-part, a matter of making the object lost (*fort*) and then found (*da*). This simple game has been claimed as a *cause célèbre* by object-relations theorists against Lacanians and by Derrideans against both.[5] Lacan and Derrida first squared

---

[2]Barbara Johnson, "The Frame of Reference: Poe, Lacan, Derrida," in *Literature and Psychoanalysis: The Question of Reading: Otherwise*, ed. Shoshana Felman (Baltimore: Johns Hopkins University Press, 1982), 457–505.

[3]See, for example, R. D. Laing's description of false and untenable positions in *Self and Others* (1961; rpt. Middlesex, Eng.: Pelican, 1969), where he describes a man who "believed that to make his presence felt he would have to go to such extremes that no one would want to have anything to do with him, and thus he came to make the central enterprise of his life to be nobody" (138).

[4]Sigmund Freud, *Beyond the Pleasure Principle* (1920), *SE*, 18:3–64.

[5]For a survey of this reading by object-relations theorists, see Jay R. Greenberg and Stephen A. Mitchell, *Object Relations in Psychoanalytic Theory* (Cambridge: Harvard University Press, 1983). The authors suggest that Freud's account of the *fort-da* game can "provide alternative explanations" for psychoanalytic theory, yet acknowledge that "Freud's concept of primary narcissism is a stumbling block for any relational/structural model, since it explicitly presupposes that the infant is at first *not* oriented toward others, thereby making object relations secondary and derivative

off in their opposing readings of "The Purloined Letter"; their opposing readings of *Beyond the Pleasure Principle*, however, offer a perspective on that relationship which displaces it.[6] Whereas Lacan always seeks to displace object-relations theory and Derrida always seeks to displace Lacan, the dynamics of Freud's text function to disarm repetition as rivalry *or as mastery*. Freud keeps on retelling his story, rethinking his explanations, offering so many different versions that these rereadings serve as yet another model of repetition. Since the process of *moving beyond* one's own thought is inscribed in the work's title, since Freud explores what keeps him from moving beyond a theory of wish fulfillment, any text unable to situate itself in a similarly circular model cannot figure the writing that is *Beyond the Pleasure Principle*. After examining the implications for *Twelfth Night* of various theories of loss provoked by Freud's text, we can in turn review these theories through *Twelfth Night*.

To the extent that a play, song, or personality can be hollowed out to incorporate another or re-present the place where loss lives on, we are led to question the status of the letter as repetition compulsion, or what Lacan terms the insistence of the signifying chain. What losses are repeated in the letter, and what is the transference involved in their translation? What is the nature of the Lacanian *objet petit a* in the context of the equally problematic return to Freud effected by Lacan? To ask how (and whether) Freud lives on in Lacan and how

---

phenomena" (205). Lacan treats this game in different seminars; see especially "The Unconscious and Repetition" (17–64), "Tuché and Automaton" (61–63), and "Of the Subject Who Is Supposed to Know" (239), in *The Four Fundamental Concepts of Psycho-Analysis*, ed. Jacques-Alain Miller, trans. Alan Sheridan (New York: Norton, 1981). Jacques Derrida offers a close reading of this section of *Beyond the Pleasure Principle* in his early essay "Coming into One's Own," trans. James Hulbert, in *Psychoanalysis and the Question of the Text*, ed. Geoffrey H. Hartman (Baltimore: Johns Hopkins University Press, 1985), 114–48. A fuller account appears in *The Post Card: From Socrates to Freud and Beyond*, trans. Alan Bass (Chicago: University of Chicago Press, 1987), in the section "To Speculate—On 'Freud,'" 257–409, esp. the section "Freud's Legacy," 292–337.

[6]Lacan, "Le séminaire sur 'La lettre volée,'" in *Ecrits* (Paris: Seuil, 1966), translated in abbreviated form in *Yale French Studies* 48 (1972), 38–72. Jacques Derrida's reading of Lacan's reading, "Le facteur de la vérité," was first published in *Poétique* 21 (1975), 96–147, and an abbreviated version appeared in translation as "The Purveyor of Truth," *Yale French Studies* 52 (1975), 31–113, in a special issue titled "Graphesis." A complete translation appears in *The Post Card*, to which I refer in the following pages.

(and whether) Sebastian gets relocated in Viola is to ask about the relation of psychoanalysis to its returns. William Kerrigan observes that for many critics today "Lacan is now the preferable model, the place where Freud has been relocated."[7] If so, we must "remain alive" to the problem of what this particular (dis)location as return means, particularly in terms of the purloined letter, the repetition compulsion, and the survivor syndrome. What to do with the blank letters that remain crumpled in one's hands? How to banish the supplement, make the past past so the present can go free of it? How to count *Twelfth Night* as the last? How to stop the transference and effect closure; how to close the system of the numerable and the repeatable; how to count one and no more? The scene of the play and of criticism, analysis terminable and interminable, all are at stake here.

II

"To him in thine own voice" (4.2.66). To repeat the story of the *fort-da* game, to relocate its many versions in *Twelfth Night* and in this text, and yet to speak as messengers are asked to speak in this play— "in thine own voice"—is it possible? The request—"Tell me your mind—I am a messenger" (1.5.205)—is for an old song, "but that piece of song, / That old and antique song we heard last night" (2.4.2–3). Whose voice shall we use? Must you ask to hear that song again? The person "is not here . . . that should sing it" (2.4.8–9). Telling one (as in a child's "first" game, as if such a thing were possible): the scene is chapter 2 of *Beyond the Pleasure Principle*. The narrative is Freud's dismissal of repetitions that do *not* challenge, do *not* move beyond that theory of wish fulfillment and the will to mastery known as the pleasure principle. Slowly, yet methodically, Freud begins to play at his game—to repeat, then repeat, and then repeat again that which does not repeat horribly, that which rather stalls off the horrible insight that there is something here which does not love what we will, something that doesn't speak mastery and pleasure. For the caption here, read "Repetition as Deferral."

---

[7]William Kerrigan, Introduction to *Interpreting Lacan*, ed. Joseph H. Smith and William Kerrigan (New Haven: Yale University Press, 1983), xxi.

The stated function of this account is to explain and so move beyond a theory of repetition as ego mastery. Freud reads the little boy's game of lost and found as an attempt to master his relationship with his mother and come to terms with her absences. Freud reminds us that the mother is the child's principal and only caretaker and adds that the boy "never cried when his mother left him." Yet the boy had been caught playing a rather curious game:

> This good little boy, however, had an occasional disturbing habit of taking any small objects he could get hold of and throwing them away from him into a corner, under the bed, and so on, so that hunting for his toys and picking them up was often quite a business. As he did this he gave vent to a loud, long-drawn-out "o-o-o-o," accompanied by an expression of interest and satisfaction. His mother and the writer . . . were agreed in thinking that this . . . represented the German word *"fort"* [gone]. I eventually realized that it was a game and that the only use he made of any of his toys was to play "gone" with them. One day I made an observation which confirmed my view. The child had a wooden reel with a piece of string tied round it. . . . What he did was to hold the reel by the string and very skillfully throw it over the edge of his curtained cot, so that it disappeared into it, at the same time uttering his expressive "o-o-o-o." He then pulled the reel out of the cot again by the string and hailed its reappearance with a joyful *"da"* [there]. This, then, was the complete game—disappearance and return. As a rule one only witnessed its first act, which was repeated untiringly as a game in itself, though there is no doubt that the greater pleasure was attached to the second act.[8]

As if this account were not in itself both the game and its interpretation, Freud *explains*—offering us not one but three related analyses, each time bringing the event closer to him.

Reading one: "The interpretation of the game then became obvious. It was related to the child's great cultural achievement—the instinctual renunciation . . . which he had made in allowing his mother to go away without protesting. He compensated himself for this, as it were, by himself staging the disappearance and return of the objects within his reach." Reading two: "On an unprejudiced view one gets an impression that the child turned his experience into a

[8]Freud, *Beyond the Pleasure Principle*, 14–15.

197

game from another motive. At the outset he was in a *passive* situation—he was overpowered by the experience; but, by repeating it, unpleasurable though it was, as a game, he took on an *active* part. These efforts might be put down to an instinct for mastery that was acting independently of whether the memory was in itself pleasurable or not." Reading three: "But still another interpretation may be attempted. Throwing away the object so that it was 'gone' might satisfy an impulse of the child's, which was suppressed in his actual life, to revenge himself on his mother for going away from him. In that case it would have a defiant meaning: 'All right, then, go away! I don't need you. I'm sending you away myself.' "[9] The last option is encaptioned here, via *Twelfth Night*, as "Go off, I discard you. Let me enjoy my private. Go off" (3.4.89–90).

Freud analyzes repetitive play in each instance as a defensive means of coping with maternal loss. Whether the defense adopted is compensatory displaced reenactment, symbolic repetition as mastery, or identification with the aggressor, in each case the loss and return of the nurturing object is the central scenario, and a preliminary working out of object relations through accepting the separateness of others is the solution. Not surprisingly, the *fort-da* game is often cited by those who wish to prove that Freud was an object-relations theorist. Arthur Modell, for example, finds confirmed in this account the following tenets: "The symbol *is* the object denoted; action upon the symbol can affect the object—a belief in action at a distance and a belief that serves the function of negating the perception of the physical separation of objects—the fact that objects can be lost."[10] Why, then, does Lacan take issue with this reading and angrily protest: "This reel is not the mother reduced to a little ball by some magical game worthy of the Jivaros"?[11] But that is to anticipate ourselves here. In question first is whether or not this reading of loss actually brings us closer to the world of *Twelfth Night*. In *Beyond the Pleasure Principle*, Freud recounts the *fort-da* narrative to explain why this version of repetition as mastery fails to move "beyond" a theory of wish fulfillment. The following reading of *Twelfth Night* repeats

---

[9]Ibid., 15–16.

[10]Arthur Modell, *Object Love and Reality* (New York: International Universities Press, 1974), 27.

[11]Lacan, "Tuché and Automaton," 62.

this gesture by working through object-relations theory in order to move beyond it.

Object-relations theory conceives of human emotional development as a spiral; at each turn, after having been seduced by the apparent acquiescence of reality to our needs, we are confronted with loss, with the need to accept the separateness of objects, and with the challenge to return to relationship. The beginnings of the sense of identity and reality are rooted in the infant's gradual differentiation from a state of at-one-ness with the mother. The infant's gradual capacity to trust in the withdrawal and return of the maternal object is therefore central to the formation and strengthening of both the ego and its object relations. The adult's capacity for autonomy and trust in turn results from the degree to which recurring phases of separation and fusion have been accepted. Following Margaret Mahler, we might term the course of human psychological development a continual "separation-individuation process" if not a "life-long mourning process."[12] Or we may think of this process in terms of what John MacMurray calls a "rhythm of withdrawal and return": at each turn of the spiral, we weigh the gains sought against the threats involved in the return to relationship.[13]

According to Modell, the message is simple: "*The acceptance of painful reality rests upon the same ego structures that permit the acceptance of the separateness of objects*" and "is identical to that psychic structure whose development enables one to love maturely." The critical disillusionment is the differentiation of self and (m)other; to accept the separateness of objects *is* to accept painful reality. Modell cautions that this is an ongoing process that is confronted at each major developmental stage: "With each subsequent deepening development of the sense of identity there is an ever-increasing capacity to

[12]Margaret Mahler, *On Human Symbiosis and the Vicissitudes of Individuation* (London: Hogarth Press, 1969); and Mahler, *The Psychological Birth of the Human Infant* (New York: Basic Books, 1975). Mahler's study of the play of separation and fusion in human development includes an analysis of the hazards accompanying each stage. For an extension of Mahler's theories to Shakespeare's problem comedies, tragedies, and romances, see Richard Wheeler, *Shakespeare's Development and the Problem Comedies: Turn and Counter-Turn* (Berkeley: University of California Press, 1981).

[13]John MacMurray, *Persons in Relation* (London: Faber and Faber, 1961), 86; his model provides the basis for my reading of *Twelfth Night* through object-relations theory.

accept the limitations of others. However, this process is not to be thought of as final and complete—separateness can never be fully accepted."[14] John MacMurray puts it most poignantly: "The rhythm of withdrawal and return does not cease with the achievement of organic maturity; it is the permanent form of the life of personal relationship. The transition from the withdrawal to the return repeats itself indefinitely, and each time . . . there is a possibility that it should be made successfully."[15]

For D. W. Winnicott, the mothering person's initial task is to mirror the infant, provide a magical environment that adapts to its needs, and so seduce the infant into an illusion of creative omnipotence. The next and most difficult task is to gradually disillusion the infant by carefully withdrawing immediate nurturance in accordance with the infant's growing capacity both to tolerate frustration and to accept its separateness. "*If all goes well,*" Winnicott observes, "the infant can actually come to gain from the experience of frustration, since incomplete adaptation to need makes objects real, that is to say hated as well as loved. The consequence of this is that . . . the infant can be disturbed by a close adaptation to need that is continued too long, not allowed its natural decrease, since exact adaptation resembles magic and the object that behaves perfectly becomes no better than a hallucination."[16] Winnicott's "mothering person" is a *Twelfth Night* playwright, seducing us through illusion into creative play with life and then disillusioning us so that we may accept our separateness.

Winnicott's work on the use of transitional phenomena as a means of dealing with separation in infancy, in childhood play, as well as in social and cultural experience emphasizes the *ongoing* nature of this process. The transitional *object* is a real object or possession, recognized as such but simultaneously invested with qualities of the self, so that it is both "me" and "not me," both "in here" and "out there." Yet in his efforts to explore "an intermediate area of *experiencing,* to which inner reality and external life both contribute," Winnicott defines transitional *phenomenon* as "an area that is not challenged, because no claim is made on its behalf except that it shall exist

[14]Modell, *Object Love and Reality,* 88, 60.
[15]MacMurray, *Persons in Relation,* 105.
[16]D. W. Winnicott, *Playing and Reality* (London: Tavistock, 1971), 11.

as a resting-place for the individual engaged in the perpetual human task of keeping inner and outer reality separate yet interrelated."[17] A play, then, is just such a transitional object for both author and audience, as Murray Schwartz reminds us.[18] And *Twelfth Night, or What You Will* presents itself as such by comparing its characters' inability to accept the separateness of others with its readers' need to project their own desires onto the play. Norman Holland concludes his analysis of projection in *Twelfth Night* with an analysis of projection onto *Twelfth Night*: "The business of the entertainer seems to be to give his audience an ambiguous thing on which they can project their desires and hungers and so be drawn in to the entertainment by their fancy."[19] Like Winnicott's mothering figure, *Twelfth Night* draws us in only to confront us with the consequences of our own desire. Like Toby, Andrew, Malvolio, Olivia, and Antonio, we too discover that that which is and what we will are distinct. Like Feste's song, *Twelfth Night* records the disillusionment experienced by the boy, the young man, the husband, and the old man alike.

Not surprisingly, psychoanalytic critics have discovered in *Twelfth Night* a variety of crises that attend any number of developmental stages charted by Erik Erikson.[20] So many different stages of

---

[17]Ibid., 2.

[18]Murray M. Schwartz first compared Shakespeare's play space to Winnicott's potential space between mother and infant; he analyzes the rupture of this space in Shakespeare's tragedies and its reconstitution in the romances in his "Shakespeare through Contemporary Psychoanalysis," *Hebrew University Studies in Literature* 5 (1977), 182–98, reprinted in *Representing Shakespeare: New Psychoanalytic Essays*, ed. Murray Schwartz and Coppélia Kahn (Baltimore: Johns Hopkins University Press, 1980), 21–32.

[19]Norman Holland, *The Shakespearean Imagination: A Critical Introduction* (Bloomington: Indiana University Press, 1964), 188. Holland's chapter on *Twelfth Night* is the most comprehensive treatment of projection in the play to date. See also David Willbern, "Paranoia, Criticism, and Malvolio," *Hartford Studies in Literature* 11 (1979), 1–23.

[20]See Erik Erikson, *Identity: Youth and Crisis* (New York: Norton, 1968). J. Dennis Huston first introduced the reading of Viola's experience in terms of an adolescent identity crisis in his essay, " 'When I Came to Man's Estate': *Twelfth Night* and Problems of Identity," *Modern Language Quarterly* 33 (1972), 274–88. In this schema, "newly acquired freedom, adventure in a realm formerly unknown, uncertain sexual identity with a tendency toward hermaphroditic . . . behavior, and experimentation with a variety of identifications" (283)—all play a major role. A year later Helene Moglen stressed the sexual component of Viola's adolescent "identity

separation and loss have been "uncovered" in this play—whether infancy or childhood, adolescence or adulthood—that these vying theories at least bear witness to the truth of Feste's closing song, "the rain it raineth every day" (5.1.392). *Twelfth Night* may never tell its grief, but critics have discovered in it at least six of the seven ages of man. The play has been championed as evidence of how the infant moves from illusions of omnipotence and fusion through disillusionment to an acceptance of separateness; how the preoedipal child begins to stand on its own as a result of further disillusionments and encouraged separations; how the child moves from a fantasized identification with parental roles to an acceptance of conscience at the resolution of the oedipal conflict; how the adolescent mourns its childhood relationship with its parents and acts out these losses in narcissistic love relationships; and how the young adult's experience of rejection in love and the mature adult's confrontation of death similarly involve the work of mourning.

For example, Coppélia Kahn accounts for the curious relationship between the identical twins by pointing to what Peter Blos terms "the transitory narcissistic stage of adolescence," which is "characterized by an overwhelming hunger for a love object of the same sex, in which the real identity of the object, the parent of the same sex, is denied."[21] According to Blos, the adolescent lets go of its parents through mourning, and employs the defensive strategy of identification common to the mourning process. But the identification, Kahn points out, is indirect; the adolescent actually seeks to merge "narcissistically with persons who can mirror him as that parent once did" and in so doing "recapitulates the symbiotic merger with the mother preceding separation and individuation." Kahn concludes that "the twin, as narcissistic mirror, represents the mother as the earliest, most rudimentary confirmation of the self."[22] According to

crisis" in "Disguise and Development: The Self and Society in *Twelfth Night*," *Literature and Psychology* 23 (1973), 13–20. Moglen analyzed Viola's disguise as "the objectification of conflict [which] allows her to act out her [sexual] ambivalence, and enables her ultimately to assume a role more appropriate to the demands of nature and society" (15). Perhaps the most useful of these analyses has been Coppélia Kahn, "The Providential Tempest and the Shakespearean Family," in *Representing Shakespeare*, ed. Schwartz and Kahn, 217–43.

[21]Peter Blos, *On Adolescence: A Psychoanalytic Interpretation* (New York: Free Press, 1962), as described by Kahn, "The Providential Tempest," 219.

[22]Kahn, "The Providential Tempest," 219, 222.

this reading we could address the mystery of Sebastian's identity by associating him with any one of the following: the betraying homosexual lover of an adult relationship (as in the sonnets and the Antonio-Sebastian relationship); the oedipal father whose place Viola unsuccessfully and only temporarily usurps; the maternal object against which one defines oneself; the maternal object with whom one experiences fusion and wholeness; one's childhood; the necessity of giving up a primary narcissism in the move toward sexual self-definition; and an "idealized" self who turns away from homosexual relationship toward decisive heterosexuality.

Rather than side with any one of these interpretations, we might explore how each of the characters in *Twelfth Night* is faced with the threat of abandonment, loss, or disillusion in relationship and is indeed *character*-ized by a particular means of responding to that threat. Orsino can gain no access to his beloved Olivia, yet chooses to fool himself with hopes rather than accept disillusionment. Olivia stops mourning the deaths of her father and brother only to engage in a fruitless battle for the heart of Viola-as-Cesario. Viola defers the mourning of her father and brother only to become the anonymous lover of the wholly preoccupied Orsino; mourning is replaced by pining, and desire remains unfulfilled. Sebastian, brother to Viola, mourns his sister's supposed death, while his companion, Antonio, pines for Sebastian and faces disillusionment when shut out from the love Sebastian so readily shares with Olivia.

The experience of being cut off from one's sustenance also threatens the subplot characters but with humorous results. First Feste and then Toby is threatened with no less than the withdrawal of Olivia's nurturance. Both shrug off her potential rejection—and its real financial consequences—with witty jests and instead replay the threat of withdrawn sustenance for others. Maria joins Toby in planning tricks that gull Andrew and Malvolio into the illusion that Olivia will "complete" them. The two enact the first part of Winnicott's game by encouraging others' false hopes; Viola and Feste play out the second part by providing others with a means of accepting the disillusionment that follows. Viola asks Orsino, "But if she cannot love you, sir?" (2.4.87), and in response to his "[I] cannot be so answer'd," she protests, "Sooth, but you must" (2.4.88). Viola counters Olivia's plaintive cry, "I would you were as I would have you be," with a skeptical "Would it be better, madam, than I am?"

(3.1.142–43). Feste meets others' needs for both illusion and disillusionment through songs that either deny mourning through fusion—"Then come kiss me sweet and twenty" (2.3.51)—or provide comfort in the form of disillusion—"Youth's a stuff will not endure" (2.3.52).

The characters in Olivia's house employ sharply delineated strategies for coping with loss and disillusionment. Olivia is the imperial-oedipal patron, both maternal figure and aristocratic lord, whose favor ensures economic and emotional well-being. Like Elizabeth, Olivia is the true double-man here; she is figured as mother and lord, mistress and king combined. Olivia determines who will be put to bed and when, who will be punished and when, who will have money and when. Fraternal rivalry for her affections or favor rules the plot—and her order rests, like Elizabeth's, on her taking one lower than herself in station.

As rivals dependent upon Olivia's protection, Toby, Feste, and Malvolio employ different survival strategies. Faced with eviction from Olivia's household, Toby misbehaves with a threatening reminder of their blood relationship, daring Olivia to forsake him while reenacting with Sir Andrew the parasitism of his own situation. Faced with the same threat, Feste chooses a more independent, if disillusioned route. He accepts separation at face value, acknowledges the degrading dependency of his untrustworthy situation, and offers a submissive cooperation that lacks authenticity. If Toby denies separation, maintaining parasitical relationships at the cost of delusion, Feste maintains awareness of delusion at the cost of intimate relationship. Feste has achieved the autonomy Toby lacks; he has left Olivia's household and survived. Yet he no longer trusts in appearances or words, and he makes a living through jests that confirm his disillusionment.

In contrast to Toby and Feste, Malvolio has yet to admit disillusionment. "The dev'l a puritan that he is, or any thing constantly but a time-pleaser," confides Maria, "an affection'd ass, that cons state without book, and utters it by great swarths; the best persuaded of himself, so cramm'd (as he thinks) with excellencies, that it is his grounds of faith that all that look on him love him" (2.3.147–52). For many readers, Malvolio's gulling constitutes the emotional center of the play, evoking both the complexity and the emotional depth of readers' experiences of loss and disillusionment. The scene plays upon the emotional disappointments of childhood and the equally harsh economic and professional losses of adulthood with which they may be confused. The betrayal of Malvolio encourages us to laugh off and yet reexperience anger at maternal rejection, as well as to celebrate the autonomy that derives from the acceptance of a rhythm of maternal withdrawal and return.

Viola emerges as the unsung heroine in such a reading, the only character in whom autonomy and relatedness join forces and in whom optimism, vitality, and faith in mutuality share pride of place with an acknowledgment of the realities of loss and disillusionment. Viola's response to the loss of her brother suggests what object-relations theorists term "trust in the reappearance of a good object": she continually affirms her faith in time, and she demonstrates the patience necessary to accept separateness and to expect mutuality. Yet the price she pays for her success is rarely acknowledged. In fact, Viola deals with loss through near-morbid overidentification, champions mutuality while withholding her own feelings, and develops clarity of vision through visual trickery and disguise. This heroine of mutuality survives by withholding, loves while refusing the role of beloved, and shares only when assured a mask of anonymity.[23] Viola's stance is a safe but suspicious compromise between the two extremes of denied and deluded love. Protected by her mask, Viola never tells her love and so never faces rejection; like Antonio, however, Viola is never acknowledged, nor is her love returned in kind. Confronted with the fulfillment of her wishes, Viola—and the play—hesitates; the negotiation of *her* return to relationship remains unsatisfactory.

At first glance *Twelfth Night* may appear to be an escapist comedy based on farcical confusions of identity. Yet the alternation of illusion and disillusionment suggests that deeper psychological work is going

---

[23]I here part company with critics who are more positive both about the conclusion of *Twelfth Night* and about its treatment of mutuality in general. Most useful among them is Marianne Novy, " 'And You Smile Not, He's Gagged': Mutuality in Shakespearean Comedy," *Philological Quarterly* 55 (1976), 178–94, rpt. in her *Love's Argument: Gender Relations in Shakespeare* (Chapel Hill: University of North Carolina Press, 1984). By the conclusion of the play, I see Viola neither as a troubled adolescent unwilling to accept her social role, as J. Dennis Huston would have it in " 'When I Came to Man's Estate,' " nor as a happy wife newly reconciled to her femininity, as Helene Moglen suggests in "Disguise and Development."

on in both the characters and the audience. When hate as well as love can be expressed, the work of accepting the separateness of others is also being accomplished. Mourning is acknowledged and ambivalence toward objects is admitted in the anger expressed by Orsino, Antonio, Viola, Olivia, Malvolio, and Toby as each comes to terms with disillusionment. Viola's usurpation of Sebastian's identity merges a fantasy of denying separation with a fantasy of oedipal displacement while enabling her to reject the rejecting maternal figure in turn. Yet despite this play of disillusionment, a deep resentment that cannot be fixed or resolved haunts this play. We may attempt to locate it in some unretrievable past—perhaps in Antonio's inability to forgive wrongs and return stolen goods from a long-ago sea battle. We may seek to locate it in the performance present—in Malvolio's inability to forgive those who tricked him so well. Or we may defer that moment, locating it precisely in the deferral of resolution, as in Viola's forestalled reconciliation with both Sebastian and Orsino.

What *Twelfth Night* leaves unfinished, undisclosed, or deliberately obscure has provided much occasion for critical speculation. In the final analysis, however, the reconciliations are withheld not from Orsino and Sebastian but from the audience. Although some critics are distrustful of forestalled reconciliations and annoyed at being excluded from them, the play encourages us to recognize that their emotional significance is, like so much else within the play, a private affair. We are encouraged, gently but firmly, to separate ourselves from the play. The answers to such questions as where Feste went, why Viola defers unveiling, who Sebastian is for Viola, or what the shipwreck or sea battles imply need not be sought so precisely. By leaving itself unfinished, by holding back what *it* will, the play derives depth and individuality, emphasizes its separateness from us, and questions our need to find completion in it. The decided and mature "otherness" of *Twelfth Night*, its gracious respect for privacy, is highlighted in Sebastian's response to Antonio: "But I perceive in you so excellent a touch of modesty, that you will not extort from me what I am willing to keep in" (2.1.12–14). *Twelfth Night* agrees to entertain us, but it reminds us that entertainment is a *profession* with very real limits. Of all Shakespeare's plays, this bittersweet comedy best conveys the sorrows and the pride that line the contours of that peculiar object, the individual.

III

Object-relations theory easily suggests an advance over both drive theory and interpersonal psychology. It differs from interpersonal psychology in that it takes into account the role of transitional objects, symbolic play, and internalized object relations in ego development. It differs from classical Freudian drive theory, which highlights repressed sexual or aggressive instincts, by stressing the internal and external object relations to which they are related. In practice, however, object-relations theory tends to elide the imaginary, representational basis of the ego and to reduce all conflict to the same issues of trust and autonomy which it always traces in the same way. The end result slights the crucial philosophical problems currently facing psychoanalysis in order to found a more experiential, existential interpersonal psychology, and lays out upon the basic grid of developmental psychology recurrent problems of loss and separation, autonomy and trust, as they structure infant-mothering interactions and later actions.[24]

Insofar as object-relations theory is basically identity theory, it is compatible with both ego psychology and New Criticism and highly useful to traditional character analysis. Whether we analyze the author's experiences as worked through in the fantasy of the text, the characters' developing experiences as they are worked out through plot and theme, or the reader's responses to the fantasy in the text as a relational conflict, we are still employing a character-oriented approach safely situated within the confines of ego psychology. Not surprisingly, then, object-relations theory may also be faulted for its failure to move beyond a model of fantasy and defense, of wish fulfillment and mastery.

Lacanian theory confronts object-relations theory with the very question that Plato raises in the *Symposium*.[25] According to the story told by Aristophanes, all human beings began as doubled; by separating us, Zeus led us to seek to unite with our other halves and so to face the trials of human individuality. In a hypothetical example, Aristophanes imagines Hephaestus addressing those lovers reunited

---

[24]See, for example, most of the essays in *Representing Shakespeare*, ed. Schwartz and Kahn.

[25]See especially Lacan, "Alienation," 205, and "From Love to Libido," 197–99, in *Four Fundamental Concepts*.

with their other halves. Hephaestus offers to use his tools to "melt and weld you together, so that, instead of two, you shall be one flesh; as long as you live you shall live a common life, and when you die, you shall suffer a common death, and be still one, not two, even in the next world. Would such a fate as this content you and satisfy your longing?" Aristophanes hastily concludes that it would: "We know what their answer would be; no one would refuse the offer; it would be plain that this is what everybody wants."[26] The renunciation of this fantasy in the acceptance of human individuality is the lesson of ego psychology which object-relations theorists preach. But the lesson is never accepted, the dream of fusion is never abandoned, and the gift of individuality is riddled with the memory of loss and desire.

Rather than deny the tremendous force of this fantasy, Lacan merely labels it as such, observing that it necessarily displaces and rereads a more primitive loss that results from our transcription in symbolic form. Lacan derives his theory from such works as "Negation," in which Freud suggests that it is only by expelling a part of itself that the subject as such is born.[27] Rather than negate the significance of object relations, Lacan stresses the means by which loss is written, re-membered, and so constituted by signifying systems, as in our inscription in a divisive gender system or in the representation of the body as one half of a complete unit. The simple act of saying or assuming "I" is not only based on "trust in the reappearance of a nurturing other" but on a fantasy of self-representation and a fantasy of the representation of the other as that which completes the self.

The instances of loss Lacan describes are less instances per se than rereadings of an origin without time or place. To attempt to chart on a developmental grid the series of lacks to which Lacan refers would obscure his attack on a theory of ego maturation and imply that there is a self that sustains losses as opposed to a self that is constructed through reference to loss. For example, Lacan hypothesizes a lack at birth from the mere fact that we reproduce and are subject to death. He refers to "the real, earlier lack, to be situated at the advent of the living being, that is to say, at sexed reproduction. The real lack is what the living being loses, that part of himself *qua* living being, in

[26]Plato, *Symposium*, trans. W. Hamilton (Harmondsworth, Eng.: Penguin, 1951), 63–64.
[27]Freud, "Negation" (1925), *SE*, 19:233–39.

208

reproducing himself through the way of sex. This lack is real because it relates to something real, namely, that the living being, by being subject to sex, has fallen under the blow of individual death."[28] For Lacan, the constitutive alienation that marks identity is recorded in the territorialization of the body, in the inscription and channeling of its libidinal zones. The loss here is a loss of full libidinal energy, a lack perceived and projected onto the *objet petit a*.

The *objets petits a* resemble Winnicott's transitional objects, yet differ in being more closely related to the drives themselves. Lacan speaks of a "pure life instinct" as "precisely what is subtracted from the living being by virtue of the fact that it is subject to the cycle of sexed reproduction. . . . The *objets a* are merely its representatives, its figures." The breast, for example, "represents that part of himself that the individual loses at birth, and which may serve to symbolize the most profound lost object."[29] What is desired there is something that is neither mother nor self-as-separate but a diffused self that the infant can never possess. The touch, voice, and look of the mother are experienced as the subject's missing complements. The desire for the *objet petit a* is therefore an impossible quest for completion based on this loss: "the subject is deprived of something of himself . . . which has . . . the value of that which binds him to the signifier. The phallus is our term for the signifier of his alienation in signification. When the subject is deprived of this signifier, a particular object becomes for him an object of desire." That which is lost is projected onto a given object, since "something becomes an object in desire when it takes the place of what by its very nature remains concealed from the subject: that self-sacrifice, that pound of flesh which is mortgaged [*engagé*] in his relationship to the signifier."[30]

For Lacan, then, the primary loss is not the splitting of the mother–infant dyad but the splitting of the subject as a result of being in symbolic form. The subject of Lacanian theory is not the stable, reliable ego of object-relations theory, which is capable of standing outside of what it sees in a relatively unproblematic relation to language and the unconscious. Rather, the subject is spoken; its

[28]Lacan, "Alienation," 205.
[29]Lacan, "From Love to Libido," 198.
[30]Lacan, "Desire and the Interpretation of Desire in *Hamlet*," in *Literature and Psychoanalysis*, ed. Felman, 28.

analysis requires a talking cure; it is divided and alienated as a function of being one. Lacan's reading of the *fort-da* game therefore draws upon an account of this game later added by Freud which includes a mirror. Freud relegates this version to a footnote because, he explains, it merely confirms the interpretations already offered. But does it? Here is the account:

> A further observation subsequently confirmed this interpretation fully. One day the child's mother had been away for several hours and on her return was met with the words 'Baby o-o-o-o!' which was at first incomprehensible. It soon turned out, however, that during this long period of solitude the child had found a method of making *himself* disappear. He had discovered his reflection in a full-length mirror which did not quite reach to the ground, so that by crouching down he could make his mirror-image 'gone.'[31]

For Lacan this reading suggests no less than Freud's confirmation of his theory of the mirror stage.[32] Freud's account confirms Lacan's suspicion that the mirror is always a part of the game of *fort-da*, and that this game is always enacting self-representation through a discovery of presence as predicated upon absence.

Lacan's rereading of Freud acknowledges its own status as a rereading and therefore seeks to repeat Freud's ideas with a difference. Lacan never rejects the reading that the *fort-da* game involves a working out of the loss of the mother: "When Freud grasps the repetition involved in the game played by his grandson, in the reiterated *fort-da*, he may indeed point out that the child makes up for the effect of his mother's disappearance by making himself the agent of it—but, this phenomenon is of secondary importance."[33] Even if the child associates his mother's absence with his playing at his own absence, the association in itself doesn't imply an effort to master maternal loss. Rather, it suggests a discovery of his own presence as predicated upon absence, and so a splitting that alone makes self-reference possible. "If the young subject can practise this game of *fort-da*," Lacan notes elsewhere, "it is precisely because he does not

[31]Freud, *Beyond the Pleasure Principle*, 15 n.
[32]Lacan, "The Mirror Stage," *Ecrits: A Selection*, trans. Alan Sheridan (New York: Norton, 1977), 1–7.
[33]Lacan, "Tuché and Automaton," 62.

practise it at all, for no subject can grasp this radical articulation. He practises it with the help of a small bobbin, that is to say, with the *objet a*. The function of the exercise with this object refers to an alienation, and not to some supposed mastery, which is difficult to imagine being increased in an endless repetition, whereas the endless repetition that is in question reveals the radical vacillation of the subject."[34] Lacan strings the fading of the real along the signifying chain through which the subject approaches it as absent. The entry into symbolization, the discovery of the unconscious, the casting out of the subject in order to assume the "I," the acquisition of language through which losses are retrieved and renewed—that is the game.

Consider: is the toy the mother, clearly differentiated from the subject who plays with the toy's/mother's comings and goings? Or is this to confuse the effects of the game (subject/object differentiation, symbolization) with the conditions upon which it is based? Again, Lacan protests: "This reel is not the mother reduced to a little ball by some magical game worthy of the Jivaros—it is a small part of the subject that detaches itself from him while still remaining his, still retained. This is the place to say . . . that man thinks with his object" and "that it is in the object to which the opposition is applied in act, the reel, that we must designate the subject. To this object we will later give the name it bears in the Lacanian algebra—the *petit a*."[35] The object, or reel, is also the subject; the infant is playing with a part of the self, playing at making the self/mother gone. The baby does not say, "Baby da" in seeing his mother; he does not seem to be connecting himself to his mother but to be playing with the relationship of parts of himself to each other, or playing at the idea of a stable entity named "baby." Rather than simply enjoying the image of himself in the mirror and identifying with it, the child is here finding himself as something that can be gone when reflecting mirrors are gone. The child is learning to play "gone" with himself, much as his mother would seem to be asking him to do. Rather than mastering the mother's absence, the child seems to be marveling at his own. *Twelfth Night* offers a caption for this reading when Feste responds to Viola's "I warrant thou art a merry fellow, and car'st for nothing" with the answer "Not so, sir. I do care for something; but in my

[34]Lacan, "Of the Subject Who Is Supposed to Know," 239.
[35]Lacan, "Tuché and Automaton," 62.

conscience, sir, I do not care for you. If that be to care for nothing, sir, I would it would make you invisible" (3.1.26–30).

Lacan maintains that the reel is the subject's object as missing complement and that the *fort-da* is a game of the subject with its parts. He concludes: "The activity as a whole symbolizes repetition, but not at all that of some need that might demand the return of the mother, and which would be expressed quite simply in a cry." Such play, of course, would entail a literal confusion of the ball with the mother, rather than a symbolic process. The play with transitional objects through which differentiation is achieved is more complex: "It is the repetition of the mother's departure as cause of a *Spaltung* in the subject—overcome by the alternating game, *fort-da*, which is a *here or there*, and whose aim, in its alternation, is simply that of being the *fort* of a *da*, and the *da* of a *fort*."[36] The infant is playing out not simply his need for the mother but his own capacity for symbolic activity. He finds himself split as a result of the going of the mother, split between himself as the object of the mother, the mother as the missing complement, and the player of games who creates these splits and then closes them up in symbolic form. In effect, the *fort-da* game is the discovery of drama, which needs no formal optical apparatus other than a single body playing out its losses and discoveries as mediated by the gaze.

Rather than reverse Freud's reading, Lacan's reading moves Freud's account of what does not go beyond the pleasure principle beyond itself. Rather than invalidate a theory of ego mastery, he *undermines* it by working at the level of the construction of the ego itself. Freud focuses on the work involved in the *fort-da* game, in particular the work done by the parents in gathering the toys and returning them to the child. He misses the joy of the game and cannot understand why the first part (*fort*) is repeated so many times without a concern for the return. Freud could not help but see the little boy working, working out his relations to his parents, and the parents working, working to unite the infant's split-off parts, but he thereby misses what is being played *out*. When the subject discovers her ability to be (gone) in different objects, she derives joy from the *fort-da* of the self, the fictional construction of the "I." The real pleasure here is what skips across the abyss and *yet* is I. The play is the play of *being loss*, of encountering that which can never be mastered.

[36]Ibid., 62–63.

The game therefore entails not only mastering loss but real-izing it, becoming (by splitting) what is lost and what is found, what is there and here, in toys and in games with words and with objects. The joy of the game lies in the mystery of that which cannot be solved, the gap that cannot be closed up. The self finds itself in meditating on its own otherness. If we can never stop—or master—the splitting of the *I* who meditates and the *I* upon which we meditate, we can play out their disjunction in a game of catching up which inevitably extends rather than closes up this distance. If the mother is the first object through which the child experiences this splitting—although "firsts" are as suspect as the ego itself—language is the place where this splitting is recorded, the deceptive mirror that recoups and re-presents those splits. The concept of deferral is crucial here, since the child is neither here nor there, but "child" is what gets played out here and there and so becomes neither here nor there. What Lacan terms the splitting of the subject in the moment of its procuring in language is realized retrospectively when the child plays at being gone only to find herself in the process as a split, speaking subject.

There is no self that is later symbolized, no mother that is later imagined as a little ball that can be lost. The rhythm of repression and representation follows a different logical schema, which recoups what was not seen before and sees it in its repetition. Freud's theory of *nachträglichkeit*, of the deferred trauma or *après coup*, was based on his discovery that in some cases it is less plausible to posit an originating trauma than to locate that trauma in its reconstruction. For example, a scene may have no significance at the time a child witnesses it but may later be associated with a traumatic event. The theory of the primal scene ultimately problematizes the concept of any originating trauma since the primal scene, like the dream, is always already the effect of unconscious reconstruction. The status of any scene becomes complicated insofar as the place of the scene per se does not exist apart from a chain of associations or traces of the past.[37] Even the scene of psychoanalysis cannot escape this problem, as Barbara Johnson well explains: "Psychoanalysis is in fact *itself* the primal scene it is seeking: it is the *first* occurrence of what has been repeating itself in the patient without ever having occurred. Psycho-

[37]Ned Lukacher, *Primal Scenes: Literature, Philosophy, Psychoanalysis* (Ithaca: Cornell University Press, 1986).

analysis is not itself the *interpretation* of repetition; it is the repetition of a *trauma of interpretation* . . . the traumatic deferred interpretation not *of* an event, but *as* an event which never took place as such."[38] Lacan attends to this problematic by acknowledging that whatever is experienced as lost must be found in the concept *loss* to be lost. Therefore it is only when the binary signifier *da* is added to the unary signifier *fort,* or only when the system of differences known as a language is called into play, that symbolization as such is possible and loss is *found.*

IV

To say that psychoanalysis is the impossible profession is to acknowledge the interminable stream of self-representations that are called into play when the subject tries to see itself from the place where it is not. To take the masks of the ego at face value, as does object-relations theory, is to fall prey to the very fictions that psycho-analysis would rethink rather than reify. To assume a fixed position in relation to a similarly stable and unified subject is to deny the role of perspective and representation in the construction of the ego, to deny the play of reflecting desires through which the ego is set up and its desire assumed. When Lacan says that "*the unconscious is the discourse of the Other,*" he refers to the fact that the subject's desire is turned upon her in such a way that she cannot assume it.[39] In placing the signifier over the subject; in identifying the unconscious as the discourse of the Other; in equating language, the symbolic order, and the Other, Lacan sets up a dialectic of desire in relationship to the signifier which is critical to psychoanalytic theory. Lacan's argument that a signifier represents a subject for another signifier assumes the fundamental problematic of desire as entangled in rivalry and representation.

Critics of *Twelfth Night* typically focus on the literal, physical confusions that result from the misidentification of one twin with the other or of one gender with another. Were the play of errors confined to physical identity, however, all problems would be resolved in-stantly with the announcement of Sebastian's presence. But *Twelfth*

[38]Johnson, "Frame of Reference," 499.
[39]Lacan, "Presence of the Analyst," *Four Fundamental Concepts,* 131.

Night postpones this happy conclusion. Viola proclaims: "If nothing lets to make us happy both / But this my masculine usurp'd attire, / Do not embrace me till each circumstance / Of place, time, fortune, do cohere and jump / That I am Viola" (5.1.249–53). Since Viola's clothes have been placed for safekeeping with a sea captain imprisoned at Malvolio's charge, and since Malvolio is notoriously unwilling to forgive anyone, such proof is unlikely to be forthcoming. The forestalled conclusion underscores the fact that the assurance Viola desires is unattainable. Regardless of "what we will," no circumstances can "cohere and jump" to prove us at one with ourselves.

Olivia may ask her supposed husband, "Hast thou forgot thyself?" (5.1.141), and Antonio may complain that Sebastian has treated him like "a twenty years removed thing" (5.1.89), but these mistakes of identity merely function as plot complications through which more complex misrecognitions are sustained. The misrecognitions that we cannot resolve are emphasized in the characters' references to themselves in the third person, in their uncanny awareness of a distance from themselves which they seek but fail to close up. Olivia asks Viola: "Have you any commission from your lord to negotiate with my face? You are now out of your text; but we will draw the curtain, and show you the picture. Look you, sir, such a one I was this present. Is't not well done?" (1.5.231–35). Antonio's query "How have you made division of yourself" (5.1.222) reminds us of the more complicated question of how a self can be constructed through division, and how one reconciles self-division and mutuality. When Orsino speaks of "One face, one voice, one habit, and two persons, / A natural perspective, that is and is not" (5.1.216–17), he is referring to the presence of twins; the doubling inherent in self-reflection, however, is less easily resolved. Insofar as Olivia, Orsino, Viola, and Feste continually refer to themselves as double, a more complex play of misrecognitions is at work. Viola informs Olivia, "I am not that I play" (1.5.184). She then asks Olivia, "Are you the lady of the house?" to which Olivia responds in kind: "If I do not usurp myself, I am" (1.5.184–86). Yet of course Olivia usurps herself endlessly, like a line of English kings, insofar as "she" is no more than a supplement in an endless series of substitutions.

Since *Twelfth Night* foregrounds gaps that cannot be closed but will not reveal and repeats our subordination to language in complex games of self-reference, it is an easy work in which to trace the play of the signifier.[40] A Lacanian reading need merely demonstrate how the characters play at representing themselves for others and how they either place themselves or are placed through the intrigues of others in relation to the displacing signifier of presence. *Twelfth Night* functions like a dramatic unfolding of Lacan's Schema L (figure 14), which charts the way in which the relationship of the unconscious subject (S) to its discourse in the Other of the symbolic order (O) is mediated by the fictional relationship of the ego (o) to the *objet petit a* (o'). The play keeps contrasting characters who acknowledge that they are not who they are with characters who seek to deny this fact through self-fashioning, idealization, and parasitism. It keeps bringing into dialogue characters who acknowledge how language prevents self-presence and characters who seek to deny this truth by presumptuous self-fashioning and masochistic flights of unrequited love. And it keeps returning us to the question of how an awareness of self-division can be reconciled with the quest for mutuality.

The activities of Orsino and Olivia function to strengthen the axis ego–*objet petit a*. Both characters send letters in order to procure objects of desire which they fail to understand as related to the missing parts of themselves. Although Orsino and Olivia recognize the same split in being that Feste and Viola do, they seek to close it up and employ two characteristic strategies to that end: idealized self-portrayal (ego reification) and obsessive romantic desire (love as self-completion). Both seek to control how they are perceived: Olivia stays inside and refuses to interact with others; Orsino tries to control his representation and passage in the letter by relying on messengers and thereby avoids any direct reflection of his image from an other. Obsessed with painting idealized images of himself, Orsino pays his servants to sustain his wavering moods through song and poetry. Malvolio's self-fashioning offers a comic example of the self-dramatizations in which Orsino and Olivia are involved, and his self-flattery is here directly related to the obsessive desire of Olivia and Orsino, the frantic gaiety of Toby and Andrew, and the hollowness registered by Viola and Feste. Each character attempts to deal with self-alienation in different ways.

---

[40]As does Geoffrey Hartman's "Shakespeare's Poetical Character in *Twelfth Night*," in *Shakespeare and the Question of Theory*, ed. Patricia Parker and Hartman (New York: Methuen, 1985), 37–53.

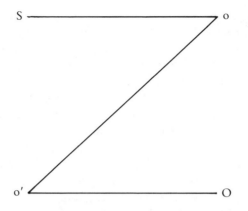

Figure 14. Lacan's Schema L, *Ecrits: A Selection*, trans. Alan Sheridan (New York: Norton, 1977), 193.

To set him (and us) straight, Malvolio is tossed a letter that consists of fragmented letters. The play of the signifier is forced into his face—the letter as definition of his desire—and yet he still cannot read it. Lacan himself tosses us a letter—the seminar on "The Purloined Letter"—but we have yet to consider the role of purloined letters in Shakespearean drama. In his analysis of desire in *Hamlet*, Lacan pays no attention to the play of the purloined letter, except to acknowledge that we find Hamlet "going about almost in a daze, breaking the seals of the message borne by Rosencrantz and Guildenstern, substituting almost automatically one message for another, and duplicating the royal seal with his father's ring."[41] Yet Maria also substitutes one letter for another when she addresses a letter from Olivia to Malvolio: "I will drop in his way some obscure epistles of love, wherein by the color of his beard, the shape of his leg, the manner of his gait . . . he shall find himself most feelingly personated. I can write very like my lady your niece; on a forgotten matter we can hardly make distinction of our hands" (2.3.155–61). Maria duplicates not a king's hand but her mistress's hand, and seals the letter not with the royal seal but with Olivia's seal of Lucrece. Editors of *Twelfth Night* usually remind us that Lucrece is a sign of chastity; given the play's interest in authentic signatures and purloined letters, however,

[41]Lacan, "Desire and the Interpretation of Desire in *Hamlet*," 24.

Lucrece would seem to signify rape and displacement as signature—
proof that one's name as well as one's desire is not one's own.

Every character may desire to become Olivia's desire but Maria
plays out the construction of that desire and transmits it to those who
would embody it. The problem, then, is not simply that there is an
absence in Olivia's house which all the hangers-on seek to fill, but that
there is an absence in that object Olivia which nothing can close up.
Similarly, there is an absence in that character called Malvolio, and it
results from the dispersal and procuring of subjectivity through the
signifying chain—from such letters as M, O, A, and even I. The self-
conscious textuality of *Twelfth Night* is evident even in its performance; its characters are floating signifiers, its subject *Hamlet*'s "words,
words, words" (2.2.192). Malvolio cries for ink, not for his lady.
Viola is a page, not a person. The characters refer to themselves as
dramatic characters, never failing to remind us that they are not who
they are. Rather than read M.O.A.I. as an anagram or as an abbrevia-
tion of the four elements, Lacan substitutes for the meaning of this
phrase the materiality of language itself.[42]

Both Feste and Viola seek to resituate the other characters in
relation to the inscription of their desire. Both emphasize how deceptive language can be, and both acknowledge their own entanglement
in words. Poets like Feste know how easily words change meanings:
"A sentence is but a chev'ril glove to a good wit. How quickly the
wrong side may be turn'd outward!" (3.1.11–13). Both Viola and
Feste seek to undermine the obsessive and futile letter writing around
them by showing others how they are both split and constituted by
the letter. Feste, for example, is wary of praise of his character. He
complains that friends "praise me, and make an ass of me. Now my
foes tell me plainly I am an ass; so that by my foes, sir, I profit in the
knowledge of myself, and by my friends I am abus'd (5.1.17–20).
Forced by a disguise to step outside of herself, Viola adopts a perspective from which she can refer to herself as another: "I am not
what I am" (3.1.141). Her physical disguise is only one aspect of her

---

[42]L. S. Cox offers the reading "I am O" in his essay, "The Riddle in *Twelfth
Night*," *Shakespeare Quarterly* 13 (1962), 360. In *The First Night of "Twelfth Night"*
(New York: Macmillan, 1954), Leslie Hotson reads the letter as follows: "*Mare*—sea,
Orbis—earth, *Aer*—air, *Ignis*—fire" (166), which J. M. Lothian and T. W. Craik
report and respond to in the Arden edition of *Twelfth Night* (London: Methuen, 1975)
as follows: "*Mare*—Sea [why not *Aqua*-Water? ed.], *Orbis*—Earth [why not *Terra*?
ed.]" (68 n. 109).

awareness that identity is a function of self-alienation and self-division. Consider her "history": "My father had a daughter lov'd a man / As it might be perhaps, were I a woman, / I should your lordship. . . . she never told her love, / But let concealment like a worm i'th'bud / Feed on her damask cheek; she pin'd in thought, / And with a green and yellow melancholy / She sate like Patience on a monument, / Smiling at grief" (2.4.107–9, 110–15). When we consider at how many removes Viola speaks, we mark the distance between a play like *The Comedy of Errors* and *Twelfth Night*.

Dialogue in *Twelfth Night* works through the interaction of these two types of characters. The following exchange is typical:

Olivia: Stay!
       I prithee tell me what thou think'st of me.
Viola: That you do think you are not what you are.
Olivia: If I think so, I think the same of you.
Viola: Then think you right: I am not what I am.
Olivia: I would you were as I would have you be.
Viola: Would it be better, madam, than I am?
       I wish it might, for now I am your fool.

(3.1.137–44)

If Olivia would be completed by Viola, Viola reveals that neither is who she thinks she is and undermines Olivia's game by exposing the masquerade. The result is a meditation on character which exemplifies Lacan's "conception of the function of the signifier able to demonstrate the place at which the subject is subordinated to it to the point of being virtually subverted."[43] And yet Viola's awareness of self-division is not one that she can reconcile with relationship any more than Lacan's thesis can be reconciled with object-relations theory. Most of the characters in *Twelfth Night* are unwilling to risk the drama of reflection by another's gaze, and Viola is no exception. Unable to risk revealing her love for Orsino, Viola chooses to hide behind the role of the masked and unacknowledged lover. Both Viola and Feste may acknowledge the play of the letter in their construction; yet neither can reconcile the truth of self-division with the need for mutuality.

[43]Lacan, "La direction de la cure et les principes de son pouvoir," *Ecrits*, 593.

V

The Lacanian reading falters at the same point that Feste errs in *Twelfth Night*. Like Feste, we are so aware of how words subvert and divide us that in always *recognizing* words as false, we err again. This amiable corrupter of words errs in mistaking Sebastian for Cesario. When Sebastian claims that he is not who Feste takes him to be, Feste misinterprets this statement as a philosophical argument. The clown who knows about dissemblance is himself taken in by the smooth blank sheet of Sebastian's face, upon which he projects Cesario's identity while seeming to guess at the ruse: "No, I do not know you, nor I am not sent to you by my lady, to bid you come speak with her, nor your name is not Master Cesario, nor this is not my nose neither: nothing that is so is so." The frustrated Sebastian wearily responds: "I prithee vent thy folly somewhere else" (4.1.5–10). Is there no avoiding the positions that Feste and Malvolio adopt? Must we either see the play as we will or mistrust it as not what it is? Is this what it means to be divided and (out)faced by the signifier?

The question of the letter remains: how not to hollow out *Twelfth Night* to make space for Lacan, how not to pass on the truth of our place as displacement? How can we beware of what Barbara Johnson terms "recognizing rather than reading"? If, as Johnson warns us, "recognition is a form of blindness, a form of violence to the otherness of the object," then "the theoretical frame of reference which governs recognition is a constitutive element in the blindness of any interpretative insight."[44] If we cannot help but recognize, like Malvolio, our image in the text, must we become "the trout that must be caught with tickling" (2.5.22)? Can we avoid the game of *We Three*, which portrays two fools and implicates the spectator as fool in the process? How can we avoid finding ourselves as displaced? *Twelfth Night, or What You Will* not only displaces us but informs us of our displacement as a result of reading it. Yet as we recognize our misrecognitions, how can we fail to *find* ourselves as erring? Does Lacan provide a way out by suggesting that we must recognize the near miss in our reading, the place where we cannot see ourselves?

The ease with which the phrase "I am not what I am" can be mapped at all points of the Schema L suggests that everything has a

[44]Johnson, "Frame of Reference," 492.

place, which is precisely why Derrida complains that Lacanian theory is reductive. What is most suspect is how easily we can perform a Lacanian reading of *Twelfth Night* and find in the play any number of Lacanian tenets: the constitutive splitting or alienation through which identity is procured; the ego as stand-in, supplement-at-the-source, or suturing of this gap; or desire as a repetition of the place of the split as the insistence of the letter. Lacan suggests that "the effect of interpretation is to isolate in the subject a kernel, a *kern* . . . of *non-sense*" and explains: "Interpretation is a signification that is not just any signification. It comes here in the place of the *s* and reverses the relation by which the signifier has the effect, in language, of the signified. It has the effect of bringing out an irreducible signifier." "What is essential," he claims, "is that he [the analysand] should see, beyond this signification, to what signifier—to what irreducible, traumatic, non-meaning—he is, as a subject, subjected."[45] But in that case, interpretation is always the same.

Since a diagram always already finds what it is looking for, a portrait may better help us to see what is always missing. Consider the portrait of *Sir Thomas Aston at the Deathbed of His Wife* by John Souch of Chester (figure 15). On the cross-staff Sir Thomas holds in his hand is, in Latin, the inscription: "The earth can be measured; grief is immeasurable." As if to prove the point, Sir Thomas appears to be leaning backward in an impossible, immeasurable perspective. Yet as he does so, he manages to occupy the same plane as his memory of his dead wife when she was alive. The portrait raises the question of how to figure immeasurable grief and equates it with the problem of how to encompass two contradictory perspectives. In question, then, is how we figure the relation of the past to its representation and how we measure that which escapes mapping. The fact of death, inscribed in memory, and the precise relation of that memory to the present cannot be so easily inscribed.

By focusing on the scene of writing in *Beyond the Pleasure Principle*, Derrida offers a different way of returning to this problem:

> The *fort:da* scene . . . is always in the process of describing, in advance, the scene of its own description. . . . it is no longer a matter of the

[45]Lacan, "From Interpretation to the Transference," *Four Fundamental Concepts*, 250–51.

Figure 15. John Souch of Chester, *Sir Thomas Aston at the Deathbed of His Wife* (ca. 1635), oil on canvas. Courtesy of the Manchester City Art Galleries.

dispatching that renders this or that absent and then of the bringing near that renders this or that present; it is a matter of the distance of what is far away and the nearness of what is nearby, the absence of what is absent or the presence of what is present. Freud recalls—his memories and himself. . . . And above all, what mirrors seem to offer is not, as is

222

often believed, merely getting back what is one's own, any more than in the case of the *da*. . . . *Beyond the Pleasure Principle* is thus not an *example* of what we believe we already know under the name of auto-biography. It writes the autobiographical. . . . A "domain" opens up in which the "inscription" of a subject in his text is also the necessary condition for the pertinence and performance of a text.[46]

Rather than seek to prove the truth of language, Derrida keeps playing at the scene of writing. Since Freud ends up repeating the theory that he aims to disprove rather than moving beyond it, Derrida reads *Beyond the Pleasure Principle* as Freud's own game of *fort-da* with contradictory evidence, which he brings close to him and then, like a child throwing away a toy, manages to "make gone" (*fort*) as well. He argues that Freud's revisions of this work suggest a theory of repetition compulsion widely at variance with the theory of repetition as wish fulfillment or mastery. Further, if Freud began work on this strange text in March 1919, he completed it in May 1919, the same month that he completed the theory of repetition entitled "The 'Uncanny.'" One year later, Freud returned to his text, revising the work in July 1920, even then uncertain that he ever could move "beyond the pleasure principle." Whereas Freud's use of the *fort-da* story is ostensibly designed to illustrate a theory of repetition which moves beyond the pleasure principle, it finally illustrates the earlier theory of repetition which remains safely within its confines at the level of content, and it moves beyond that theory only at the level of the scene of its writing. After completing *Beyond the Pleasure Principle*, Freud began work on "Supplement to the Theory of Dreams," a paper delivered in the same month of that year to the International Psycho-Analytical Congress. In that essay he continued to assert that punishment dreams as well as other anxiety dreams safely fall under the category of wish fulfillments.

Beyond the Pleasure Principle is also the site of Freud's outrageous hypothesis that death is not a natural phenomenon but further evidence of the strength of wish fulfillments. This hypothesis comes as less of a surprise in the context of Freud's many declarations concerning his refusal or inability to mourn. His response to the death of his daughter, the mother in the *fort-da* story, is typical in this regard.

---

[46]Derrida, "Coming into One's Own," 134–35.

With a flippancy more characteristic of *The Importance of Being Earnest*, Freud responds: "The loss of a child seems to be a grave blow to one's narcissism; as for mourning, that will probably come only later."[47] Freud later adds a note describing Ernst as equally inept at mourning: "When this child was five and three-quarters, his mother died. Now that she was really 'gone' . . . the little boy showed no signs of grief. It is true that in the interval a second child had been born and had roused him to violent jealousy."[48] Since Freud's younger brother died when Freud was five, it is possible that Freud was projecting his own feelings of jealousy onto his grandson Ernst.[49]

The scene of writing provides yet another way of figuring the relation between *Twelfth Night* and *Beyond the Pleasure Principle*. Both texts describe a denial of death and a refusal to mourn at the level of content, and both employ repetition as a fantasied return at the level of style. As a crossroads for psychoanalysis, *Beyond the Pleasure Principle* is a curiously liminal text; it shows Freud unable or unwilling to accept evidence that subverts his theories of wish fulfillment and ego mastery, evidence that will prove decisive for resituating psychoanalysis on a tragic level. *Twelfth Night* also refuses to admit evidence that proves decisive for moving Shakespearean drama in the direction of the tragedies. Lacan correctly observes that *Hamlet* is about interrupted mourning.[50] But *Twelfth Night* stages the interruption of mourning from a comic perspective, compulsively repeating comic plots and themes as a way of denying death. *Twelfth Night* is not only the last of Shakespeare's romantic comedies but, as

[47]Freud, in a letter to Oscar Pfister dated 27 January 1920, as quoted in Max Schur, *Freud: Living and Dying* (New York: International Universities Press, 1972), 330, and as translated and quoted by Derrida in "Coming into One's Own," 142. Derrida reminds us that Sophie died in January 1920 and that within the space of two weeks Freud wrote to Sandor Ferenczi of "the feeling of a deep, irreparable blow to my narcissism" (141)—trans. modified by Derrida from Ernest Jones, *The Life and Works of Sigmund Freud*, 3 vols. (New York: Basic Books, 1953–57), 3:40–41.

[48]Freud, *Beyond the Pleasure Principle*, 16 n. 1.

[49]Freud writes to Oscar Pfister that "Sophie leaves behind two boys, one aged six and the other thirteen months [the one Ernst was jealous of, as he was of his father]"—as edited here by Derrida in "Coming into One's Own," 142.

[50]In "Desire and the Interpretation of Desire in *Hamlet*," Lacan studies the role of "insufficient mourning" in *Hamlet* and observes that "in all the instances of mourning in *Hamlet*, one element is always present: the rites have been cut short and performed in secret" (39, 40).

its title suggests, self-consciously situated as the last. Both titles remind us of their liminal status: Freud peers over the precipice as if trying but unable to move beyond it, whereas Shakespeare tries to forget what he knows is on the other side. Like *Beyond the Pleasure Principle*, *Twelfth Night* recapitulates earlier work and serves as a site for its repetition.

Twelfth Night is not only a performance script; it self-consciously stages its own repetition as ritual performance. Its fondness for ritual repetition is evidenced by the characters' interest in repeating a song just as it was sung, as in: "That strain again, it had a dying fall; / . . . Enough, no more, / 'Tis not so sweet now as it was before" (1.1.4, 7–8). Or: "Now, good Cesario, but that piece of song, / That old and antique song we heard last night" (2.4.2–3). Or again: "O fellow, come, the song we had last night" (2.4.42). *Twelfth Night* even refers to its performance as an uncanny doubling: "If this were play'd upon a stage now, I could condemn it as an improbable fiction" (3.4.127–28).

At the simplest level, *Twelfth Night* foregrounds a number of prosaic, literal returns. The play figures physical, visual, and auditory doubling through identical twins, identical "handwritings," and identical voices. It repeats "catches" that fail to catch up with themselves, and recalls sad old ballads to keep loss alive. It asks such questions as who can leave Illyria and who can return. Why has Feste left? Can he return? Why can't Toby leave? What is the cost of Antonio's return? What are the implications of Sebastian's return? If Sebastian returns, must Viola leave? Is there any way to stay without displacing someone else or any way to leave that allows one to return? Repetition in time is also figured as a return—whether in the sea's tide or in the flow of object relations as a similar rhythm of withdrawal and return. Finally, *Twelfth Night* is concerned with psychological acts of repetition, whether in the form of repetition compulsion, identification with the aggressor, or transference. By staging its writing and performance, presentation and representation, *Twelfth Night* is always in search of, yet unable to re-cover, itself, to catch up with the losses that occasion its namings.

Twelfth Night is not only a pastiche of experiences of loss but a study of the more complex problem of *recording* and *presenting* loss. The comic theme of surviving in the face of loss is here complicated by the ideas of surviving as constituted by loss and of surviving loss as a repetition or incorporation. The last stanza of the song "On the First Day of Christmas" derives the twelfth day by repeating the previous eleven. The twelfth night, hollowed out as a space where the preceding eleven live, exemplifies the deferral of that revelation known as the Epiphany. The twelfth night of Christmas also marks the last night of a repetitive ritual, or the close of repetition which is death. Re-presentation is thus figured as a performing of loss which attempts to resurrect or make present that which is gone, a performance that, through words, music, and masks, weaves a presence from repeated traces of absence.

The guilt of the survivor syndrome permeates *Twelfth Night*: "Perchance he is not drown'd— / what think you, sailors?" Viola asks, to which the Captain responds: "It is perchance that you yourself were saved" (1.2.5–6). The subtexts of the survivor syndrome, so prominent throughout *Twelfth Night*, include such events in Shakespeare's life as the mourning of his sisters and the death of his own son, Hamnet.[51] William Shakespeare was the eldest son of John Shakespeare and Mary Arden, but he was not their first child. One year before his birth the Shakespeare family could be found at the burial grounds, mourning their infant daughter Margaret (1562–1563); four years before, they had buried their first daughter, Joan (1558–ca. 1559–60). In view of the high infant mortality rates in Elizabethan times and in the Shakespeare family, there must have been strong pressure to abandon mourning and to seize the day.[52] At

[51] W. Nicholas Knight, "Shakespeare's Mourning for His Son in *Twelfth Night*," presented at the 1984 Shakespeare Association Seminar on the play, is an excellent treatment of this subject.

[52] In *The Family, Sex, and Marriage in England, 1500–1800*, abridged ed. (New York: Harper and Row, 1979), Lawrence Stone observes: "The most striking feature which distinguished the Early Modern family from that of today does not concern either marriage or birth; it was the constant presence of death. Death was at the centre of life, as the cemetery was at the centre of the village. Death was a normal occurrence in persons of all ages, and was not something that happened mainly to the old" (54). After observing that in the seventeenth century the average age at death was thirty-two and that "between a quarter and a third of all children of English peers and peasants were dead before they reached the age of fifteen" (55), Stone concludes that "to preserve their mental stability, parents were obliged to limit the degree of their psychological involvement with their infant children. . . . Nothing better illustrates the resigned acceptance of the expendability of children than the medieval practice of

the age of fourteen, Shakespeare would have watched his parents bury their fourth daughter, Anne, age eight. Like Viola, William was all the daughters if not all the sons of his father. Like her, too, he carried the burden of his dead siblings on his shoulders, as if his survival could make up for their loss.

The guilt and responsibility that accompany survival function as a viable biographical source of *Twelfth Night*. Compounding the survivor syndrome here is its repetition in Shakespeare's adult life, when the guilt of surviving a sibling may well have been complicated by the guilt of surviving a child. Shakespeare was a father of twins— Judith and Hamnet—and his son Hamnet died at age eleven. Like her father, and like Viola, Judith was the image of her dead sibling, the place where loss was recorded and preserved. Like them, Judith had to respond to the question regarding the loss of a sibling—"Perchance he is gone?" with the answer, "Perchance I was saved."

Given a play that dances jigs on coffins and flirts in black, we are emboldened to ask how it is that the other comedies "live" in *Twelfth Night* and how the phenomenon known as identification through incorporation operates here. We are encouraged to consider how a play can mourn and mark the absence of those that precede it. We wonder if Shakespeare was a mark for his parents to represent his siblings Joan and Margaret. We wonder if his persona as everyone and no one, his fascination with making others live on in him and through him is not unrelated here. We wonder how Shakespeare's parents could name their fifth child Joan without feeling that they were resurrecting their first, or how Shakespeare could fail to mourn his son Hamnet in Hamnet's living twin, Judith. Finally, we begin to wonder how theatrical representation, so tied to a rhetoric of presence, works through recording or repeating loss. As both Freudian and Shakespearean texts play out a game of *fort-da*, both end up trapped in the very web of desire, loss, and repetition they would untangle. Both seek to analyze repetition in relation to objects they cannot seem to get hold of, move beyond, or leave alone. *Twelfth Night* not only incorporates the earlier comedies but hollows itself

---

giving the same name to two living siblings in the expectation that only one would survive. The sixteenth-, seventeenth- and early eighteenth-century practice of giving a new-born child the same name as one who had recently died indicates a lack of sense that the child was a unique being, with its own name" (57).

227

out to keep them alive, much as Viola hollows out her personality to keep her lost brother alive, much as we hollow out literary texts and fill them with theory to keep them alive.

VI

Ideally, we would conclude by exposing the critic's desire to purloin the letter, but what letter do we exchange for the letter we identify as the critic's desire? The critic's desire is a series of desires, not unrelated to those of Orsino and Olivia, Toby and Andrew, Viola and Feste. Like them, we employ an object (literature) parasitically in order to complete ourselves, to define ourselves, to idealize the other and so ourselves, to set up oedipal dramas we can win through claims of truth and mastery. But how can we read otherwise? Further, how can we repeat these readings without seeking to master them?

The readings we have explored may be summarized simply. First, object-relations theorists read the author's (or character's or reader's) desire, and seek to prove that drives cannot be separated from object relations, whether external or internalized. Lacan in turn criticizes early object-relations theorists for being oblivious, in their desire for completion by the other, to the impossibility of self-completion by the letter. Finally, Derrida criticizes Lacan for employing literature to locate and complete psychoanalysis: "Literary writing, here, is brought into an *illustrative* position" and the "text is in the service of the truth, and of a truth that is taught." Derrida adds: "The displacement of the signifier, therefore, is analyzed as a signified, as the recounted object of a short story." The "truth" of psychoanalysis which Lacan finds is the very problematic of representation that literature pronounces. Therefore, the discovery of the purloined letter as the *objet a* suggests a psychoanalysis that completes itself through that recovery, a psychoanalysis that refuses to admit that there is always another crumpled letter to take the place of the first one. Derrida explains: "There is missing here an elaboration of the problem of the frame, the signature, and the *parergon*. This lack permits the scene of the signifier to be reconstructed into a signified . . . permits writing to be reconstructed into the written, the text into discourse, and more precisely into an 'intersubjective' dialogue."[53] Derrida criticizes Lacan for closing the play of meaning by always finding a theory of loss in the letter and so resuscitating the specular name of literature as the transcendental signified. But what is the alternative?

Barbara Johnson intervenes, asking pointedly: "If Derrida criticizes Lacan for making the 'signifier' into the story's *signified*, is Derrida not here transforming 'writing' into 'the written' in much the same way?" "Derrida, by filling in what *Lacan* left blank," she adds, "is repeating precisely the gesture of blank-filling for which he is criticizing Lacan." "While thus criticizing the *hypostasis* of a lack—the letter as the *substance* of an absence—(which is not what Lacan is saying)," Johnson continues, "Derrida is *illustrating* what Lacan *is* saying about *both* the materiality *and* the localizability of the signifier *as the mark of difference* by operating *on* the letter as a material locus of differentiation." How are we to avoid the undeniably repetitive and parasitical aspects of the scene of writing? In reframing Lacan, Johnson observes, Derrida necessarily repeats Lacan's mistakes: "According to Derrida, at the very moment Lacan is reading the story as an allegory of the signifier, he is being blind to the disseminating power of the signifier in the *text* of the allegory, in what Derrida calls the 'scene of writing.' . . . Therefore it is all the more noticeable that Derrida's own reading of Lacan's text repeats precisely the crimes of which he accuses it." Yet how is one to conclude? Johnson reasons "otherwise": "But the question of the seemingly inevitable slipping from the signifier to the signified still remains. And it remains not as an *objection* to the logic of the frame, but as its fundamental *question*. For if the 'paradoxes of parergonal logic' are such that the frame is always being framed by part of its contents, it is precisely this slippage between signifier and signified—which is *acted out* by both Derrida and Lacan against their intentions—which best illustrates those paradoxes."[54]

If Johnson is right, then she is framed by what she frames as well. For example, she adds: "The fact that the debate proliferates around a *crime* story—a robbery and its undoing—can hardly be an accident. Somewhere in each of these texts, the economy of justice cannot be

---

[53]Derrida, "Le facteur de la vérité," *The Post Card*, 426, 428, 432.
[54]Johnson, "Frame of Reference," 484, 464, 495, 465, 484–85.

avoided. For in spite of the absence of mastery, there is no lack of *effects of power.*"[55] By concentrating on the effects of power, Johnson addresses a point that fails to make its way back into her argument: from a feminist standpoint, "The Purloined Letter" is a narrative that assumes, in advance, that the queen is not only guilty but sexually guilty. Since her sexual guilt must be inferred from the story and is not the only plausible reading, Johnson unwittingly repeats a sexist assumption and so is also guilty of "recognizing" rather than "reading."

That critics are necessarily framed by the terms of their argument does not, however, simply return them to that argument. Rather, in repeating what we would deny, we can trace a difference. Johnson is aware that she is framed by what she describes, just as Derrida is aware that he is framed by Lacan when he writes about him. But is Lacan aware of how he is framed? By transferring the problem of representation from content to style, Lacan manages to evade the mastery he claims for his theories. He answers Derrida's critique by demonstrating that writing and reading can never stand for or in the place of any given truth pronounced from a position of mastery outside them. Literature can never simply function as an allegory of the truth of psychoanalysis. Literature is not the truth of the person or of writing, of the signified or of the signifier; rather, it is the game of *fort-da* in which each is found in and resists being found out by the other.

For Lacan, this otherness emerges in the peculiar form of repetition known as the analytic transference, in which the analysand projects a primary relationship onto the analyst. Lacan describes the transference as a repetition that differs from itself, that misses in the right ways; he thus claims: "The function of missing lies at the centre of analytic repetition."[56] He explains: "If the transference is only repetition, it will always be repetition of the same missed encounter. If the transference is supposed, through this repetition, to restore the continuity of a history, it will do so only by reviving a relation that is, of its nature, syncopated. We see, then, that the transference, as operating mode, cannot be satisfied with being confused with the efficacity of repetition, with the restoration of what is concealed in

---

[55]Ibid., 458.
[56]Lacan, "Presence of the Analyst," 128.

230

the unconscious, even with the catharsis of the unconscious elements." Accordingly, the transference is evidence of the reality of the unconscious, not of the progress of therapy: "What is certain is that the transference is one thing, the therapeutic end another. Nor is the transference to be confused with a mere means."[57] Whereas Freud reads repetition as a form of mastery over the abyss, Lacan reads it as a missed encounter that can only speak of where we are not.

Repeating things in another way is at the core of the transference, in which one compulsively repeats in order not to face one's desire but to defer the repressed—to talk and talk while saying nothing, smiling at grief. Dialogue in *Twelfth Night* proceeds almost analytically, so that the characters always get their reactions returned to them in a way that places them in a different relationship to their desire. When various characters complain to Viola, for example, she helps them hear themselves differently and asks questions that move them beyond what they have said to what they have not. In the same manner, one can write on and about *Twelfth Night* more than once and each time hear the play, or one's responses to it, differently. Just as the presence of the analyst suggests to the analysand the presence of the unconscious, so this play evokes the place where we are not.

Despite its focus on repression, on doubles, on the compulsion to repeat, *Twelfth Night* is canny rather than uncanny, precisely because it assumes both a gap and a letter that covers it. It brings the cold otherness of the gap into the field of desire and forces us to see it as our own. *Twelfth Night* not only places us in a position of inevitable delusion, but forces us to confront the desire to own the place of our look. By both encouraging and mocking inappropriate projections onto it, *Twelfth Night* finally stages and so resists transference. Whereas the play stages doubling as a compulsive warding off through automatic repetition or incorporation to avoid loss, it also figures doubling as a return with a difference, a repetition that hears the first because it is in another place.

Rather than attempt, as does *The Comedy of Errors*, to re-cover what has been lost in time, *Twelfth Night* seeks to find one self in relation to loss as other. Deferral and distance, masks and performances forge a space between past and present, present and future, to expel ghosts or to render their return less uncanny. Marking time

---

[57]Lacan, "Analysis and Truth," *Four Fundamental Concepts*, 143, 145.

until Viola can be revealed, the play is concerned with what that entails. We are not really waiting for Sebastian's return, nor are we anticipating Viola's self-discovery. Rather, in marking (the) time we are working out the repetition involved in (Viola's) self-representation, and in that form of (mis)identification known as character. Lacan notes of the unconscious: "Its essence is to mark that time by which, from the fact of being born with the signifier, the subject is born divided."[58]

Derrida criticizes Lacan for reading literature as an allegory of the desire for completion by the other and for failing to recognize how his own desire is implicated in the reading he performs. He claims that Lacan stalls the play of meaning by always writing on that blank piece of paper the letters of Freud's name. Yet if Lacan uses the purloined letter to demonstrate that literature proves the truth of psychoanalysis, Derrida employs the same letter to demonstrate that, like literature, psychoanalysis can never claim a position of mastery but undoes itself and so is never on its own. Moreover, Lacan's poetic style allows him to convey the endless disruption and displacement that he denies at the level of content. Lacan's role as a poet or corrupter of words is as much a part of the letter he would deliver as a factual account of his theory. If Lacan seeks truth, he seeks a truth that he can never name. If he keeps finding our subjection to the signifier, he finds it in different ways, as we do, in different texts. Moreover, if Derrida seeks the textuality of experience, he would appear, despite claims to the contrary, to employ the *mise en abyme* as if it offered a final, inescapable truth: "I have never wanted to abuse the abyss, nor, above all, the *mise 'en abyme,'*" he protests apologetically.[59]

Lacan identifies the problem of reading as transference when he identifies a theory based on a loss of the other and a theory based on loss in signification as two points on the triangle that constitutes the scene of transference. These two points are the two glances described in his reading of "The Purloined Letter"—the look of the prefect, who cannot see the letter, and the look of the queen, whose desire is either to hide it or to find completion through its (re)possession. The first point is illustrated by Malvolio's self-love ("it is his grounds of faith that all that look on him love him")—which is the position of a

[58]Lacan, "From Love to Libido," 199.
[59]Derrida, "Freud's Legacy," *The Post Card*, 304.

232

man who will soon be crying out for pen and ink. The second point is depicted in Orsino's insatiable and destructive longing ("But if she cannot love you sir? [I] cannot be so answered")—which is the point of obsessive letter writing and reading. These points can be located in the transference as it functions within literary and psychoanalytic theory. Lacan explains:

> I mean that the operation and manipulation of the transference are to be regulated in a way that maintains a distance between the point at which the subject sees himself as lovable—and that other point where the subject sees himself caused as a lack by *a*, and where *a* fills the gap constituted by the inaugural division of the subject. The *petit a* never crosses this gap. . . . This *a* is presented precisely, in the field of the mirage of the narcissistic function of desire, as the object that cannot be swallowed, as it were, which remains stuck in the gullet of the signifier. It is at this point of lack that the subject has to recognize himself.[60]

Reading (analysis) must maintain a distance between these two points as well. The place of the critic's desire is suggested by the first reading of *Twelfth Night*, which denied our construction in signification, denied the process of reading and interpretation, and took the characters as mirror images of ourselves. Both Lacanian and Derridean readings mark the second point when they turn a theory of loss-in-the-letter or a theory of subversion by the scene of writing into a truth that completes the text at hand, a truth whereby psychoanalysis finds itself in literature, or philosophy finds itself in literature. The reader must, therefore, maintain a strict distance between these two different points. In question is whether we can theorize a place outside these points or whether we can continually displace and defer the fulfillment of our own desire.

Twelfth Night holds out as the salve the subject's recognition of itself as split by the letter or *objet a*, as in the statement "I am not who I am." This is the point of ironic wordplay, the ideal position of the messenger who knows how letters appear and disappear, who carries the "truth" of the letter's subversion of the subject. But to fully identify with this character is to deny the level at which literary characters operate. If it is at this point of lack that the subject has to

---

[60]Lacan, "In You More than You," *Four Fundamental Concepts*, 270.

recognize herself, this recognition must be a misrecognition, a repetition that succeeds by missing the mark. The role of the enigmatic *objet petit a* assumes paramount importance here and returns us to the problematic with which we began, to that which is caught in the gullet of the signifier, what Lacan would term the insistence of the letter or what *Twelfth Night* speaks of as "the tongue of loss" (5.1.58).

If these three moments are points on the triangle of that transference known as literary criticism, what is the desire of the literary critic? Is our self-recognition tantamount to an acquiescence in our own subversion? To read theory as an allegory of the desire of theory is yet another means of deferring through repetition the foreclosure of the critic's desire. But how long can this throat clearing in the face of the unary signifier continue? Moreover, if we ever do separate out the participants in this curious game of *fort-da*, what will be resuscitated when we succeed in being made gone by it? In question, as Joel Fineman suggests, is the desire of the critic:

> But criticism, whose things are not words but the meanings of words, meanings forever foreclosed by words, will find in silence only the impetus for further speech and further longing, which it will thereupon thematize as its own responsibility for the loss of meaning. Whereas a poem can be closed poetically even by a gesture of self-abandon, criticism, discovering the futility of its pro-ject, can only go on and on, frustratingly repeating its own frustration, increasingly obsessed with its own sense of sin—unless, of course, in the psychoanalytic sense, it projects its own critical unhappiness onto literature, whose self-deconstructions would then be understood as criticism.[61]

The current fad of playing gone with the text in its retelling betrays the critic's desire to turn literature into truth by rediscovering it as philosophy or psychoanalysis. We therefore find ourselves engaged in an interminable mourning that, having renounced its object, cannot bear to renounce its desire.

What we desire in our play with theater is not to master hidden places but to keep the game going, to play with loss as that which cannot be mastered. And so we return to our beginning: "In a field / I

[61]Joel Fineman, "The Structure of Allegorical Desire," in *Allegory and Representation*, ed. Stephen Greenblatt (1981; rpt. Baltimore: Johns Hopkins University Press, 1986), 50.

am the absence / of field. / This is / always the case. / Wherever I am /
I am what is missing. / . . . We all have reasons / for moving. / I
move / to keep things whole."[62] Our passage through language can
never be mastered; we can neither step outside of it nor become
synonymous with it. The disjunction we experience alone permits
play and residence. Our mourning can never be completed, our
losses closed up. And it may be that through our play with literature
we attempt to restore the fullness of language that we distort by
passing through it. As we move through language we seek to trace
that passage in a way that preserves its mystery and allows for empty
spaces to be on the move. Perhaps this language of desire is the desire
of literature? And perhaps it is true that an "analysis terminates only
when the patient realizes it could go on for ever."[63]

[62]Mark Strand, "Keeping Things Whole," *Reasons for Moving: Poems* (New
York: Atheneum, 1968), 40.
[63]Hans Sachs, quoted in Anthony Wilden, "Lacan and the Discourse of the
Other," in Jacques Lacan, *Speech and Language in Psychoanalysis*, trans. with notes and
commentary by Anthony Wilden (Baltimore: Johns Hopkins University Press,
1968), 311. See also Freud, "Analysis Terminable and Interminable" (1937), *SE*,
23:209–53.

Index

237

Index

Index

Kamuf, Peggy, 153
Kaplan, E. Ann, 117n
Kavanagh, James, 156
Keppler, C. F., 90n
Kerrigan, William, 36n, 196
Knight, W. Nicholas, 226n
Knowing unknowingness: in deconstruction, 43, 47–48, 157, 175, 190–91; in delusional belief, 78; in film vs. theater, 66–70; and learned ignorance, 11, 15–16, 41; vs. myth of not-knowing, 112, 157, 190–91; psychoanalysis as study of, 37–43, 174–75; in Shakespearean comedy, 10, 80–81, 112, 172, 189–91; and theater, 6, 41–43, 56, 74–77; in the uncanny, 80–84, 112–13
Kristeva, Julia, 116

Lacan, Jacques, 3, 7, 19, 30–35, 39–42, 52–66, 69–78, 110–11, 116, 127–28, 130, 135–38, 149–50, 158, 174, 190–98, 207–21, 224, 228–33; analyst's presence and position, 40, 231; analytic dialogue and Socratic dialogue, 39–42; analytic transference, 230–34; attacks on Cartesian *cogito* in, 61; attacks on object-relations theory in, 135–37, 150, 207–14; binary vs. unitary signifier, 214, 234; on castration, 138–39, 148–50; critique of as framed by what it frames, 136–38, 230; critique of by Derrida, 221, 228–29, 232; cultural-materialist attack on, 138, 158; of deferred vision or *après coup* in, 53, 60, 213; drives, invocatory and scopic, 50n; *fort-da* game and critique of repetition as mastery, 59, 208–13; gaze, 1, 40, 52, 61–66, 76–77; gender ideology in, 116–17, 127–31, 135–38, 148–50, 158; identification (primary vs. secondary) in, 32–35; imaginary and symbolic orders in, 57–60, 135–36; *jouissance,* 58–59; *méconnaissance,* 53; Maurice Merleau-Ponty and, 61–66; mirror stage, 31–33, 52–54; myth of non-knowledge, 190–91; object a (*objet a, objet petit a*), 54, 64–65, 208–11, 216, 233; other vs. Other, 53–54, 214; paternal metaphor and name of the father, 135–37; phallus, 116–17, 129–30; schema L, 216–17; sexuality and signification, 127–30; *spaltung* (splitting of subject), 53, 209, 212–13, 218; struc-

tural anthropology and, 130, 135–36, 158; subjectivity and signification, 208–9, 213, 218–19; subject supposed to know, 42; subversion of subject by signifier, 219; suture, 55n; unconscious, 137–39, 214, 232
Works: "Agency of the Letter in the Unconscious," 72, 110, 127–28; "Aggressivity in Psychoanalysis," 54; "Alienation," 136, 207–9; "Analysis and Truth," 34, 110–11, 230–31; "Anamorphosis," 19, 30; "Concept of Analysis," 39–41; "Cure Psychanalytique," 53; "Desire and the Interpretation of Desire in *Hamlet,*" 70, 209, 217, 224; "La direction de la cure," 219; "From Interpretation to Transference," 221; "From Love to Libido," 207–9, 232; "Function and Field of Speech and Language in Psychoanalysis," 39, 111; "Guiding Remarks for a Congress on Feminine Sexuality," 137; "In You More than You," 233; "Knowledge, Truth, Opinion," 40; "The Line and Light," 66; "Maurice Merleau-Ponty," 66; "La méprise du sujet supposé savoir," 174; "The Mirror Stage," 31–32, 52, 210; "Les non-dupes errent," 190–91; "Presence of the Analyst," 214, 230; "Propos sur la causalité psychique," 78; "Remarque sur le rapport de Daniel Lagache," 59; "Seminar on 'The Purloined Letter,' " 195; "Split between the Eye and the Gaze," 61–63, 69–70, 76–77; "Of the Subject Who Is Supposed to Know," 42, 195n, 210–11; "Tuché and Automaton," 195n, 198, 210–12; "The Unconscious and Repetition," 195n; "What Is a Picture?" 55, 63, 70–71
See also Gaze; Optics; Psychoanalysis
Laing, R. D., 194n
Langer, Susanne, 108
Laplanche, Jean, 31, 104–5
Learned ignorance, 11, 40–42. *See also* Knowing unknowingness
LeClaire, Serge, 40
Levao, Ronald, 16n
Levin, Harry, 82–83
Lévi-Strauss, Claude, 130, 136
Lloyd, Harold, *Safety Last,* 97–98

Library of Congress Cataloging-in-Publication Data

Freedman, Barbara, 1952–
    Staging the gaze : postmodernism, psychoanalysis, and Shakespearean
comedy / Barbara Freedman.
        p.   cm.
    Includes index.
    ISBN 0-8014-2279-5.—ISBN 0-8014-9737-X (pbk.)
    1. Shakespeare, William, 1564–1616—Comedies.   2. Psychoanalysis in
literature.   I. Title.
PR2981.F65   1991
822.3′3—dc20   90-55117